# THE CENTRAL SCHOOL OF SPEECH AND DRAMA

## UNIVERSITY OF LONDON

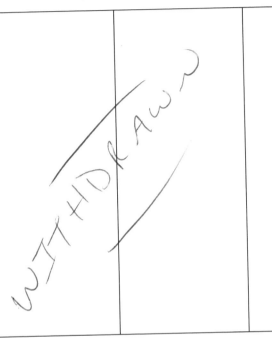

**Please return or renew this item by the last date shown.**

The Library, Central School of Speech and Drama,
Embassy Theatre, Eton Avenue, London, NW3 3HY
http://heritage.cssd.ac.uk
library@cssd.ac.uk
Direct line: 0207 559 3942

*The Great Betrayal*

# *The Great Betrayal*

## Brian Cox

CHAPMANS

Chapmans Publishers Ltd
141–143 Drury Lane
London WC2B 5TB

BRITISH LIBRARY CATALOGUING IN PUBLICATION DATA
Cox, Brian
Great Betrayal
I. Title
370.92

ISBN 1–85592–605–9

First published by Chapmans 1992

Photoset in Linotron Ehrhardt by
Falcon Typographic Art Ltd, Fife, Scotland
Printed and bound in Great Britain by
Butler & Tanner Ltd, Frome and London

*For Jean*

# Contents

# *Acknowledgements*

I am especially grateful to my wife and children, who during my educational campaigns have put up with frequent absences, numerous telephone calls and persistent journalists. I am also grateful to the Black Paper contributors who courageously supported me when this meant public obloquy. I should particularly like to thank Margaret Smith, without whose administrative zeal the National Council for Educational Standards would have never survived so long. I must also thank the members of the National Curriculum English Working Group, who helped to make our Report so spectacularly successful; Jane Benham, our Secretary, has efficiency and tact which saved me from many mistakes.

Throughout the 1970s and 1980s, while I was busy with political activities, *Critical Quarterly* continued regular publication, and our conferences for sixth-formers continued to attract large numbers. I am grateful to Bryan Loughrey, who has kept the *Critical Quarterly* sixth-form conferences going into the 1990s, and who is now editing a new version of our journal for teachers, *Critical Survey*. Professor David Palmer, Professor Ronald Draper, Professor Dick Watson, Mrs Felicity Currie and Dr Bill Hutchings also provided invaluable assistance during those difficult years. I should like to thank all my friends at Manchester University, whose kindness meant so much when I was being reviled in the Press. I think particularly of my squash partners, Trevor Myers from our Metallurgy Department, and Mike Yates from Town and Country Planning. On bad days hitting a squash ball hard proved a great relief.

Tony Dyson, Katharine Perera, Michael Schmidt and Rivers Scott read chapters of this book, and offered invaluable advice. Shelagh Aston, Maxine Powell and Mary Syner of the Manchester University English Department assisted the preparation of the manuscript in a variety of ways. I particularly thank Shelagh, who has been my secretary for twenty-six years, and survived with me many crises.

# Introduction

When in the early 1950s I was a young man I believed that British State education would get better and better, and that private schools would gradually wither away. This has not happened. During the last decades independent education has thrived, while State education, for various ideological, political and financial reasons, has faced a series of crises. This book is not intended to be an attack on teachers in State education. I respect the great zeal and dedication among the hundreds I have met and talked with in recent years. I remain hopeful too that the 1990s may yet witness a resurgence of State education so that parents will wonder whether the fees for the independent sector are worth the sacrifice. My purpose in *The Great Betrayal* is to make clear what went wrong since the 1950s, and why.

My first six chapters are autobiographical, describing my life up to 1969, when the publication of what are called the Black Papers on education hurled me into the centre of great national controversy. After 1969 my marriage with Jean remained idyllic, while my children after university courses left home for their own careers. My own time has been dominated by the educational problems in our schools which made headline news in the 1960s and which have not been resolved today. Chapters 7 to 12 are mainly concerned with my involvement in this national crisis, and with my campaign to bring about major educational reforms in the British school system.

Why have I included autobiographical material alongside analysis of educational controversies? When I first planned this book my intention was to limit the personal details to my educational background, but I soon realised this gave a false impression. Important events in my life – my mother's early death from tuberculosis in 1938, my brother's suicide during the weekend

1

in 1975 when a Black Paper was published – very much influenced my fundamental beliefs and attitudes. As I drafted and redrafted the chapters, I decided to include as much detail as possible about my upbringing and early years as a teacher; even trivial details and anecdotes provide the cultural contexts in which I made my decisions about educational issues. Many false notions are current about the Black Papers and about the proposals of the Working Party on the National Curriculum in English, which I chaired. In addition to my personal memories I also provide description and evaluation of what was written and what actually happened.

These events imposed great emotional stress on me, and I have not found this book easy to write. However, I wanted to tell the truth as I see it about events which to some degree changed the ethos of British schools. I possess a treasure trove of primary material: letters from Mrs Thatcher when she was Secretary of State for Education, from the Poet Laureate, Ted Hughes, and from Dr Rhodes Boyson, whose Black Paper activities ended in ministerial appointments in Mrs Thatcher's Government. In his first letter to introduce himself to me, sent in April 1969 after the publication of the first Black Paper, he firmly criticized some of its contents.

I lived too close to these events for me to claim to be objective. I have quoted letters, manifestoes and articles at length so that primary material can speak for itself. Total evaluation of the Black Paper campaign must be left to historians who were not so emotionally involved. Similarly it is too early for a full assessment of my work on the National Curriculum: we need to wait to see how it is implemented in practice.

During his last years, before he died at the age of ninety-one, my father embarrassed me by repeatedly saying that as a professor I was now 'somebody' in the world. My family existed on the borders of the working and lower middle classes; in the years before 1914, when my father started work, he was desperate to escape from poverty, and to establish himself as 'somebody'. In the popular consciousness of our times, images of the working classes have been dominated by Richard Hoggart's *The Uses of Literacy* (1957) or the Granada Television stories of Coronation Street. We hear about warm, closely integrated communities in cities such as Leeds or Manchester. Like Mrs Thatcher I come from Lincolnshire. In Grimsby, my home town, we lived cheek-by-jowl with middle class families whose style of life attracted us by its comforts and prestige. We met them at our non-conformist churches where their clothes and accents and manners witnessed to their different social standing. They were somebodies; we were nobodies, unless by hard work or education we dragged ourselves away from the poverty in which we were born.

My father partially accomplished this transformation in his own lifetime, at least in economic terms, starting as an office boy and ending with a satisfactory income as treasurer and director of a small company. His family knew the harshness of working-class life in the first decades of this century, the inadequate houses, domestic drudgery and long hours of poorly paid work. Not surprisingly most of them sympathized with their children's attempt to escape. The two other chief protagonists in the Black Paper campaign, Dr Rhodes Boyson and Tony Dyson, were reared in comparable backgrounds, working-class, but with determination not to submit to its penuries and repressions. We learnt we could only survive by competitiveness and realistic assessment of what was possible in our circumstances.

In my first chapters I describe how as a boy I tried to succeed in the educational system of the 1930s and 1940s. I learnt by my failures the need for contacts with the best teachers and with other children of similar interests and abilities, and for order and structure in the class-room. I survived partly by ability, partly by my desperate need to escape from my unhappy home and partly by good fortune. Children today succeed or fail largely according to the quality of their schooling. An average child who attends an inner-city comprehensive will probably never be accepted at polytechnic or university. An average child trained in good private schools stands a reasonable chance of a university place. I want to see State education improved, but this can only be achieved when misplaced ideologies, particularly the egalitarian ethos, are banished from our schools.

My personal story illustrates the problems facing a child from a home without books and without knowledge of university requirements. Much educational discussion of the last thirty years has ignored these realities, the actual needs of children in difficult social situations. The Black Paper opponents were often from middle- or upper-class families (Anthony Crosland, Professor Brian Simon, Shirley Williams, for example) and from public schools. Their reforming zeal thrived on misunderstandings of the real needs of the working-class child. My autobiographical chapters provide an intimate account of the kinds of educational problems which face such children. When I became a teacher I was fortunate for many years to run a little literary business which taught me much about the economic realities which utopian thinking neglects. In California I witnessed the problems of neighbourhood schools and the disastrous effects of student sit-ins on the status of the university. By 1969 I had gained first-hand experience of the difficulties created by progressive and comprehensive education, and by student rebellions; this made me unusual among British academics.

The publication of two Black Papers in 1969 marked a major shift in British attitudes towards education, and indeed towards the whole ethos of the 1960s. The extent of the influence of our pamphlets is difficult to assess, for, obviously enough, many factors were involved in the radical transformations of society which took place during the next decade. The Black Papers included little that was original, but on the other hand they served to express the hidden feelings and thoughts of thousands of ordinary teachers and parents. They broke down taboos among educationalists and politicians who for years had been cabined and confined by the popular fashion for progressive education. The campaign brought together people who had never met, though they shared similar anxieties. It made it easier for individuals to take courage to speak out when they had previously felt isolated and kept quiet.

The Black Papers liberated a repressed ideology which eventually was to play a part in making Mrs Thatcher Prime Minister in 1979. Their success in transforming the educational scene was a triumph for the ordinary, the obvious, the instinctive and the natural over the theorists and utopians of the 1960s. Our pamphlet war was part of a much larger movement, particularly associated with Lord Harris and his colleagues at the Institute of Economic Affairs, which converted Sir Keith Joseph and Mrs Thatcher to competitive markets and monetarism in the 1970s. This movement helped persuade the electorate to vote Conservative in 1979.

In his address to the National Union of Teachers on 8 April 1969, Mr Edward Short, Labour Secretary of State for Education, described the publication of the first Black Paper as 'one of the blackest days for education in the past 100 years'. The situation created by this 'backlash' against progressive education, he said, had provoked 'the crisis of the century'. He labelled our criticisms of informal teaching practices 'archaic rubbish'. Mr Short was followed by many others who poured abuse and scorn on the first Black Paper. In the *New Statesman*, Christopher Price – Labour MP for Perry Bar, Birmingham, later to become Director of Leeds Polytechnic – described the authors as 'a decrepit bunch of educational Powellites' (18 April 1969). *The Times* reported that Michael Duane, the famous ex-head of the progressive school, Risinghill, had called us 'fascist' (14 July). The *Evening Standard* called the pamphlet 'a trivial document by some elderly reactionaries which has so far remained suitably underpublicised' (9 April). Such vilification continued for many years, with the leading figures in the campaign continually treated as pariahs by left-wing educationalists.

In 1969 our ideas were treated with contempt by the leaders of intellectual fashion who had lost touch with those ordinary people, many from the working classes, who do not attend conferences or read the latest articles in progressive magazines. The hate directed towards us showed the inability of the progressive orthodoxy, like any other orthodoxy, to tolerate earnest and practical dissent.

Over the years our views have gradually prevailed. After the first two Black Papers in 1969, further pamphlets were published in 1970, 1975 and 1977, and there were many other associated conferences and publications. In October 1976, Mr Callaghan, the Labour Prime Minister, repeated in his famous Ruskin College speech our assertions that money was being wasted, standards were too low, and children were not being given the basic tools of literacy and numeracy. *The Times Educational Supplement* said of Mr Callaghan's speech: 'He has gathered his Black Paper cloak around him.' In 1987 Mr Baker, the Conservative Secretary of State for Education, put forward proposals for tests at seven, eleven, fourteen and sixteen, and these are now incorporated into the National Curriculum, and for city technical colleges – central Black Paper ideas.

Even the Labour Party began to ask why the schools in inner cities were so much criticized. In the *New Statesman*, 16 October 1987, the editor, John Lloyd, wrote that the Labour Party had failed to ask the hard questions: 'they have been waiting to be asked for at least a decade, since the James Callaghan "great debate" on education ran into the sand. The Left did not face up to failures and to the manifest alarm of the mass of parents.' In an interview in the *Sunday Times*, 1 November 1987, Neil Fletcher, Labour Leader of the Inner London Education Authority, said that 'mixed ability and progressive teaching methods have failed to equip children with basic skills of literacy and numeracy'. He made a list of parents' worries: 'Concern about tables, concern about spelling, concern about handwriting, concern about homework, even just simple things like learning poetry, the old ways of absorbing culture, hymn singing, all the things that used to happen. Parents say, "Why don't they do that any more?" There's a feeling that progressive teaching methods have achieved something but also that they've lost a lot.' These are the kind of comments which are typical of the Black Papers in 1969, and which provoked scorn and contumely from left-wing educationalists and politicians.

Educational battles, however, are never finally won; they continue from generation to generation. I regret most that the Black Paper campaign helped to promote a public reaction against the teaching profession, and in recent articles and speeches I have tried to reverse this trend. We brought into being a number of extreme right-wing groups whose ignorance and prejudice still dominate the headlines in newspapers. If we are to help the children of the 1990s, we need parents, teachers and politicians who understand the history of the education crisis of the last thirty years, and who do not make the same mistakes.

My father wanted me to be christened 'Charles Brian', but my mother preferred 'Brian', so that is what I was called. When I first started to publish literary criticism I signed myself C.B. Cox, for at that time it was conventional to use initials, not Christian names. I continued in this fashion until 1985, when I was asked to contribute a regular monthly back-page article for *The Times Educational Supplement*. The *T.E.S.* printed my article under the name 'Brian Cox', and I was not sufficiently bothered to object. The series became popular, and after two years I had become well-known among teachers as 'Brian Cox'. Some readers failed to connect this person with the supposedly right-wing C.B. Cox who edited the Black Papers. When the National Curriculum English Working Group Report was published, newspapers commented that I had moved from an authoritarian to a liberal stance. The change from C.B. Cox to Brian Cox reflects this change in public perceptions, so for this autobiography I have retained my new image. My own belief is that C.B. Cox and Brian Cox have much in common.

Why have I called this book *The Great Betrayal*? Since the 1960s British education has been betrayed, for a variety of reasons, so that in the 1990s the difficulties facing all levels of education, from primary schools to universities, have assumed alarming proportions. In the 1960s a great wave of utopian ideology swept across British schools, undermining the authority of the teacher, damaging to the real needs of children. Some traditional teachers succumbed to nervous breakdowns; others took early retirement or left the profession. While this was going on, the violent student sit-ins permanently damaged the reputation of universities, lowering the esteem in which they had been held by the general public.

After Callaghan's speech, the teaching profession gradually pulled itself back from the worst excesses of the 1960s and 1970s. The Conservative Party introduced the National Curriculum, which imposed modern ideas of structure on the schools. Kenneth Clarke, Secretary of State for Education, commissioned the 1992 Report on primary education of the 'three wise men'. This Report showed that although too many primary schools were still using shapeless discovery methods, with children wasting time on unco-ordinated activities, there was a growing consensus among experienced teachers in favour of a sensible balance between formal and informal methods of instruction.

In the 1980s and 1990s, though, the great betrayal of education continued in new forms. Over the years the breakdown of structured learning in many State schools had led to a fierce reaction from the media, supported by many Conservative politicians. Teachers in State education were repeatedly reviled in the Press, and this has gone on unabated to the present day. The Conservative Party felt no political necessity to commit itself to substantial increases in the money allocated to State education, and the morale of teachers deteriorated rapidly. The success of the National Curriculum depended on a considerable injection of extra cash to help teachers to adapt to radical changes: this was not forthcoming. The burden of administration persuaded more teachers than ever to take early retirement, and these were often the best in their profession. At the same time the standards of universities declined rapidly, with Conservative financial cuts leading to crowded classes, underfunded libraries and many early retirements.

I believe passionately in education, particularly in the Arts. As a teacher I want to promote an improved quality of life for as many people as possible. From the 1960s to the 1990s I have watched the teaching profession beset by false ideologies and by the present crisis of low morale. Teachers in State education today are underpaid, overworked and often exhausted. During this period I have fought for higher standards at all levels of education by editing pamphlets, addressing rallies, organizing conferences, lobbying MPs, chairing committees, and by teaching students. I hope this autobiography will encourage politicians, parents and the general public to think hard about our educational needs, and that as we move through the 1990s we shall see a surge of new confidence that investment in education will bring all members of our community a great enrichment of life.

# 1

# *A Humberside Childhood*

The river's level drifting breadth began,
Where sky and Lincolnshire and water meet.
'The Whitsun Weddings', Philip Larkin

I was born on 5 September 1928, in Grimsby, then a thriving fishing port on the cold east coast of England. My mother's pains began soon after dawn, but in those days my father, after contacting the midwife, could not even consider taking a day off work. He departed as usual soon after 8 a.m., travelling fifteen miles by bus to Louth to sell consignments of coal and coke to Lincolnshire farmers. Neither we nor our neighbours could afford a telephone, so it was not until his return that he discovered that the new baby was a boy. Derek, my brother, was then four years old.

All my grandparents died before I was born. My grandfather on my father's side worked as a bricklayer, in continual financial difficulties because of his large family of five girls and two boys. The two boys, Albert and Hedley, my father, were the youngest, and much spoiled by their elder sisters. My mother's parents were drunkards. My grandfather was an engineer on a merchant ship, who in his cups quarrelled violently with his wife. They had four children, Isa, Emily, Ethel and Rose, my mother, and then separated in anger. After a few years they came together again and produced several more children. Perhaps because of their early sufferings, the four elder sisters were emotionally very close to each other, and all their lives quite separate from the younger group of children born after the reconciliation. I do not even know

9

how many children there were in the second batch, for we have had almost no contact with that part of the family.

My father missed the 1914–18 war through ill-health. When he was fifteen he was told he was suffering from tuberculosis of the bone, and could not hope to live for more than a couple of years. A tenacious survivor, he lived to a great age, mentally alert until he died, and eloquent about the hard conditions on Grimsby docks when he first started work in 1911. His brother, Albert, volunteered in 1914 to serve as an officer in the Grimsby Chums (the nickname of the 10th Battalion, the Lincolnshire Regiment). In May 1915, after a period in training camp at Brocklesby Park in Lincolnshire, the Chums staged an emotional farewell parade through the streets of Grimsby and Cleethorpes before leaving for advanced training and the Western Front. In his first week in France my uncle fell off his horse and broke his arm. The accident probably saved his life, for on 1 July 1916, the 1,000-strong battalion was decimated by German machine-gun fire in Sausage Valley on the Somme. The official casualty list was seventy-one killed, 162 missing and 269 wounded, just over half the strength. After going out to Murmansk with the British expeditionary force to Russia, Albert survived to serve in India during the Second World War, and to be twice Mayor of Cleethorpes.

Grimsby's name is of Danish origin, meaning Grim's town. Primary school children, from my father's day to my own, were taught the legend of its foundation. The thirteenth-century poem 'Havelock the Dane', recounts how a Danish fisherman, Grim, ordered to murder Havelock, the baby heir to the throne, fled instead to England; there the boy eventually married an English princess. As king of both England and Denmark, he rewarded Grim with lands, and so Grimsby, according to the story, took his name.

When I was at school we were proud that Grimsby had established itself as the largest fishing port in the world. Its sudden rise to prosperity dates from 1848, with the arrival of the Manchester, Sheffield and Lincs. Railway Company (popularly known as 'Mucky, Slow and Late'), and the development of improved dock facilities. The foundation of the new Royal Dock was laid by Prince Albert in 1849. When my father began work as a clerk for a trawler owner, the fishing fleet was made up of over 500 steam trawlers and a few sailing ships. The fishermen were a tough breed, accustomed to icy conditions and fierce storms as far north as Iceland, the Faroes, Bear Island and the White Sea.

Tragedy was commonplace. When my father was still in his teens, a trawler capsized in the Humber just outside the docks; many of the sailors were below deck to change their clothes, and seven were drowned. The father of one of the drowned sailors came into the shipping office to ask if his son was dead. My father looked down at the ground, and suggested he should ask the manager. The man immediately picked up the implication, and broke down into desperate weeping. In his later years my father told this story again and again; it haunted his dreams.

While on shore trawlermen were notorious for drinking, fighting and spending sprees. The pay for the hard-working deckhands was poor. In 1901 the great fishing dispute was precipitated by the demand of the Grimsby Federated Owners' Protecting Society Ltd. (the Federation) that the previous system of straight wages paid to the crews should be replaced by a mixture of wages and 'poundage' (i.e. part payment by results). The men went on strike, even though the deckhands had nothing, not even the dole. As soup kitchens were set up for their wives and children, rioting broke out, and the Federation's offices were wrecked. A large crowd on the docks was charged by eighty policemen brought in from Sheffield, and Mr Joseph Hewson, JP, read the Riot Act in Riby Square. Not surprisingly, my grandparents were most anxious that Albert and Hedley should not go to sea, and both were persuaded to look for office jobs.

Grimsby and its adjacent seaside resort, Cleethorpes, run into each other. As a boy my father and his friends pranced up and down the middle of local streets, shouting that they were half in Grimsby, half in Cleethorpes. Grimsby's football ground, Blundell Park, is in Cleethorpes; an old radio teaser was to ask contestants which football team never played at home. Cleethorpes boasts a long, flat, sandy beach at the mouth of the river Humber seven miles wide as it flows past Spurn Point and Lighthouse into the North Sea. In winter the north-east winds strike cold into every vein; the locals say the winds blow straight from Russia. When I look back on my childhood I recall innumerable days pushing my bike against cold winds, thankful in this flat landscape that there were no hills. At home we sat crouched over small coal fires, draughts freezing our backs, wet feet and chilblains a constant irritation.

A single track railway arrived in Cleethorpes in 1863, and soon thousands of trippers from inland towns such as Sheffield, Doncaster and Leeds were arriving to breathe in large gulps of bracing air. Steel-workers and cotton-mill workers arrived who had never seen the sea before, overwhelmed by its breadth and moving colours. The beach is dangerous, for the tide flows in fast, silently entering the hollows between the sand-banks. On one occasion I was playing too long by the water's edge, and with my friends was forced to wade up to my neck through a gulley which had filled with water behind us. Fifteen minutes later we would have been stranded, and in need of rescue. In 1968 a riding mistress named Tasker and three young children were drowned with their horses in thick fog when they presumably could not decide which stretch of water led towards land and which towards the sea.

Although my father did not go to sea, we felt very much part of a fishing community. He brought home gifts of fresh cod or haddock or plaice from the docks. On hot days the stink from the fish meal factory at Pyewipe would infiltrate every cranny of our home, polluting the air as we tossed in our beds at night. On Fridays we took sandwiches to school; after a short break at 12 noon, school continued until 1.30 p.m., when we were released so that children of trawlermen could go to the docks to collect their father's wages.

My parents married in 1921. On the marriage certificate my father is described as an accountant's clerk. My mother worked as a lady's maid in middle-class houses in Grimsby, and once was forced to change jobs when her employer tried unsuccessfully to seduce her. Both of them left State schools at the age of fourteen, and spent the first years of their married life in a terrace house near the centre of Grimsby. My father's mother refused to agree to his marriage until he had accumulated sufficient money to pay the deposit on the house. She also refused to attend the wedding because the drinking habits of my mother's parents were notorious.

Their early years together were intensely happy, with their

social life centred on Ebenezer Methodist Chapel, where my
father acted for several years as secretary and treasurer of the
large Sunday School. About 500 children would enrol at both
morning and afternoon sessions; one of my earliest memories
is of disappointment at not being given a prize because I only
attended in the afternoon. Without radio or television, my mother
and father spent their evenings in a continual round of parties,
playing charades and singing traditional romantic ballads around
the piano. They paid a few pennies to watch silent films with
Charlie Chaplin or Laurel and Hardy, and waited in long queues
for seats for performances of Gilbert and Sullivan at the Prince
of Wales Theatre in Freeman Street. In some ways it was a
period of lost innocence. Not long before he died, my father
told me that he never saw my mother naked. With due modesty
she always undressed in the dark, or during the summer months
pulled on her night-dress in the bathroom. Two of my mother's
sisters never married; they were born into the generation whose
prospective husbands were killed during the war. All the sisters
were socially ambitious, determined to escape from the working
class. Aunt Isa ended her career as Matron of the Blind Institute
in Edgbaston, Birmingham. Aunt Emily, a saint if ever there was
one, slaved for decades as companion to an irascible, crippled old
lady, Mrs Hossell, who presided over a gloomy Victorian house in
Abbey Road, not far from the Old Market Place in Grimsby. When
I read Dickens's *Great Expectations*, I immediately associated Miss
Havisham with Mrs Hossell. My aunts were immensely kind to
me when I was a child, determined that through my successes at
school I would find my way into the middle classes.

Tragedy destroyed my parents' world when two years after
my birth my mother contracted tuberculosis. In 1932 my father
managed to scrape together sufficient money to put down the
deposit for a mortgage on a new three-bedroom, semi-detached
house in Laceby Road in fields beyond Nunsthorpe, on the
outskirts of Grimsby. The house was named 'Coniston' in memory
of a short holiday my parents had spent in the Lakes soon after
they were married. He hoped the country air would suit my
mother's failing health, but she died on 29 September 1938,
when I was ten.

There was no National Health Service, so my mother's illness made us very poor. Out of a wage of six pounds a week my father was forced to pay ten to fifteen shillings a week for a daily maid to prepare food, clean the house and look after Derek and me. Once to help pay his bills he took us to the Post Office Savings Bank to withdraw a few pounds from our children's tiny accounts. As we signed the forms I sensed his awkwardness, his unnecessary shame.

When I was four my mother was sent for two weeks to a sanatorium at Bournemouth, but my father could not afford to pay fees beyond this period. During this fortnight I stayed with my godmother, Mrs Blaker, on Carr Lane. I retain two memories of this visit. Mr Blaker brought home a live crab from the docks, and my godmother dropped it straight into boiling water. On another occasion she smacked me for disobedience. For many years the two incidents were linked together in my dreams. From later years I know my godmother was a kind woman, but my mother's absence must have troubled me sorely. My brother Derek was naturally generous, and in those years I found his company a great solace. At night after our bedroom lights were out he regaled me with complicated adventure stories, whose twists of plot he concocted to lead on from night to night.

My earliest memories of my father are of a small, blue-eyed and good-looking man who every morning in the bathroom sang his favourite romantic ballads as loudly as possible. He enjoyed playing the clown, and on departure from an aunt's house would always don the ladies' hats, and make faces. After my mother's death, however, he fell into depression, and abandoned his social activities. He sent Derek and me to the local Methodist Church, but never attended himself. He often took me to the Bird's Nest Cafe overlooking the Boating Lake at Cleethorpes, where he would order a pot of tea, with chocolate biscuits. On these occasions I welcomed his affection, the privilege of being alone with him, but he spoke little, and I knew he was thinking of my mother, whom I resemble.

My father was a very shy, diffident man. Once when I was eight I overheard my aunts condemning a girl who was pregnant. I thought babies grew naturally in young women over eighteen, so when later that evening he tucked me up in bed I challenged him on my aunt's morality. 'Why blame the girl?' I asked. 'Don't you know?' he replied evasively. I looked up at him, bewildered, and he left hastily. We never discussed sex again.

As I look back I wonder what my mother must have felt as she realized she was almost certain to die and to leave her boys without her love. I have few memories of her. Once standing by her bedside I watched her spit green phlegm into a little china bowl, and then replace the lid. In 1986, when my stepmother died, I became responsible for looking after my father, who spent his last three years in a nursing home at Davenport, near Stockport. As I used to help him undress, I often felt my mother was present, waiting for him to join her. She was only forty-one when she died, so the figure I imagined was much younger than me. In my fantasy I saw her husband restored to her as he was in the 1920s. Sometimes she seemed very close, really present; the face of the woman I almost saw, though, was taken from her wedding photograph, in shapeless white medium-length dress and broad-rimmed hat, not from childhood memories. After she died my father never talked about her, not until his last years at Davenport. As an adolescent I had to piece together information about my parents, to work out for myself what happened and when.

When my father moved to Davenport I took over his personal documents, and found my mother's death certificate. I had always thought she died in 1937, when I was nine; I was strangely troubled when I discovered I had been a year out in the calculation made so long ago. I'm surprised that I remember so little about my mother, and conclude that for many years I suppressed her image in order to forget.

Fifty boys and girls were sitting in battered double desks at Nunsthorpe Elementary School in Grimsby, all of them silent and very still. It was my first day at school. At the front, lit by shafts of sunlight from long windows, the lady teacher had flung a recalcitrant girl over her knee, revealing black woollen knickers. She spanked the girl hard, but the child at first stubbornly refused to cry. The battle of wills continued for about twenty seconds, when the girl let out a yell, and the teacher desisted.

From this episode I learnt a simple lesson: it would be wise to obey the teacher. In those days it was customary for teachers to assert their authority forcefully on their first meeting with a class. Afterwards, they could relax, for the children would never step out of line. At Nunsthorpe the cane was available, but rarely brought into action. One young bully called Waters was always being caned, but usually corporal punishment was confined to a quick smack. I was never caned at Nunsthorpe, although I recall Miss Williamson, my favourite teacher, cuffing me over the head to stop me waving scissors in the air.

Nunsthorpe mainly served a new working-class housing estate on the outskirts of Grimsby. In 1919, 128 acres were bought from the Earl of Yarborough for £19,200. The layout provided for almost 1,000 houses, all with little gardens, and the school where I started my academic career in 1933. Fictional accounts of such elementary schools often portray scenes of brutality, vicious repression of the children, as in Dennis Potter's television serial, *The Singing Detective*, or the film, *Hope and Glory*, about school-days during the bombing of London in the Second World War.

In D.H. Lawrence's *The Rainbow*, Ursula tries to treat her class with kindness, but the inflexible school routines defeat her. As at Nunsthorpe, she is confronted with long rows of desks, and with teachers whose hard authoritarian voices appal her. The head, Mr Harby, bullying and threatening, behaves like an inhuman machine; the school becomes for her a hideous prison, blocking out the sunlight. Ursula only survives when she thrashes the rat-like Williams, whose grinning insolence at last snaps her self-control.

Schools like Brinsley Street, where Ursula underwent her ordeal, undoubtedly existed, particularly before 1914, but Nunsthorpe was very different. Lawrence thought that oppressive routines killed all spontaneity, that the great effort of the teacher of a large class to subjugate the children to his or her own will necessitated the abnegation of the personal self. In revolt against such disciplined class-rooms, A.S. Neill, the famous head of Summerhill, the ultra-progressive school, wanted his children to live without fear, leaving his pupils free all day to choose their own activities, to work or play as they pleased.

Nunsthorpe offered me a sensible balance between Brinsley Street and Summerhill. I was afraid at Nunsthorpe, but not of the teachers as individuals: I was afraid to break the standards of behaviour which they imposed. I remember my teachers – Miss Thicket, Mr Terry, Miss Williamson – with affection. Miss Williamson, whom I knew later in life when my wife taught in her school, inspired great respect in me when I joined her class at the top of the Juniors. She imposed her will on her class not for personal survival or pleasure, but because she was determined to teach her children civilized values.

The curriculum at Nunsthorpe was not just rote learning and tests. We acted in dramatized stories, particularly in the weeks before Christmas. One evening Miss Thicket took a group of children to perform *Dick Whittington* before old people in a church hall. I played the part of the cat, dressed in a black garment contrived from a hearth-rug. My role finished about five minutes before the final curtain, so, perspiring, I returned to the changing-room and took off my costume. Clad only in my vest, I heard Miss Thicket call us back on stage to enjoy the audience's applause. Taught never to disobey a teacher, I dashed on stage, and brought the house down. It was my most successful stage appearance.

We also sang in choirs, and were encouraged to draw and paint. I was always bottom of the class in Art, a failure rate which continued unabated through all my years in secondary school. On one occasion we were asked to design a poster for a Grimsby Fair. On the left of my sheet I drew a black minstrel in green pantaloons, with space on the right for the lettering. When Miss Thicket looked over my shoulder, she saw a splodgy muddle of lines. She bent over, her brown hair touching my cheek, and with firm black strokes drew the outline of my minstrel and his banjo. I was good at lettering, so all I had to do was colour her drawing. Prizes were awarded for children's art at the Grimsby Fair, and my offering was chosen for display. As with my proud father I gazed at my minstrel mounted on a board, I knew in my heart that my success was entirely due to Miss Thicket. From this moment I date my mistrust of course assessment examinations, where marks are awarded for a student's work in class.

Nunsthorpe school was built in the typical style of the 1930s, with a quadrangle of class-rooms around a central courtyard of grass and pathways. We were rarely allowed into this enclosed space, reserved for the crowning of the May Queen, or for Empire Day, when we sang 'I vow to thee my country'. I soon learnt that some spaces were reserved for the privileged, for teachers, for example, and that in this world of boundaries, limits and enclosures, I would succeed only by self-discipline and hard work.

In 1938, when I was nine years old, I kept a little diary which I still possess. We were trained to be always punctual, to finish every task in due order, so I wanted to keep a diary for a whole year. I lasted out until 8 July, when the temptation of summer evenings persuaded me to forget my voluntary task. A few years ago I read bits of this diary to a conference of educationalists at Llandudno, for comic relief, telling my audience that my spelling was superior to that of most present-day university students. I thought that no representatives of the Press were present, but I had failed to notice a local man in the back row. The next day my offhand remark made headlines in the popular newspapers.

By Easter my entries had become perfunctory. On Monday, 9 May the diary reads: 'Went to school, had Spelling, Drill, Arithmetic, Science and Poetry in the morning. In the afternoon had Painting, Games and Singing. Played Monopoly in the evening.' On Tuesday it is much the same: 'Bought the Rover. Went to school, had Scripture, Spelling, Drill, Composition and Arithmetic in the morning. In the afternoon had Poetry, Handwork and Geography.'

Each day at school was carefully planned, with clearly defined slots for each subject and a work programme monitored by the head. On Monday 4 July we began exams: 'Had Grammer (sic – my spelling wasn't perfect) Exam with Miss Thicket from 9–11.20. After that had Silent Reading. In the afternoon had History Exam, forty questions. After History Exam had Reading.' In those days children of eight or nine were quite used to a series of tests covering a period of over two hours, and to returning in the afternoon for more. We were encouraged to compete with each other and rewards of golden stars were given to those who scored high marks. When the teacher told us to rest with our heads on the desks we obeyed without question. When we were instructed to fold our arms and listen silently to a story we accepted this as normal ritual. New teachers of average ability fitted into these routines easily without discipline problems. Our minds were filled with traditional verses, ballads such as 'Sir Patrick Spens' or the strong rhythms of Masefield's 'Cargoes', which we learned off by heart; and with classical stories, such as Perseus and Medusa, Roland and Oliver, Theseus and the Minotaur. At morning assembly we sang hymns and listened to Bible stories. I recall a vivid image of God as a tall man dressed in a kind of black wet-suit, his white face leaning over a balcony to peer down at us.

In his poem, 'The Best of School', D.H. Lawrence creates the atmosphere of a disciplined class-room, typical of Nunsthorpe, completely unlike Ursula's Brinsley Street. Boys and girls in white summer blouses bow their heads over their books, awakening to the power of language, occasionally looking up at the teacher, seeing and not seeing as they ponder their next sentence.

> Touch after touch I feel on me
> As their eyes glance at me for the grain
> Of rigour they taste delightedly.
>
> As tendrils reach out yearningly,
> Slowly rotate till they touch the tree
> That they cleave unto, and up which they climb
> Up to their lives – so they to me.

At Nunsthorpe I felt I was being initiated into a colourful world of literature, mathematics, music and history; its disciplines entered my blood stream and became a source of great joy. I learnt that outside myself there existed an invulnerable world of learning and aesthetic pleasure, available for consolation even at the darkest moments of failure or sickness.

I was just as fascinated by the sounds and shapes of words as by what they represented. As a boy, and to a lesser extent even today, I picture all letters and words in colour. Brian is red and Derek is blue. Dunfermline in the ballad of Sir Patrick Spens appears dark blue, while Patrick is silver. York and Cleethorpes are yellow, and Humber a dark brown. These word associations depend on arbitrary factors – the colours in my word-book, for example, when I first started to read. These colours are personal to me, part of my unique self, so that when I read a poem such as Coleridge's 'Kubla Khan' I visualize scenes different from those of any other reader. 'Damsel' and 'dulcimer', for instance, appear to me as the darkest blue.

We were fortunate that our teachers had not been indoctrinated with the pernicious notion that a child should not be taught to read until he or she is ready. Great emphasis was placed on the formal teaching of reading and writing, with much use of phonics and word-building exercises. In spite of the progressive revolution of the 1960s, many schools with features like those of Nunsthorpe continue to exist. In the 1970s, while preparing a new Black Paper, I visited Mr Beard, headmaster of Waterloo County Junior School in a working-class area in Ashton-under-Lyne, near Manchester, and published a description of his school in *Black Paper 1977*. He expected each teacher to hear each child read at least once a week. He himself heard every pupil twice a year, in February and July, and tested them. Problems were discussed with class teachers.

My childhood diary included references to tests administered to us by Mr Neal, the head at Nunsthorpe. The tests were old-fashioned, only measuring ability to recognize and pronounce isolated words, but at least they drew attention to children with problems, and provided an organized framework for reading progress.

In my diary I kept a list of books I'd been reading, with marks for 'good', 'not good', and 'not bad'. Jackson's *Air Spies of the North Sea* and *Air Gold Hunters*, and Foster's *The Captive King* were rated 'good'. Charles Kingsley's *Westward Ho!* was marked 'not good'. Regular visits on my bike to Grimsby Public Library were a major part of my schoolboy life; I read avidly. There was no television, of course, and how that would have affected me I do not know. I never came across Beatrix Potter, and most of what I read was junk. I read all the Biggles stories by W.E. Johns, and felt slightly guilty when in 1988 my English Working Party for the National Curriculum did not include him in its list of recommended authors (I 'put my boot into Biggles', the tabloid Press announced). Biggles, an air-man hero, typified the fictional characters whose adventures stimulated my boyhood fantasies. In his stories it is taken for granted that the British Empire existed as a glorious force for the promotion of civilized values, and that black people were backward and dangerous. As a young reader I never doubted that this was true.

At Nunsthorpe it would not have occurred to the teachers that accurate spelling, punctuation and grammar might inhibit a child's creativity. They took for granted that a child's imagination cannot work in a vacuum, and that he or she must come to terms with the nature of form, whether it is language, music, paint or clay. They would have been astonished if anyone had suggested to them that accuracy is a middle-class virtue, or that it is only appropriate in training courses for jobs. They believed that in a democracy everyone should be able to use words precisely, to speak clearly, to develop a lucid argument, and that such attainments are essential for personal growth. They accepted the traditional view that children who cannot use language accurately are denied major forms of self-exploration and fulfilment. Mr Terry told us about the dangers of prescriptive rules: 'Never end a sentence with "with"', he wrote on the blackboard, and took it for granted we would see the joke.

This approach to learning, taken for granted at Nunsthorpe, has profound moral, psychological and cultural implications. The emphasis is on service and self-discipline, a true attention to the realities of the social world. Instead of writing disorganized personal prose we learnt the rules of civilized discourse. At Nunsthorpe we were invited, indeed compelled, to submit ourselves to the disciplines of study. The rules we learnt were a means of understanding the demands of the outside world, and of controlling them in the service of the community and our own desired forms of personal fulfilment. There was too much rote learning, and oral abilities were neglected, but the children profited in a rich variety of ways from the traditional teaching. We memorized great verse, we read extensively, and learnt to write accurate prose. These were rare gifts for the working-class children who formed the majority of the pupils.

I was nervous and over-sensitive, but school helped me to gain self-confidence. After a few weeks I understood its rituals, and knew how to cope with its demands. On the morning my mother died, my father came into the bedroom I shared with my brother and told us what happened in the next bedroom during the night. I cried, but my brother just stared out of the window. After breakfast we went off to school as usual.

Nunsthorpe was a safe place where my mind was occupied with the usual routines. School became my castle, where I could grow and develop in conditions fully controlled by adults who took responsibility for the world; it became a substitute home. Not surprisingly, women teachers acted for me as surrogate mothers.

On Sunday afternoons I attended Bradley Cross Roads Methodist Church. These one-hour Sunday school sessions were the limit of my visits to church until I was adolescent. Only on holidays in Hull with Aunt Annie, my father's sister, was I subjected to the boredom of sermons, passing twenty minutes adding upwards and sideways and down again the numbers of the hymns on the board near the preacher's head. To travel to Hull meant taking a train up river to New Holland, and then crossing the Humber by paddle-steamer, a romantic twenty-minute journey. This was so enjoyable that I always looked forward to my Hull visits, in spite of the sermons. On those Sunday afternoons at Bradley Cross Roads we learnt famous psalms off by heart, and became conversant with all the main Bible stories. This background no longer exists for most of my students today at Manchester University. Undergraduates taking English Honours often do not know the story of Job or Lazarus or the parable of the talents. Those Sunday school years were relatively happy, with annual outings and sports meetings. My brother played in goal for the Sunday school's first soccer team; they lost 25–0. It was later, when I was at secondary school, that the puritan, evangelical quality of the Methodist Church wreaked some harm on my young imagination.

Both at Sunday school and at Nunsthorpe teachers insisted on punctuality as a form of courtesy, an attention to the rights of other people. This reliability rooted itself in my nature. I still feel ashamed if I am late for a meeting, even if I have due cause.

My father's shortage of money meant we had no spare cash to buy books. As a young man he had bought H.G. Wells's *The Outline of History* in monthly instalments, but this was almost the extent of his library. My Aunt Emily brought me a comic every week, first *The Rainbow* and then *The Rover*, with long serials which I followed eagerly. My brother and I listened regularly to Children's Hour on the radio, particularly Romany's dramatized accounts of his country walks. My brother announced that he wished to work in a bank when he grew up, because they closed early, so he would be home in time for Children's Hour.

Nunsthorpe School was indeed regimented. When playtime ended we marched in lines class by class back into school, and we were expected to stand when the teacher came into the room. Yet outside the school we engaged in activities of great diversity and richness. Without television we were forced into the streets and fields for our entertainment.

Sir Alec Black, a local landowner, conceived grandiose schemes for developing private housing in an area of open fields with sporting and cultural activities. In the meadow behind our house he placed a wooden structure intended, so we were told, as the pavilion for a sports complex. This building had three large covered spaces, open to the fields on one side. According to gossip the shed had previously been owned by the defunct Grimsby Zoo, so it was named the monkey house. The building remained unused for twenty years, until after the war it was demolished to give way for a garage development.

The monkey house was of great importance to the children of the neighbourhood, and on rainy days it became our community centre. We could swing from the rafters, or devise ball games against the rough wood; we could play darts or marbles or cards. Most games were highly competitive, which seemed as natural to us as the tests and rewards of Nunsthorpe School. We leant a cigarette card against the wall and then flicked our own cards turn by turn to try to knock it down. The player who succeeded picked up and kept all the cards previously thrown. Like all boys in country areas, we prized tough horse-chestnuts on a string which could break to pieces an opponent's conker, and so add to our tally of successes. I recall betting an acquaintance sixpence that I could score more than forty with three darts. I failed. I didn't have sixpence or any chance of finding such a large sum. For weeks the boy plagued me for payment and even haunted my dreams: I've never gambled for money since.

Outside the monkey house the fields were our playground in fine weather. We picked blackberries from the hedgerows, fetched home bluebells from Bradley Woods, and rolled down the hills in what we called the up-and-down field. We never lacked opportunity for self-expression.

When I drive through the new housing estates in Hulme and Moss Side at Manchester, so carefully and disastrously planned by specialists, I acknowledge that the deprived children of these areas inhabit an environment inferior to Nunsthorpe. When I visited Darjeeling in 1977, the sight of very poor children on a rocky hillside playing all kinds of games with sticks and stones reminded me of my childhood. Unfortunately, children of the television age reared in the cruel high-rise flats of inner cities need more opportunities for self-expression in their schools than we did in the 1930s.

The housing estates of the 1918–1939 period often adjoined large playing fields. Beside Nunsthorpe stood Barrett's, with bowls, tennis courts, football and cricket pitches. An area with goal-posts was left free for children to create their own games. Saturday mornings often ended for me in a scuffle as I fought to reclaim my ball when it was time to return home.

When I was nine I shared with another boy, Peter Kemp, a craze for climbing trees, and then daring each other to drop from high branches. One morning in bed I noticed my arches had fallen, but gave the matter little thought. We also loved playing with catapults, and hurled stones considerable distances. One evening a group of boys, including my brother's friend, Brian Larmour, barricaded themselves in the monkey house, while the rest of us attacked them from different angles. I can still see the stone from Brian Larmour's catapult whizzing towards me as I tried to dodge. I was hit in the mouth, my front tooth broken. I was never taken to doctor or dentist. I've often wondered why, although I presume my father could not afford the fees.

A.S. Neill says that 'in an ordinary school obedience is a virtue, so much so that few in later life can challenge anything'. As far as Nunsthorpe School is concerned, this is absurd. Outside school we stole apples from orchards, lit fires on waste lots and baked potatoes, explored the countryside on our bikes. I was only ten years old when with a friend called Eric I cycled to Louth, a round trip of thirty miles. On the way home, near North Thoresby, Eric grew tired, so I forged ahead. When I was out of sight, I hid behind a high hawthorn hedge and watched him peddle by, puffing and blowing and cursing. I then cycled up quietly behind him, and touched him on the shoulder. This prank gave me great pleasure, but he was not amused. When I arrived home hours later than expected my father was so relieved that he did not punish me. We were independent, and our strict school did not turn us into robots.

Another escapade brought more serious consequences. My father persuaded me to join the cubs at Flottergate Methodist Church in the centre of Grimsby. I detested uniforms and regimentation, so I preferred to spend my evenings cycling through the Wolds with Eric. One evening I hid my bike in long grass behind our house, and then caught the bus as usual to Flottergate. Soon afterwards I returned with Eric to retrieve my bike. Unfortunately my father witnessed my return from the back window, and hurried out to catch me red-handed. He sent me to bed in disgrace, insisting that my real crime had been that Eric and I had bought sweets with my weekly sixpence subscription for the cubs. I never returned to Flottergate.

Cycling for me became a means of escape from our house of sickness. Just as Nunsthorpe School was introducing me to poems and stories, to the power of language, my physical explorations took me further and further away from my home and from Grimsby. We often cycled to Cabourne, nine miles away, just to free-wheel down the only steep hill in the area, to rush at twenty miles an hour between the hedges at a time when there were few cars, few dangers on the roads.

On summer evenings I would cycle with Eric or some other friend to Irby Dales or Barnoldby le Beck, where a running stream with watercress or an old-fashioned water pump down a by-road became my possessions, part of my secret knowledge, independent of my home. I was attracted to hidden places, to sheltered chalk-pits, hollows, ditches, a special glade in Bradley

Woods. In E.M. Forster's *The Longest Journey* Rickie Elliot, a Cambridge undergraduate, discovers near Madingley a secluded dell, paved with grass and planted with fir-trees. When the snows melt, fiords and lagoons of clear water are left, like a miniature Norway or Switzerland. For Rickie, the dell becomes a kind of church, where you are free to do anything you like, but where anything you did would be transfigured. Irby Dales became such a church for me, where I felt my life expanding beyond the home I wanted to forget.

I cycled repeatedly to Cleethorpes, attracted by the great stretch of the Humber to Spurn Point and beyond to the North Sea. The sea has always fascinated me, with its ever-changing colours, emerald green, cobalt blue, indigo. After dark the lighthouse at Spurn winked at me across the water. I was not taught to swim until I went to secondary school. In the 1930s none of my parents, aunts and uncles could swim, and on our seaside outings we were limited to splashings at the tide's edge.

As a child I spent hours watching a variety of beach entertainments at Cleethorpes: pierrots, song-and-dance acts, Jimmy Slater's famous Super Follies. We would stand on the promenade and watch the shows from a distance without paying the admission fee for seats in the enclosure. Along the front an extraordinary array of booths and game parlours attracted us by their posters, though we could rarely afford to go inside. In the summer of 1939 Madame Zillah took £300 a week with her mind-reading and future-foretelling act on the sands. We children preferred Wonderland, the largest amusement park on the East coast, with its dodgems, dip-the-dips, water-chute, helter-skelter and ghost train.

Another great annual attraction was Grimsby's Statute Fair (the 'Stattus') which dates back to the town's first Charter, granted by King John in 1201. Huge crowds were attracted by swings, roundabouts, side-shows with animal freaks, boxing-booths, candy shops, games with darts or quoits with teddy-bear or doll prizes. I once discovered a machine with colours in a clock formation. You paid a penny, chose a colour, and whirled the clock. If the pointer rested on your colour you won twopence, threepence, or even ninepence, according to how frequently the colours appeared on the sequence. I discovered that when the machine stopped you could tap it gently until the pointer reached your chosen colour, and then push the button for your winnings. I returned home with sixteen pennies, a magnificent sum, which I hid under my clothes in a drawer so my father would not ask questions. I went back the next afternoon, but all the machines had been withdrawn.

My father could not pay hotel prices, so we spent our annual two-week holiday with Aunt Ethel in Penwortham in Preston, Lancashire. She had married a handsome Welsh electrical engineer, and settled in a semi-detached three-bedroom house. My Uncle Percy worked shifts, so when he was on nights our laughter would disturb his day-time sleep, and he was cross. But at Penwortham I was granted my one experience of a normal home. Like her sister, Aunt Ethel drew on deep reservoirs of kindness, transporting us by bus and train for day excursions to Southport and Blackpool, to public parks where we cavorted on swings and slides and climbing ropes. Most important, her daughter, Diana, attracted numerous friends who were encouraged to play in the garden. The fact that they were girls and three or four years younger than me added to the attraction. In contrast to my home at Laceby Road, people were continually coming and going, with cups of tea and glasses of mineral water always available. At Penwortham there was great festivity and easy informal friendships, which became my own preferred ideal.

At Nunsthorpe classes were streamed. I have no doubt that a system of setting for individual subjects would have helped the less favoured children in the lower groups to overcome any sense of failure. Eventually we were faced by the scholarship examination. Grimsby operated a system of selection at eleven for Wintringham Secondary School (what we would now call a grammar school), and then at thirteen for the Grimsby Technical School. Failure at eleven-plus meant the end of any hope of academic training. Transfer from Nunsthorpe Senior School after the age of eleven was almost unknown. Those children who passed for the Technical College could expect only vocational education. I have always been convinced that selection at eleven is too early, and that all systems must allow for late developers. My dislike of the eleven-plus exam does not mean that in principle I oppose selection, however.

In my year at Nunsthorpe eleven children passed the scholarship. The head, Mr Neil, came specially to the class-room to read out the list of successful candidates. As each name was called out, we were told to stand up. I remember looking down at the blank, despairing face of Audrey, a girl of some intelligence whose name was not on the list.

# 2

# *Co-Education in Wartime*

You would think the fury of aerial bombardment
Would rouse God to relent; the infinite spaces
Are still silent. He looks on shock-pried faces.
History, even, does not know what is meant.

Richard Eberhart

Like many other people, I recall vividly the events of 3 September 1939. After Chamberlain in his radio broadcast announced that we were at war with Germany, my father and I set off for our customary Sunday walk across the back fields. Near Toothill he chatted to an old friend, while I listened. They conversed in subdued tones, fearing an immediate outbreak of trench warfare, as in 1914. In the afternoon the gloom was dissipated by a visit from Uncle Albert, whose army service gave him the authority to pronounce that Germany would be defeated by Christmas. On that day my brother Derek was only fourteen, and I doubt whether it occurred to my father that before the war ended his eldest son would be conscripted.

That night the air-raid sirens sounded for the first time, a false alarm which I slept through. My father, an incurable optimist, refused to build an air-raid shelter, and during the raids of 1940 and 1941 stuck his head out of an upstairs window to watch for German bombers caught in the searchlights.

Those early weeks of the war were very happy for me. The head of my new school, Wintringham, feared that the school's dark Victorian buildings, near the centre of Grimsby, would be in danger from daylight bombing raids. He decided to move the whole school to Highfield, a farm near Barrett's Recreation Ground. Wooden huts were erected, partly by the teachers themselves; this construction work took about six weeks, during which we were granted an unscheduled holiday. When people say children would be bored if there were no school, I can categorically reply that we were joyous, free to roam the fields and hide in bracken when aeroplanes (in fact British) flew low overhead.

When the huts were ready there were insufficient class-rooms, so we settled down to a makeshift regime, with half the school attending in the morning and half in the afternoon. The huts had been constructed too hastily, so the roofs leaked, particularly after falls of snow. We watched with delight as the drops grew worse, pinging into buckets, until the teachers were forced to send us home. In the wooden class-rooms the heating was confined to one smoky coke-stove. Miss Greenfield, our white-haired history teacher, made us jump up and down every fifteen minutes to restore circulation. Lessons were disturbed by air-raid drill, when we evacuated to brick shelters and played with hose-pipes, and by gas-mask practice. When I pulled my gas-mask over my face I could not breathe, so during drills I stuck a finger in the rubber over my cheek to let in the air. This seemed to me more sensible, in my shyness, than to draw the teacher's attention to my plight. After two years, when daylight raids failed to materialise, the senior school returned to Eleanor Street, near the centre.

In January 1941, I started once again to keep a diary, and this time I lasted out the whole year. The diary begins, ominously, with a record of 'Sirens this year'. On Wednesday, 1 January, the siren sounded at 6.20 p.m., to be followed by the All Clear at 7.10 p.m. At 10.30 p.m. the night was again disrupted by wailing air-raid sirens, and this time the relief of the All Clear was not heard until 1 a.m. Such interruptions of our sleep were normal.

Grimsby was not bombed as badly as Hull or Coventry, but its position near the mouth of the Humber meant that German bombers used the river's sheen as a guide to their destinations inland. At the entrance to the Humber stood two heavily fortified structures. Bull Fort was about two miles south of Spurn Lighthouse, while Haile Sand Fort was less than a mile offshore from Humberstone, where we went for excursions when

I was a child. Their construction, planned in 1913, was not completed until 1918, too late to be of any use in the Great War; they became of considerable strategic importance after 1939. Their object was the defence of the Humber, with an anti-submarine chain linking them. In the 1930s, as I paddled at the tide's edge at Humberstone, I would gaze in awe at these huge inverted buckets of steel, capped with concrete. The forts stood forty-five feet above the high waterline, with three floors and a basement, roughly eighty-two feet in diameter. I used to long to walk out to Haile Sand Fort, but even at low tide this was dangerous. During the Second World War they carried garrisons of 200 men, and were equipped with six-inch and six-pounder guns. They were subject to continual attack from German planes, U-boats and E-boats. There were also many other anti-aircraft batteries on the Lincolnshire coast, near the boating lake at Cleethorpes, and, only a mile from my home, at Broadway near Bradley Cross Roads. I used to cycle to these two batteries to watch the men at drill, loading the shells into the breach, and smartly standing back as the gun jerked backwards.

My brother and I shared a bedroom, with two single beds, at the back of the house, overlooking fields and the monkey house. After the air-raid siren sounded at nights I would lie very quiet, listening to the distant mutterings of the guns from the forts at the mouth of the Humber. I prayed that the bombers would continue on their way inland, and leave us undisturbed. When we peered out the bedroom window we could see the search-lights interweaving their shafts over Grimsby Docks, and sometimes an enemy flare would light up the whole sky. Laceby Road was two miles inland from the docks, so usually, as the noises moved down river towards Hull, we would stay in bed.

When the battery at Broadway opened up, however, we would rush downstairs, while the windows rattled, and the noise grew deafening. Early in 1940 I heard for the first time the whistling of two bombs which landed harmlessly in mud near Bradley Cross Roads Methodist Church. As I heard this swishing sound I reminded myself of the supposed fact that because of the time noise takes to travel you do not hear the bomb which kills you. The flight path for German bombers en route to Grimsby Docks lay over Laceby Road. We could crouch down over the electric fire, listening to the beat of Heinkel engines growing louder and louder. As the sound diminished over the back fields, we relaxed until the approach of the next plane made us tense once again. I consoled myself that the aircraft would be two miles off target if they dropped a bomb on us. I knew there were mistakes, though, as a huge crater in a road only half-a-mile away proved to me one day as I cycled to school. My father had to spend nights as a fire-watcher in Royal Dock Chambers, near the fish-docks, where his firm, Nickerson and Company, rented offices. After particularly bad raids, I would look across the fields at the fires which lit up the sky over the Docks, the huge bulk of Spiller's Flour Mill silhouetted against the flames, and wonder if he was dead. The possibility excited rather than upset me.

One night I awoke from a deep sleep to find the bedroom as light as day from German flares. My father rushed me downstairs; as Broadway guns shattered the silence, we cowered under the heavy mahogany table in the front room, while a German bomber, for no explicable reason, machine-gunned Laceby Road. A neighbour was killed at a doorway opposite our house. My father never talked about such tragedies, and I only found this out weeks later. On my way to school next day I was jealous of friends whose houses boasted bullet scars; we had not been hit. During those raids I learnt the meaning of fear. I often thought how wonderful it would be to go to bed knowing there would be no air-raid. My war memories make me a happy man, for even today I appreciate pleasures such as sleeping at night without the fear of bombs.

After my mother died I was looked after for a few weeks by a long-serving maid, Barbara Austen, whom I adored. Unfortunately for me she was supplanted by my Aunt Suie, my father's sister, a small gaunt spinster who welcomed this escape from her previous work as a companion and housekeeper in middle-class families. Sharp-tongued and short-tempered, she never seemed to care for me. She never touched or kissed me, and I began increasingly to spend as much time as possible away from home. At Christmas in 1939 my father withdrew from the family guests into our back sitting-room, where I joined him, knowing how desperately he missed my mother. Aunt Suie entered the room to chide him for not entertaining his guests, and there followed a noisy argument.

Such scenes became commonplace in 1942, when my father started courting a young widow, Nellie Clarkson, who sang in the choir at Flottergate Methodist Church, and had worked as a cashier in a local drapery shop. She had one daughter, Christine, aged five. When Aunt Suie realized she was to lose her safe berth and would have to return to work, she was furious.

The marriage took place in August at Welholm Congregational Church after a courtship lasting less than a year. Only months after the wedding the house was riven by new conflicts, initially caused by my brother. At the end of 1942 he received his army call-up papers. He had left Wintringham at the age of fifteen, before the School Certificate Examination, to take up a position as clerk at Forrester-Boyd, Chartered Accountants in the centre of Grimsby. My father's decision that Derek should leave school proved an absurd error. Because of his memories of the unemployed (his brother Albert had great difficulty in finding work after he left the army at the end of the 1914–18 war) my father thought the opening at Forrester-Boyd was too good to be missed. If he had stayed at school for one more year Derek's School Certificate would have given him exemption from the Preliminary Accountancy examinations. Instead he was forced to attend night classes after work for nearly three years, which meant he slaved away in our back bedroom with virtually no social life. In the exam he took first place in all England. He had registered with the Institute of Incorporated Accountants, having chosen this qualification because he could not afford to take articles at Forrester-Boyd, for no pay, as required by the more prestigious Institute of Chartered Accountants.

After my mother died, when he was thirteen, Derek's academic work suffered, and for one term he was bottom of the class; but he had great force of will, and soon pulled himself together. Alone in his evening studies, while his friends were still at school, he developed a vigorous independence of mind, and so when his army call-up papers arrived he determined to register as a conscientious objector. Derek had no religious beliefs, but held that it was absolutely wrong to kill.

My new stepmother, whom I called Auntie Rene, opposed

this decision vehemently, and my father too was distressed and uncomprehending. There were shouting matches over the mid-day meal, and I would often set off on my bike for afternoon school with tears in my eyes. But my brother was inflexible, and after appearing in court at Lincoln was allowed to join the Non-Combatant Corps. He spent his army service in England, mainly working as a clerk in prisoner-of-war camps. These years in the N.C.C. were lonely and hard, for he was ostracized and treated with contempt. On more than one occasion, when he entered a cafe, he was bundled back out onto the road, and cuffed and spat at. Always an eccentric, on several occasions he took a little torch to the cinema so he could read a book while waiting for the main feature film. In the army he started Gibbon's *Decline and Fall*, and would read it while waiting for roll-call on cold, early morning parades.

After he had departed for service in the N.C.C., I enjoyed taking possession of our bedroom for myself, but the new marriage never recovered from this early upset. A baby was stillborn during an air-raid. My father was forty-five and Rene thirty-six when they married. He was middle-aged, tired by overwork, and after my mother's death abjured company. Rene was at the centre of Methodist social life, loved singing in choirs, and was often invited out by herself, leaving her husband to look after her young daughter. It was a recipe for conflict. I became accustomed to long-drawn-out battles of tongues, particularly soon after they retired to bed. I longed for a divorce, but because of their Methodist background they feared scandal. I often became involved in their disputes, when, for example, they arrived home to find that, wrapped up in my books, I had allowed the fire to die down.

When I was sixteen I made up my mind never to become involved in their arguments again, to try to keep the peace, and to leave home as soon as financially possible. These painful nightly outbursts frightened me. To this day I would do almost anything to avoid the slightest altercation; my wife and I, after thirty-six years of marriage, have never exchanged a cross word (except, I must confess, a few times when confronted by a tense driving situation in our car). It amazes me that someone as averse to conflict as I am should have been at the centre of so much public controversy.

From 1942 until I was conscripted into the army in 1947 I kept away from home as much as possible, and stopped inviting friends to the house. The night before I was married, in 1954, I entertained three friends from Cambridge, Tony Dyson, Geoff Roberts and his new wife, Helen, together with my fiancée, to dinner at the Kingsway Hotel in Cleethorpes. After dinner I took them for a drive to view the gentle, undulating Lincolnshire Wolds. On the way back I needed to pick up a book from Laceby Road to hand to one of my friends. After I stopped the car I did not invite them into the house to meet my father. Later he told me he was made miserable by this, but it had not occurred to me to introduce them to him. By 1954 many years had passed since I last invited any friends (except my fiancée) into the house.

I created a separate life, partly at church but mainly through my friends at Wintringham. Retrospectively I regard my adolescence as very happy. Outside the home I committed myself to every available social, cultural and sporting activity with an almost fanatical determination to live as fully as possible.

At Bradley Cross Roads Methodist Church I eventually graduated as a Sunday School teacher. This work involved giving short talks, such as a five-minute introduction to the life of Henry Francis Lyte, who wrote 'Abide with me'. The puritanism of the Methodist church penetrated deep into my blood; I have never completely rid myself of this inheritance. When I go on holiday I justify my pleasure as a valuable preparation for work on my return. My year in California in 1964 helped me to become more relaxed, less earnest, but such a puritan upbringing can never be entirely eradicated.

I found a boys' club in the centre of Grimsby where I could play billiards and table tennis. The penalty was that membership involved attendance at King's Terrace Mission in Garden Street on one Sunday evening per month. I soon began to attend regularly, encouraged by Mr Dalby, a church leader. When I was fourteen he acted as a surrogate father for me, taking me on excursions to Cleethorpes or Mablethorpe, encouraging me to help him count the Sunday collections and keep the financial records. After a few piano lessons at the age of eleven from my Uncle Norman, husband of one of my father's sisters, I had learnt to play the air of all the hymns in the Methodist hymnal, and to follow this with one finger of the left hand. When the organist was absent I accompanied the singing, pumping away with my feet to keep the music flowing. Mr Dalby was unmarried, a manual labourer, who sponsored a series of boys in this fashion. Today we would take it for granted that he was homosexual, but I witnessed no sign of it. In those days the word 'homosexual' was never used in the Grimsby non-conformist co-educational circles in which I moved, and few people gave the matter a thought. Indeed most of us hardly knew the phenomenon existed. Mr Dalby was an immensely kind man, devoted to King's Terrace Mission, and to his evangelical faith. He never touched the boys he befriended.

The worshippers at King's Terrace Mission were all working-class, and some were very poor. The chapel was destroyed long ago. The sermons were often rant. On one occasion a British Israelite, who believed the lost tribe came to Britain, had been invited by mistake, and this zealot's sermon lasted fifty minutes. Half way through a lady in the front row broke into uncontrollable laughter. She walked out down the centre of the aisle, with her hand over her mouth, and the preacher hurling insults at her back.

Several older people in the congregation smelt, particularly on hot summer evenings; at first I was nauseated, but they were all very kind to me. I learnt to appreciate the genuine friendliness of the evangelicals, even as I began to lose my faith in their Christian dogmas. I learnt from these old people the true meaning of love. When later I read T.S. Eliot's *Murder in the Cathedral*, in which the Chorus of Canterbury women are said to be 'living and partly living', I was angry at Eliot's sense of superiority. The regulars at King's Terrace Mission sang the last verse of their favourite hymns twice, such as 'Will your anchor hold in the storms of life, When the clouds unfold their wings of strife?' They stood up to offer impromptu prayers (very boring) and helped each other out when times were hard. My belief was, and still is, that they knew more about Christian love than T.S. Eliot's Thomas Becket: they had the right to sing about their hopes of paradise.

At Bradley Cross Roads Methodist Church preachers often invited members of the congregation to come up to the front to bear witness that they had been saved. On one occasion no one came forward. Afterwards, as I was counting the collection, the preacher thrust a pamphlet into my hand, and asked me to bear witness. I was far too diffident to oppose his will, so replied in the affirmative, and then escaped into the night as soon as possible. The following week I received a long emotional letter from the preacher congratulating me on my decision, and welcoming me into the blessed company of the elect. As my father insisted on reading this letter, I was both enraged and embarrassed.

As months went by I drifted away from the churches both at King's Terrace and Bradley Cross Roads. By the age of sixteen I found it impossible to believe in the physical reality of the Resurrection. Increasingly too I could not understand how a good creator could be responsible for the suffering of animals or children. In the sixth form I read Aldous Huxley's *Point Counterpoint*, with its bitter denunciation of a world in which a child can suffer excruciating pain before dying of meningitis. But I never forgot what the old people at King's Terrace taught me about love. For the rest of my life I have been half in, half out of the Christian Church, deeply religious in my belief that life has ultimate meaning, in despair at the sermons I have heard in Methodist chapels; there the preacher's rhetoric glossed so easily over the problem of pain, the apparent meaninglessness of the suffering of little children.

During those years I felt most at home while I was at school. I was usually in the top three or four in my class, so this helped my self-confidence. At Wintringham, a co-educational secondary school not granted the prestigious title of 'grammar' school until after the 1944 Education Act, my educational opportunities did not rival those of famous schools such as Winchester or Manchester Grammar. In its out-of-the-way situation at the end of a railway line, the school did not attract the most ambitious teachers; after the outbreak of war all the young men under forty were called up. The arrangements at Highfield reduced the time available for lessons. Our French teacher, Mr Wheatley, complained that our whole year was behind because the foundations of the subject were never properly laid in the truncated first year.

Teaching was often just rote learning, followed by long tests while the teacher watched us from behind his or her desk. When

I was in the sixth form, the history teacher spent the lessons reading aloud from the textbook on Tudors and Stuarts, making occasional comments as she went along. We were also made to specialize too early. I abandoned Physics and Chemistry at the age of thirteen; we learnt to read French and German, but were given few opportunities to speak the languages. I studied Latin only in the sixth form, an enforced labour because Latin was an entry requirement for university courses in English. I passed the school certificate examination in one year, and then took a subsidiary exam in Latin for Higher School Certificate. With my natural ability in mathematics I found the precision of Latin grammar easy to comprehend, although a year after I left school I had forgotten almost all the Latin I had learnt.

The teachers were friendly, however, and the co-educational atmosphere created easy, informal relationships between boys and girls, children and staff. In my second year a new headmaster, Dr J.H. Walter, imposed what were thought to be progressive methods of teaching. The time-table was built on a new framework, day one to day six, so that if Friday was day five, Monday would be day six, Tuesday day one and so on. This meant that the sports afternoon kept changing, and double periods in Art, for example, did not appear for some children regularly and tediously every Friday afternoon when they were tired. Day six afternoon was assigned to cultural activities. A debating society offered me the opportunity to declaim a couple of formal speeches; but in general the staff were not ready for this liberal regime. Music lessons from Mr Wheeler (notorious because he smelt of alcohol after lunch) often consisted of gramophone records of popular classical music, and nothing else.

When I was in the sixth form, my English teacher, Miss Jesse Bemrose, invited us to choose any work of literature we liked for discussion in the day six slot. In the school library I had discovered *The Waste Land*, and responded immediately to its rhythms and imagery, although I could not understand their meaning. When I asked if we might discuss *The Waste Land*, Miss Bemrose looked surprised. I doubt whether she had read any T.S. Eliot. Next week she gave me a strange look, and announced that instead of *The Waste Land* we would discuss the medieval morality play.

Presumably the clerk carbuncular's seduction of the typist in *The Waste Land* was thought unsuitable.

Miss Bemrose was a dedicated teacher, however, organizing a play reading society in the evenings, and an annual Shakespeare production. I took part in this on three occasions, playing Borachio, a minor villain in *Much Ado About Nothing*, the Welsh Parson Evans in *The Merry Wives of Windsor*, and Theseus in *Midsummer Night's Dream*. The boy who played Benedick in *Much Ado* later became a famous actor, taking part in successful television drama, after changing his name from Patrick Cheeseman to Patrick Wymark. In *Much Ado*, Borachio is accused of seducing Margaret in the guise of Hero (after one look at me at the age of fifteen the audience would have known I was innocent of the charge), and Claudio is tricked into repudiating his future bride, Hero, at the church ceremony. Later, Benedick, Claudio's friend, falls in love with Beatrice, and demands that she should ask him any favour; 'Kill Claudio!' she replies. For Miss Bemrose these words changed the whole tone of the play, and she rehearsed them repeatedly. I learnt more about Shakespeare from taking part in this play than from her repetition in class of conventional ideas taken from the critics.

In my first year at Wintringham we attended compulsory swimming lessons in the school baths. Mr Latto, a young martinet, forced us to duck our heads under water during the very first lesson; during the third lesson those who could not dive were made to lie on their stomachs at the edge, and then he gripped our legs like the handles of a wheel-barrow and trundled us head first into the water. I learnt to fear swimming lessons, and was glad when Mr Latto disappeared for the war. Eventually I taught myself to swim. In the large open-air bathing pool at Cleethorpes I managed to swim breast-stroke in a yellow rubber-ring, and soon could cover thirty or forty yards without difficulty. I crossed the deep-end in this fashion, before I dared take my feet off the ground without the rubber-ring. I tremble to think what would have happened if for some reason the ring had deflated. By the age of thirteen I loved swimming, and on Saturday mornings cycled to Orwell Street Swimming Baths, hoping to change quickly and be the first to dive in.

Tennis was only played by the girls at Wintringham, but I learnt

to play in the evenings at Barrett's; with a good eye and fast
footwork I became one of the best players in the school. With
considerable confidence, a group of us entered for the under-18
county championships at Lincoln. In our sparsely populated county
there could not be many boys who played tennis. So sure was I
of winning the trophy I had already decided where to place it in
my bedroom. At Barrett's the grass courts were very bumpy, so it
was wise to take the ball late so you could react to the wayward
bounce. We learnt by trial and error, and none of us took lessons.
At Lincoln my opponent in the first round was a public school
boy from Grantham (Mrs Thatcher's birthplace). I was wearing
long white flannels and old tennis shoes streakily blancoed. He
wore carefully pressed white shorts, and played with an expensive
racquet. He had been taught to play strokes properly, hit the ball
early and hard, and all my scampering along the back line proved
of no avail. The courts at Eastgate lie close to the cathedral; its
towers looked down on me with disdain as I mis-hit and poked
my way to defeat: I lost 6–2, 6–2. This was my first meeting with
a public school product, and I was amazed by his self-confidence.
For the first time I became aware that Wintringham and Grimsby
were not the whole world.

Mr Wilson, our games master, insisted on discipline. He
instructed us that when chosen to play for a school team on
Saturday afternoon we should turn up whatever the weather,
even if there were two feet of snow. We took his regime for
granted, and I was never late. Mr Wilson also acted as Captain
of the Officers' Training Corps, and I am proud that with only
three other boys in my year I refused to enlist. We were forced
instead to participate in country dancing lessons with the girls,
a fate which at the age of fourteen embarrassed me but already
seemed not altogether too unpleasant. Like most of my friends,
from the fifth year onwards I became obsessed with girls, falling
in love once a week. Ballroom dancing lessons were held in the
gymnasium, to prepare for the annual Christmas dance. Boys and
girls rarely went out with each other regularly, and only one or
two couples formed a permanent relationship. A year after I left, a
sixth-form girl with a regular boyfriend became pregnant. We were
all shocked; we had not believed such goings-on were possible.

I attended all the school dances, and when in the sixth form spent every Saturday evening at a dance in a church hall at Scartho. At least the old quicksteps and waltzes, however lugubrious the music, gave me the opportunity to dance with any girl I chose. For a girl to refuse an offer to dance was almost unknown. Conversation was stilted, but by the time I was eighteen I found no difficulty in making conversation with strangers.

Wintringham's courtship rituals now seem innocent and antiquated. You tried to dance the last waltz with the girl of your choice, and then asked her if you might accompany her home. If she agreed, you might be allowed to put your arm around her waist, and to kiss her at the gate. There the relationship usually ended. My first success in this game took place after a school dance when I was sixteen. I was no Don Juan, however; at the gate of the girl's house I stood nervously for several moments, wishing the occasional passer-by would disappear. Eventually my courage evaporated, and I fled, leaving the girl unkissed. But on the way home this trivial success exhilarated me, like the outburst of profane joy experienced by Stephen Dedalus in Joyce's *Portrait of the Artist as a Young Man*, when he witnesses a girl wading in a rivulet, like a strange and beautiful seabird. When in the sixth form I read this novel, I found Stephen's adolescent desires exactly like my own – his epiphanies, his longing to travel far away from home, to make himself an artist, 'to forge in the smithy of my soul the uncreated conscience of my race'.

After this first failure I was more successful in my attempts at courtship, often walking a girl home for two or three miles in the wrong direction for me, and then jogging home through the night, intoxicated by my success. Beside the lake in People's Park, off Weelsby Road, I would sometimes meet my friends after we had taken girls home. We flicked stones into the water, disturbing the moonlight, and felt very pleased with ourselves. Even during the black-out in the war, girls as well as boys walked about quite safely after dark. I never heard of anyone being attacked, or even considered the possibility. Today Grimsby is different; no sensible girl walks alone late at night.

In the sixth form I learnt to talk at ease with girls, and for me, a shy not particularly good-looking boy, this facility was a great boon. Later at Cambridge I felt very superior to grammar and public school boys who were tongue-tied when a girl came into the room. I still believe in co-education, even now that manners are more relaxed. I made a fool of myself when I was sixteen, whereas many of my friends were committing the same absurdities in their mid-twenties; several made hasty, foolish marriages. In his unfinished poem, 'The Dance', Philip Larkin describes a function at Hull University in 1962 or 1963 at which I must have been present. By this time he was in his late thirties, yet he confesses his inability to talk at ease with the woman he is pursuing ('And I wish desperately for qualities Moments like this demand, and which I lack'). By this time I was married with three children. Philip was an excessively shy man, of course, but if I had not attended a co-educational school I might have remained similarly maladroit.

At the age of fourteen I decided I wanted to become a teacher. It was the only profession I knew anything about. One evening I nervously broached this subject with my father, and told him I wished to stay on into the sixth form. The departure of younger men to war had opened up opportunities for him, and he had become secretary and director of Nickerson and Company Ltd., so he had sufficient money not to oppose my plans. Although disappointed because he wanted me to work in a bank, after a day of reflection he agreed. Mathematics was my best subject at school, but I wanted to teach English Literature, my secret passion.

Much of my response to literature was something I kept to myself, unconnected to my studies in the class-room. My imagination was first seized by great literature when at the age of thirteen I read *Great Expectations*; for weeks my thoughts were haunted by the convict Magwitch and the half-crazed Miss Havisham. In the fourth and fifth forms I undertook a course in novel reading for myself, and learnt to enjoy Sir Walter Scott, Dickens, Galsworthy, Charles Reade and Trollope. I never discussed my enthusiasms with anyone else, though I had plenty of friends, and my secret reading programmes involved some peculiar habits. To skip seemed to me a sin, and so I read every sentence with care. If my attention wandered, when reading a page of Scott's *The Bride of Lammermoor*, for example, I would conscientiously start again from the top of the page. Not necessarily a bad practice, this inculcated in me the habit of close reading.

In a red notebook I kept a record of each book, with brief critical comments and a grade: excellent, very good, good, satisfactory and poor.

Among books I read in the sixth form, Pope's *Essay on Criticism*, George Eliot's *Silas Marner* and F.R. Leavis's *Revaluation* shared the distinction of being rated 'poor'. These critical comments were trivial, but the whole venture satisfied the puritan instincts inflicted on me by my Methodist upbringing. I felt that I was collecting great books rather like postage stamps, so investing for future profit in the educational world. Fortunately I enjoyed a good deal; at the same time, though, my natural responses were perverted by this sense of preparing for some final test, to be adjudicated by future examiners, by society or by God – I wasn't sure who. My main problem was that my commitment to reading never found expression in school work, and so I received no advice or criticism. My brother provided some opportunities for talking about books, but he was away in the army for most of my adolescence. My father and stepmother were not readers, so my enthusiasms were never shared. Rather like Leonard Bast in Forster's *Howards End*, my selection of books was dominated by my belief that I must read the classics. I therefore ploughed my way through Carlyle, Ruskin, Hazlitt and Macaulay, not enjoying them very much, but feeling there must be profit in it for me somewhere.

This secret life became even more important to me in the sixth form. When I read Milton the experience was like religious conversion. During those years at the end of the war, I used to work in the evenings in a back bedroom, only heated in winter by a small one-bar electric fire. I used to place it near my feet for a quarter of an hour or so, and then on the table to warm my hands. My room overlooked a flat Lincolnshire landscape, with fields often waterlogged after rain, and about half a mile away a farm partially obscured by a line of fir-trees. In this room I enjoyed much adolescent self-pity and romantic inspiration. I read Milton's *Il Penseroso*, and then proceeded through *Lycidas* to the famous examples of personal feeling in *Paradise Lost*. Although I had previously studied Wilfred Owen and Siegfried Sassoon for the matriculation examination, this was my first absorbing experience of poetry. My obsession with Milton recalled my earlier reaction to *Great Expectations*. I learnt off by heart lines from *Il Penseroso*:

> But let my due feet never fail
> To walk the studious cloister's pale,
> And love the high embowed roof,
> With antique pillars massy-proof,
> And storied windows richly dight,
> Casting a dim religious light.

Captivated by their heavy, melancholic rhythm, I had little idea what visual picture was intended. I developed a theory that aesthetic experience derived not from the 'content' of the poem, but from the poet's 'mood in creation'. The style of the poem conveyed the poet's transcendental insights into truth, beauty and goodness, and it did not matter whether he was describing a garden, a cathedral or an individual. This theory mattered a great deal to me because it explained my own aesthetic experience. Reading Milton constituted for me what Wordsworth called 'a spot of time', an entry into a brave, new world, an epiphany. At such times, like so many adolescents, I felt overcome with exaltation, which must be expressed in both literature and life. For me this creative mood came first, and afterwards I tried to find a particular mode of expression for it.

I enjoyed many such 'spots of time' in my teens – listening to Brahms or Rossini, reading Milton or Marvell or Shakespeare, walking home from a dance gazing through branches at the stars. Such Wordsworthian experiences are common, of course. As an undergraduate at Cambridge, Sylvia Plath claimed that the stimulus of literature and music induced mystical experiences. After an Advent service at King's College Chapel she connected her feelings with moments when literature struck her hard: 'as if an angel had hauled me by the hair in a shiver of gooseflesh'. For me it seemed extraordinary that the most educational and fulfilling experiences of my life were never mentioned or expressed at school.

At this time, as might be expected, I began to write verse, always sonnets at first because this was almost the only form I knew much about. Later I tried both free and blank verse. An early sonnet included these haunting lines:

> The wailing howl of some stray dog
> Reminds me of the dead.

I was deeply moved by my own callow, lyrical fancies, and felt reasonably certain that I was destined to become a genius. I showed my poems to no one, and was slightly ashamed of them, another curious result of my grammar school education. Just once I determined to express my secret thoughts in a school essay. We had been studying Sidney's *Apologie for Poetrie*, which helped me to articulate more precisely my Platonic idea of art. I began my essay in my usual fashion, but towards the end I inserted two paragraphs in which I explained my theory about the artist's 'mood in creation', 'spots of time' and the transcendental value of aesthetic experience. I found these thoughts difficult to explain, for I had never tried to put them into prose before, and so I crossed words out and even ruled out a whole sentence, an unusual practice for me. The two paragraphs thus stood out from the others. I handed in the essay with some trepidation, and waited nervously for its return, finding myself wishing I had not exposed myself in this manner. When the essay was returned no comment had been written near the two paragraphs. At the bottom I received a good mark and a brief remark, which I now forget. I never again tried to express my real feelings in a sixth-form essay.

Although at Wintringham study of set books provided me with useful information and widened my literary horizons, I was never encouraged to write verse or fiction or to use any form except the traditional essay; this, of course, was typical of secondary schools at that time. Essays were marked with 'A', 'B' or 'C', with comments usually not extending beyond a couple of sentences, and we were never asked to revise or to prepare new drafts. In the sixth form we were occasionally encouraged to take part in a seminar, but for most of my school career discussion was almost unknown during lessons in class.

My own first contacts with university life were not fortunate.

When I was in my second year in the sixth form, I travelled to London to be interviewed by Professor Sisson of University College. After he had welcomed me he asked: 'Are you interested in philology?' After a short pause I nervously admitted I did not know what the word meant. He motioned towards a dictionary on a shelf behind me. After a few desperate moments worrying whether the word really did begin with 'ph', I found 'philology', and looked up at the Professor. There was a silence, so I replaced the dictionary; he then asked me for the definition.

The interview then went from bad to worse, and I was not surprised when University College turned me down. Like many grammar school students I had received almost no advice on how to conduct myself during an interview, and afterwards felt furious that my answers were so brief and foolish. Professor Sisson's incompetence as an interviewer was very common in the universities of those days.

During my second year in the sixth form my only other application was to King's College, London. I was not granted an interview, and in early October after my Higher School Certificate results were known I received a short circular letter rejecting me. My H.S.C. results were a great disappointment to me. I had worked hard, obeyed my teachers' instructions, and could not understand why I had scored only 'B' in English and History and 'C' in French. In the Shakespeare paper I scored only fifty-six per cent, and in my special period paper on Elizabethan England fifty-one per cent, marks lower than those now demanded for entry by my own English department at Manchester. I had compiled copious notes on Bradley's *Shakespeare's Tragedies* and the appropriate Granville Barker *Prefaces*, and regurgitated them in the examination. I had no knowledge of *Scrutiny* or the work of L.C. Knights. At this time it never occurred to me that any other policy was possible. In the sixth form I had learnt to distrust my own judgment, and to prefer secondhand material. On one occasion I was required to write an essay on Pope's *Essay on Criticism*. I detested Pope, and composed a vigorous condemnation of his cold, self-conscious style. I preferred the exuberance of Shelley. My teacher gave me the lowest mark I ever received for a sixth-form essay, and tried to explain to me what I had missed. His efforts were unavailing, for I was not sufficiently mature at this time to respond to Pope, and remained convinced he was dull. I learnt from this episode that I must repeat my teacher's views in the exam and repress my own. This sequence of events is still commonplace among sixth formers studying English 'A' level.

Although the war was over, conscription still existed, so after the H.S.C results were published I would be forced to join the army within a couple of months. I applied for deferment to take university scholarships, and with a vanity which now amazes me I began to study the Oxbridge entry requirements. These arrangements have now been abandoned, but they gave Oxbridge dons the opportunity to look carefully at students from unusual backgrounds. Today my low scores at H.S.C. would have made entry impossible. My plan was to be offered a place I could take up after my two years in the forces. My one success in H.S.C. had been in the practical criticism paper, where I scored seventy-six per cent. In discussing passages of prose and verse I found it easy to express my response to literature. I discovered that the scholarship papers at Oxford were very similar to H.S.C., with general questions on Chaucer, Shakespeare and Milton, and I still had little idea how to attain high marks in this kind of exercise. Instead I turned to Cambridge, where practical criticism and the dating of unseen passages of prose and verse were major elements in the papers of some groups of Colleges. I chose the examinations set by Jesus and Pembroke Colleges, for these included most questions of this kind. The exams took place in early December, so I was able to devote three months to preparation. I particularly concentrated on the dating question, and found this work stimulating and enlightening. Previously I had known something about Elizabethans and Romantics, but the intervening periods rested under a haze. To date passages accurately demands not only wide reading and knowledge of the development of style, but also some awareness of economic, social and political history, and the changing ideas in philosophy and theology. I could find few books to assist me with this question, and so began to make chronological tables and to collect specimen prose and verse from each period. All this work I carried out on my own, and I was forced to read unfamiliar poems and to develop ideas for myself.

In another regular question, a number of passages from Shakespeare's plays were to be analysed and assigned to their correct periods in his development. I read all Shakespeare's plays and examined their verse structure with care. Fortunately Miss Bemrose possessed an intimate understanding of Shakespeare's language, and allocated one lesson a week to personal tuition on this topic. Over-worked sixth-form teachers will appreciate her generosity, and I owe her a great deal. By the end of November I was ready, with much revision completed for the compulsory Latin and French questions, the Chaucer translations and the few required literary questions on major authors.

I determined that for this exam I would adopt a new policy. Instead of regurgitating the ideas of my teacher and the famous critics, I would reveal my secret life. In the interviews I would not remain silent, but explain in detail why the study of literature had become so important for me. In the written papers I would express my enthusiasms, the secret system of thought I had worked out in my cold bedroom. I travelled down to Cambridge, where all candidates were required to assemble, resolved to be as daring and provocative as possible. After my average H.S.C. results what had I to lose?

I have heard some university teachers describe the four or five days of the entrance examination as like an entry into Hell. Lonely, with butterflies in the stomach, they felt like country cousins among the other candidates, mostly from public schools, all apparently so knowledgeable and sophisticated. My own wretchedness lasted a long half day, until it was ended by a stroke of luck. The man in the next room, called Peter Ahn, was full of self-confidence, and years ahead of me in maturity. He deliberately befriended me, and my short visit became an entry into the world of intellect of which I had always dreamed; we talked and argued. My brother, who was stationed near Norwich, came up one afternoon and showed us round the Colleges. We walked everywhere, particularly to the bookshops, to David's where I bought cheap and useless eighteenth-century editions, fingering their covers with reverence. Peter and I delighted in a room of our own, and in the prospects of liberty suddenly revealed. I felt like David Copperfield with Steerforth.

The night before the Shakespeare paper, my new friend was

very put out when I started discussing the compulsory question on Shakespeare's development of style. He had not heard of this question, and though he had read most of Shakespeare's plays he had never thought seriously about their chronological sequence. He asked if he might take my notes to bed with him. I'm glad to say that I agreed, and I hope my face did not show how much I was feeling that this was a competitive examination. Peter had been sent to Cambridge by his school with little advice on what to expect, and he started each paper almost totally ignorant of its nature. When the results were announced, my friend's name appeared nowhere, and I never saw him again. When I went up to Cambridge, after conscription, I discovered he had gone up before me and taken a first in geography.

In contrast, all my preparations paid off. The examination took place in the Old Library at Pembroke, and there were about 100 candidates. After some initial difficulty with the high quality, unlined paper which I had never used before, I settled down to my enthusiasms. The practical criticism and dating papers were as I expected, but the Shakespeare paper started with a surprise. In the question on the development of his style, the rubric was changed from a straightforward request for analysis of passages to these tantalizing words: 'If the following passages were only ascribed to Shakespeare on internal evidence, at what period in his writing would you take them to have been written? Comment on their verse, imagery and literary merit, pointing out whatever seems to you to be authentically Shakespearian.' I had carefully studied all the long speeches in Shakespeare, and was surprised that I could not recognise any of the three passages set. The words 'authentically Shakespearian' gave me a clue, so I hazarded correctly that the passages were not by Shakespeare. I tried to demonstrate this by internal evidence, concluding tentatively that they might be by contemporary dramatists. On the three-hour essay paper, among topics such as 'The future of the English countryside' I found 'The artist as citizen'. I inserted my concept of the artist's 'mood in creation' and its social value in moving readers toward truth, goodness and beauty.

Winners of awards were sent telegrams, and we were told the day these would be dispatched. Nothing happened until the early evening, when suddenly there was a telegram boy at the door. 'It must be from Derek,' my father guessed. 'It had better not be,' I replied, and rushed to the door to find that I had been awarded an open exhibition. This was worth only forty pounds a year, but the award meant I would also receive implementation for fees and maintenance from the government. I assured my father that the money would cover all my needs, but he was so delighted he was determined to make any necessary sacrifice.

# 3
# *Teaching in the Army*

All day it has rained, and we on the edge of the moors
Have sprawled in our bell-tents, moody and dull as boors,
Groundsheets and blankets spread on the muddy ground . . .

Alun Lewis

On Thursday 20 February, I caught the early morning train from Grimsby to Lincoln to begin my army service. After my months of hard work for the Cambridge examinations, I looked forward to the experience. A friend from school, Fred Chamberlain, was joining up at the same time, so I enjoyed his companionship on my journey. I envisaged a two-year holiday in the open air, with lots of football and cross country running: I could not have been more wrong.

My first day turned into an endless nightmare. In retrospect it is easy to laugh about peacetime army misfortunes, and undoubtedly my adolescent sufferings helped me to mature. I am now glad I went up to University at the age of twenty-one rather than eighteen; in the army I learnt to become self-reliant and independent.

February 1947 was the year of the famous winter when the Labour Government faced a major fuel crisis, and the whole country was paralysed for weeks by heavy snow falls. After we arrived at Lincoln the weather grew worse, and all roads and rail lines between Lincoln and Grimsby were blocked for three weeks. On that first day it was bitterly cold, the large barrack blocks and parade grounds covered with snow and ice, as if we had been magically transported into a Russian film; there was no heating. We started the day in a freezingly cold gymnasium, with water dripping through the roof, where we hung about for an hour, waiting to be kitted out. As soon as our lance-corporal and corporal arrived, they began to shout and abuse us with four-letter words I had never heard before. We were made to run across the snow, clutching our new khaki uniforms, stumbling and slipping while Corporal Hutchinson swore at us from the rear.

At an early briefing meeting, I was sitting at the edge of the front row. When the captain arrived, he slipped on a piece of ice, and fell heavily, knocking me sprawling onto the floor. The corporals and sergeants rushed to pick him up. He was unhurt, but swore vigorously. I had bruised my forehead, but no one took any notice of me, or apologized; I began to learn about army hierarchies.

Most of the other conscripts in my batch were from Glasgow, many from deprived homes in the Gorbals, south of the Clyde, and they were certainly very familiar with Corporal Hutchinson's vocabulary. I found my first meal uneatable. There were burnt potatoes, with black eyes, and a mess of minced meat with lumps it was difficult to cut. Army cooks sploshed the food into our mess tins, plus a round of plain bread, but when I arrived at the table to sit down the twelve pats of butter had all been grabbed by the Glaswegians. After the meal I cleaned my metal knife, fork and spoon and my mess tin in a tank of dirty lukewarm water. Large mugs of tea were supposed to be heavily laced with bromide, to reduce our sexual drive, Corporal Hutchinson informed us. He asked us why there were red lights on Lincoln cathedral towers, and then explained that if we used the Lincoln prostitutes we would catch venereal disease. It all seemed a long way from my reading of Milton in the quiet library at Wintringham.

We spent the first day being taught how to wear our equipment, the denims, belt, gaiters and ammunition packs. I am a clumsy person, mechanically inept, and was usually among the last to complete each task. We were taught how to march in threes, how to clean our boots and brasses, how to fold our blankets into neat bundles. The day ended with Corporal Hutchinson mounted on a table throwing ammunition packs at anyone (often me) who was behind in learning how to lay out our beds. After lights out I settled down to sleep in the crowded barrack-room, clutching the rough blankets to my chin to keep out the cold (we were not issued with sheets). I listened to the breathing of many sleepers, and felt very hungry. The silence was broken by a bugler playing the Last Post. It ought to have been a romantic moment: it was not.

I sometimes wonder if I exaggerate our suffering, but I recently read Alex Robertson's *The Bleak Midwinter: 1949*; Robertson recalled for me the extreme conditions through which we struggled during those late February days. On 20 February heavy snow fell all over the country, followed by spectacular blizzards. The weather from January to the middle of March established various records for unpleasantness, most of which still stand. There was constant cold, one of the longest sunless periods ever chronicled, extreme frigidity lasting for days on end. The mean maximum temperature recorded for February 1947 by the Greenwich Observatory was the lowest for any month for well over 100 years. As we recruits stood about waiting for orders, our hands were red with cold, our faces lashed by raw, penetrating winds.

When at 6.15 a.m. the first morning the duty corporal woke us up, with loud shouts of 'Wakey Wakey', we were ordered to put our feet on the ground before he arrived at our beds. In the wash-house we had to queue at each basin and then shave as quickly as possible in cold water. I soon learnt to get up fifteen minutes early to shave in peace, without someone jostling me from behind. The lance-corporal marched us to the cook-house for breakfast, where I picked at lumpy porridge and burnt bacon, all in the same tin. It was freezing cold in the toilets, so I became constipated. Each day repeated the first: regular drill, square-bashing, lectures on army routines, and then, in the evening, fatigues when we would peel potatoes for three hours or more. Physical training was particularly gruesome. The instructors behaved like sadists, partly as a comic act, but the consequences were not funny for those who fell foul of their displeasure. For example, they ordered us to lie on our backs on the rough wooden floor, raise both legs twelve inches in the air, and then informed us that the first two to lower their legs would clean the gymnasium that evening. Fortunately several of the Glasgow contingent were puny and ill-nourished, and they gave in quickly. Cold showers afterwards were compulsory, with the instructors pushing anyone back under the jets who tried to emerge too quickly. Everyone soon learnt to count the days until our six weeks preliminary training was over; for me the ending of each slot in the time-table was a step towards liberty. It occurred to me to wonder why, like my brother, I had not chosen to be a conscientious objector. I had never given the matter serious thought, for like most of my generation I took the idea of a just war against Hitler for granted.

The training in the use of firearms was of very low quality. After sixteen weeks of infantry training I still fumbled when loading a magazine with cartridges. There were no models on which we could practise, and at Lincoln and Oswestry, where I was posted for the next ten weeks, we were given few opportunities to fire either rifle or bren-gun. I failed to hit the target in the final test on these weapons. Nobody explained to me why, or suggested how I might improve my performance. The failure was simply recorded in my records. I wondered how the young men from Glasgow fared when they were posted to areas where real fighting was going on. Presumably, as during the war, they learnt quickly, or died.

At Lincoln Fred Chamberlain and I left the barracks on every possible opportunity. When we were not on fatigues we journeyed each evening by bus to the NAAFI club in central Lincoln, and bought ourselves succulent meals of fried eggs, sausages and chips. We were paid only twenty-eight shillings a week, and for my first seven months in the army I spent most of this on food.

A couple of other events enlightened my darkness. A local school advertised a performance by the Ballet Rambert. I had never seen a ballet before, and so with Fred paid one shilling for a ticket. I was overwhelmed, and converted to ballet for life. I cannot remember now what pieces they danced; my memory is only of glorious colours, greens and reds and blues and whites, of exquisite rhythmic shapes and romantic music. On another occasion I went alone to the Cathedral to hear Bach's St Matthew's Passion. Crouched deep in my army greatcoat (the nave seemed to have no heating) I stuck it out to the end, savouring each chorale with rapture. For me ballet and Bach reflected the world of art, of beauty, goodness and truth, which awaited me at Cambridge, after demobilization 708 days ahead. I survived by always looking forward to my alternative world of literature, dipping occasionally into a little Penguin anthology of poetry which I carried in my pocket when we went out in the evenings.

Most of my time at Lincoln I was suffering from a mild sense of shock. If you made an error in infantry training, such as not cleaning your webbing properly, you were put on a charge, and would probably be punished with seven days' jankers. This meant being forced to parade each morning at the guard-house in full kit ready for inspection, and then spending the evening on fatigues. If you were guilty a second time, perhaps turning up late at the guard-house, your punishment might be extended. All my time at Lincoln and Oswestry this penalty loomed close; several of my friends suffered the indignity. I hated every moment in the Lincoln barracks. Over a year later I befriended the orderly-room sergeant in my company, and he suggested I should read my confidential records. On the record card for Lincoln P.T.C., Corporal Hutchinson had summarized my achievements in one word: 'lifeless'.

At Lincoln I enjoyed the intelligence tests, during which I escaped from the humiliation of my incompetence as a soldier. I recall a test where you were given a definition, and then asked to complete words beginning with PAR. One definition read: 'A heavenly place'. After my studies in literature, the first word I thought of was 'Parnassus'; I was cross when I was told the correct answer was 'paradise'. Ever since I have felt a healthy scepticism for IQ tests. As a result of my high marks (I checked this when I consulted my confidential records) I was assigned, together with Fred, to the Royal Army Education Corps. Like me, Fred had opted out of the Officers Training Corps at Wintringham. Our other friends, with their training certificates from school, were posted to infantry regiments, and would be lucky to be promoted to the rank of corporal. If we passed our course successfully, Fred and I would be sergeants within seven months. The irony of this pleased me, and bucked up my spirits. After the war thousands of troops in Germany or the Middle East needed some way to pass their time profitably, and so when I enlisted there was an urgent need for more education sergeants.

The course began with ten weeks of infantry training at Oswestry in Shropshire, not far from the Welsh border, two weeks at Kington

Battle Camp, near Hereford, and then three months' Royal Army Education Corps training at Buchanan Castle, near Loch Lomond in Scotland. The theory was that the young men we taught would respect us more if we were well-trained soldiers. After a few days' leave, during which I appreciated the comforts of Laceby Road, we arrived at Oswestry, where the regime was not quite so brutal as at Lincoln. The conscripts at Oswestry divided into two distinct groups. About a third were like me, waiting to go to University, and candidates for the R.A.E.C. In addition to Fred Chamberlain, I now made many friends of my own ilk. The other group were almost entirely scousers from Liverpool, training as infantrymen in the King's Regiment. A wild crew, they continually boasted of sexual triumphs, and their language was just as full of four-letter words as the Glaswegians at Lincoln. On one occasion I was awoken in the early hours when two of them, both drunk, wrestled each other onto my bed.

My new friends, often just as nervous and timid as I was, gave me much needed moral support. A small man called Harold was going to Caius College, Cambridge. When the officer asked us all, including the scousers, to prepare short five-minute speeches for a discussion group on something we particularly liked, Harold chose as his topic: 'The Pleasures of Afternoon Tea'. The scousers did not laugh at him, but admired his pluck. Three years later I had the pleasure of joining him for afternoon tea in his rooms at Cambridge.

On my first day at Oswestry it turned out I possessed the largest head among the new intake, and the store contained no steel helmet large enough for me. A special order was sent to depot, but it was two weeks before I was fitted out. This was a great boon. While my friends sweated in full kit on route marches, I wore a light beret. On several occasions an officer demanded: 'Why isn't that man wearing a steel helmet?' The corporal explained: 'His head's too big sir.' I did not mind the leg-pulling. The R.A.E.C. candidates formed a coherent group, all opposed to army routine, and I did not feel so isolated. The weather improved; every morning, before reveille, I could hear one of the corporals singing 'Take me back to Sorrento', while performing his ablutions, and the days until demobilization were down below 700.

In the army I learnt cynicism, however, for often the hardships we endured were absurd. There was every rational reason to cheat and avoid duties, to skive, in the jargon of that time. In the 1950s it was sometimes argued by politicians that the work-shy habits of my generation were developed when we were conscripts. A good example of such imbecilities occurred when Field Marshal Montgomery inspected the Oswestry camp. For days before he arrived we were made to dig over the allotments, and to remove every weed. One afternoon, as there were no gardening tools available, ten of us were ordered to use our army scissors to trim the grass verges. On the day Montgomery arrived, red curtains were mounted at every barrack-room window; the work was completed after first parade so the curtains could not be damaged before they were inspected. At the mid-day meal, for the first time, we were offered a choice of three menus, and luxury of luxuries, a water-jug and tumblers were supplied for each table.

At the ceremonial parade, Montgomery cut short the proceedings by walking quickly through the lines, rather than inspecting each soldier row by row. As he approached my platoon, I was standing in the front row; he was wearing the famous black beret, with two cap badges. After looking me up and down, he sniffed and marched sharply off to his car. Montgomery demanded to be driven to the most distant part of the camp, our huts, where he inspected the facilities, including the new red curtains. We were told later that he complained that the washing areas were inadequate. A few weeks after his visit, we reverted to set meals at mid-day, the water-jugs and tumblers disappeared, and docks and dandelions congregated where we had dug so vigorously. About this time, though, Montgomery ordered that all soldiers should be issued with sheets for their beds, which made us in this respect a little more comfortable.

We learnt how to survive. On one occasion we were allocated to fatigues, and sent round the camp to pick up bits of paper. After thirty minutes there was no more paper to be found, so we hid inside a garage for two hours until it was time to report back. I felt angry at what I thought of as the waste of my youth. We dared not even sit on the grass outside the garage, lurking instead in the shadows, for if spotted we should have been given another meaningless task.

When we were assigned to guard duty we were not prepared for our task; if the IRA had attacked we would have been nonplussed; we carried rifles, but no ammunition. We patrolled around the guard-house for two hours, an interminable period of time in the middle of the night when you are sleepy and have no occupation except to stay awake. One recruit patrolled at the front, the other at the back, and we were forbidden to talk to each other. Harold and I used to exchange a few words in the darkness under an awning, while looking out watchfully for the duty officer, then march round the other side and continue the conversation. Again I felt angry at the absurdity of it all (only 660 more days to go).

At Kington Battle Camp, army incompetence became seriously dangerous. Some of our fears were deliberately provoked by the officers for their own enjoyment. At a lecture on the Mills bomb we were informed that one in a thousand develops a hair-line crack during manufacture, and would explode too early. Each recruit marched up to a forward trench where he was handed a Mills bomb. The officer pointed to a scarred tree stump as the target. 'Good shot', he said to me, only to turn with surprise to find I was already slumped down at the bottom of the trench. When we handled the piat anti-tank gun we were informed that it backfired dangerously, and might break your shoulder if held incorrectly. The corporal, perhaps wisely but against orders, left Fred Chamberlain and me alone in the forward trench to fire on our own. Having satisfied myself I was holding the piat correctly, I was about to fire when I realized it was pointing at the ground only a few yards ahead. I raised the gun, pressed the trigger, and the recoil took the skin off my nose.

One officer was certainly crazy, perhaps as the result of wartime pressures. He adopted the insouciance of a James Bond, explaining the use of gun cotton to us, and then going outside our sandbagged hut to light a fuse. 'If you hear an explosion before I return,' he quipped, 'come out and collect my body.' After his lecture we were divided into two groups. Fortunately for me I was not allocated to him, and so from a hillside watched him force his squad to double-march up a hill, while he fired a sten-gun into the soft earth behind them. We did not laugh. A few moments later ricochets from the nearby range, where men were being taught to fire from the hip, whizzed over our heads. For five minutes we hugged the earth, flat on our faces, until in a lull in the firing sequence the officer ordered us to run over the crest of the hill.

That night we were issued with one blanket, and told to return in the morning. Harold, Fred and I tied our rain-capes together as a ground sheet, and snuggled together under the three blankets hoping to keep each other warm. Fortunately it was now June, and a clear summer night, but our makeshift bed was only large enough for two, and so throughout the night one of us would wake up on the damp ground. We said afterwards we started the night friends and ended up enemies, though as we shaved in a cold stream at dawn the miseries of the night were soon forgotten.

During escapes from the barracks I was intensely happy, perhaps more so than ever before or since. While at Oswestry I travelled by bus with Fred to Llangollen, where we spent the night in a hotel. The Welsh mountains entranced me, and I was in a high state of excitement. We shared a room (today two young men in this situation would joke about being gay; that possibility never occurred to us). Fred was astonished when I lay on my back in my pyjamas and bicycled my legs wildly in the air, delighted to be back in civilized surroundings.

By the time we arrived at Kington, army training had transformed the wild young men from Liverpool. After sixteen weeks in the army, its routines had sunk deep into their thinking. They took for granted that they must clean their equipment according to regulations, and they took pride in shining their boots. Obeying orders without question, they began to talk as if army discipline were a natural phenomenon everyone must accept. I witnessed at first hand how an education based on authority and punishment could reduce its subjects to willing subservience. The purpose of army drill and discipline is to make men march towards the enemy guns when rational human beings would run away; I detested this indoctrination. But, in later Black Paper days, when educationists pronounced that moral standards depended entirely on the development by children of their own personal values, I knew from my army experience that ideals of reliability and service and duty can be instilled by teachers so that children never forget them for the rest of their lives. This was the kind of teaching I received at Nunsthorpe.

At Kington we were invited to compete in the Western Command Sports. A chosen team would travel to a camp near Birmingham, stay the night and compete on the following day. I volunteered for the three miles, because I thought few others would choose this event. I proved right, and so I joyously set off by army lorry knowing my fourteen days at battle camp had been reduced to twelve. In the three-mile race the other entrants turned out to be real athletes from the regular army. I jogged around as fast as I could, but soon I was being lapped and lapped again. No one spoke to me after I finished minutes later than everyone else, but I did not care a hoot. I had escaped from Mills bombs and piats, and pride did not matter.

After ten days leave we all travelled by train to Glasgow, and then by lorry to Buchanan Castle at Drymen, where Rudolf Hess was imprisoned in a military hospital in 1941 after his famous flight to Scotland. The wooded landscape, part of the Duke of Roxburghe's estate, offered occasional glimpses of Loch Lomond.

The training included drill in the charge of sergeants from the Guards regiments. Like the soldiers who stand on sentry duty in Whitehall, we were taught to raise our knees high and stamp our feet down hard. Like our infantry training, this was supposed to enhance our prestige, but when three months later I reported for duty on attachment to the Royal Signals the officers looked distinctly startled as I stamped and saluted. No one else behaved like that, and I soon adopted a less sensational style.

Only a few people failed at Buchanan. We soon learnt that the Guards sergeants would recommend two or three for R.T.U. – return to unit. This meant that you returned to the stage you had reached when you left Preliminary Training Camp (at Lincoln, in my case) and started training in some new unit all over again (probably as a clerk). We also soon discovered that the two or three failures were chosen haphazardly according to names taken for an error during drill parades. For someone as awkward as me, this meant every drill session became a nerve-racking ordeal, for one slip could mean R.T.U. I used to try to lose myself in the middle row, but among this group of intelligent young men there were many others playing the same game. Fortunately I survived until the last drill parade, when a red-faced lout of a sergeant took my name, too late, as his report had already been submitted.

To prepare us for our duties as teachers we were given lectures, and then practised our skills in small groups. The lectures were mainly about army routines, such as how to fill in forms, and were almost useless. However, small groups (about fifteen recruits) took it in turns to give a short talk and to organize discussions. We then criticized each other's performance, and I found this of great value. I gave a talk on literature and platonism, heavily criticized by a young man called Busby, who later became a well-known literary agent and publisher. Busby was a leading figure among the recruits; after dark, during that hot summer of 1947, he encouraged us to sing the Red Flag in voices loud enough to be heard in the Officers' Mess.

One evening with Fred and two other friends I booked for a show in Glasgow. After I had changed into my best uniform I visited the toilet. As I was sitting there, a corporal arrived and ordered Fred and my friends to join a coal fatigue. I waited until the coast was clear, and then quickly slunk away to catch the bus to Glasgow. Hours later, when I returned, I could see Fred still lumping coal. I learnt then something about the arbitrariness of fate.

At Lincoln I was converted to ballet; at Buchanan Castle I was converted to opera. I bought a standing ticket for Verdi's *Il Trovatore*, my first opera. The short melodic arias swamped me in emotion, and for weeks afterwards I went around whistling the gypsy Azucena's last song, in which she recalls lost happiness in the mountains of Biscay ('Ai nostri mosti'). It brought back memories of my own lost happiness when cycling through the Lincolnshire Wolds. As at Oswestry escapes from the prison-house of the army camp were times of exhilaration, promises of a future civilian life. Fred and I visited Balloch and Balmaha, and rowed on the loch where our skills learnt on the Boating Lake at Cleethorpes proved invaluable. One summer evening we were rowing back to Balmaha to catch the last bus when we realized a strong current was holding us back. We pulled and pulled, knowing that to return after 'lights out' would have dire consequences. We docked at the jetty with only minutes to spare; later we heard that the apparent placidity of Loch Lomond can suddenly be transformed by a huge, dangerous swell.

At last we sewed on our three stripes as new sergeants, and, proud of our status, we were posted to units in North Yorkshire. After a few weeks Fred was drafted to Singapore, and, except for one brief meeting after demobilization, I never saw him again. For me he was a trusted and supportive companion as we struggled through those early conscript days. I had no desire to go abroad; soldiers were being killed in Palestine and Malaya. A more common fate was to face a year of boredom in a camp in the North African desert.

I was posted to the Royal Signals at Dalton, near Thirsk, in Yorkshire. This was a draft camp where hundreds of men, after Signals training at Catterick, spent a few weeks before setting off for postings overseas. The education sergeants taught both the draftees and the men on permanent staff who had not reached school certificate standard. Soldiers with higher educational qualifications were exempt from regular education, a curious decision.

I became expert at coping with huge audiences, some over 100 men, often sent to us because their sergeants could not think of anything else for them to do. A.B.C.A. (Army Bureau of Current Affairs) pamphlets provided us with topical information, on the nationalization of the coal mines or the National Health Service, for example. Other sergeants, particularly those with teaching qualifications, found it difficult to control the men, who only wanted entertainment or a good laugh. I started by inviting those in the audience who did not want to participate to put their heads back, go to sleep, and not to interrupt the rest of us. As many of them had been revelling late at night this was a welcome order, and created for me an easy rapport with this adult audience. Many were so surprised they stayed awake as I gave my introductory talk, which I kept as short and lively as possible, before organizing questions and discussion. The qualified teachers found it difficult to be so unscrupulous. I believed my technique was the only way of surviving to teach some of the men, a limited but possible goal. Things did not always go my way, however. Once after I had pontificated for about ten minutes on the coal mines, a man in the front row informed me he was a coal miner, and my pamphlets were wrong; I had no answer.

By chance the education sergeants senior to me were all due for demobilization, so very soon, at only nineteen years old, I found myself in charge of the education centre, with four sergeants under my command. Within a month I was in trouble. It was customary for us to go on leave together, so all classes could be cancelled, and it had never occurred to me to check the security of the building. When we returned the gramophone had been stolen, and a Court of Enquiry was set up. For the first time I examined with care the rooms for which I was responsible. I discovered broken windows and rusty, unusable locks; I already knew we had loaned keys to friends so that they could retreat to the centre while the sergeants were on leave. The flat-roofed, low building was shaped in a rectangle, with offices, class-rooms and library grouped round a little central courtyard. When the officers arrived for the Enquiry, I explained to them that we had realized it was possible to climb over the roof and enter from the courtyard, whose door possessed no lock. They tested my theory by climbing over the roof from different entry points, and departed, satisfied they had discovered the burglar's entry point. They did not ask about keys, or examine the defects of the rest of the building.

I was charged, marched into the major's office without my hat (a form of disgrace) and punished by being made to pay for the estimated cost of the gramophone (only five pounds). Signalman Clarence, who worked in the orderly room, privately told me he did not dispatch the order to dock my wages of the five pounds. Years later at Cambridge, I picked up a newspaper with a large photograph of Signalman Clarence; he had been convicted of an absurd attempt to sell secrets to the Russians. I hope my pleasure when he helped me out over the gramophone did not contribute to his decision to embark on a life of crime.

In the spring of 1948 the Royal Signals draft camp was moved from Dalton to an old prisoner of war camp at Ripon, where I was allocated three huts at the far end of a long, narrow site overlooking the valley of the River Ure. We were anxious not to be forced to sleep in a barrack-room with the transit sergeants. The last hut, a long way from the camp's busy central offices, had previously been used as a chapel. After dark on the Friday of our arrival we stole a number of high cupboards from unallocated huts, and built ourselves cubicles where we could each sleep with some privacy. Very pleased with ourselves, we slept well on Friday night, and spent Saturday cycling to Ripon Cathedral and Fountains Abbey. At about midnight, after we had finished playing snooker in the Sergeants' Mess, we glanced at the Orders for the following day. (This would make a much better story if we had failed to do so.) To our astonishment we read that at 9 a.m. the army chaplain would be conducting a service in the prisoner of war chapel at the end of the camp. We jumped on our bikes, and spent the next two hours shifting beds, mattresses, wardrobes, lino and pieces of carpet into our other two huts. I still fantasize about what would have happened if on the Sunday morning the chaplain had arrived with his entourage to find us all in bed.

At Ripon I had my first experience of teaching illiterates. Three were allocated to me, and I tried very hard to help them to read. Two of them seemed quite intelligent, but another, called Brown, sticks most vividly in my mind. He was very small, almost wizened, with yellow, unhealthy skin.

I introduced Brown to the army text-book, and after four weeks he was able to read back to me the simple words on the first ten pages. I was very pleased with myself. It occurred to me to buy the *Daily Mirror* and to help him to pick out the simple words he could read. As he held the newspaper close to his nose, a bead of sweat rolled down his narrow forehead. He could not read any of the words; he had learnt off by heart the sequence in the text-book, and could not recognize even words such as 'man' or 'cap' in another context. I had been given no training in teaching illiterates, and had no notion about what to do next. In civilian life he was employed in a factory in Birmingham, where he served tea to the women factory workers, who fussed and coddled him. In the army he was desperate, and I like to think that one day he was happy again, serving tea in the familiar factory routines. Later during the Black Paper campaigns I often thought of Brown. In the crowded formal class-room of fifty children he endured in Birmingham in the 1930s he did not learn to read. He would not have learnt to read if left to his own devices in the noisy, fashionable class-rooms of the

1970s, where he would have been free to choose his own activities. Someone like Brown needed carefully structured programmes of work supervised by a professional teacher trained in remedial work for illiterates.

On my first day in the army I stopped writing verse. At Ripon I completed about a third of a novel about my conscript days, with material akin to that in David Lodge's first novel, *Ginger You're Barmy*, but I could not manage dialogue. I had plenty of free time for reading, particularly when I became an education sergeant. I consumed avidly most of the classic English novels, from Fielding's *Tom Jones* to Dickens's *Little Dorrit*, and long poems such as Wordsworth's *Prelude* and *Excursion*. By the time I went up to Cambridge I was conversant with a wide range of literature, including Tolstoy and Dostoevsky. I was an extremely well-read first-year undergraduate.

The hard-bitten Royal Signals sergeants were always kind to me. Most of them had enlisted in the late 1920s because of unemployment, and throughout the war had lacked the ability to be promoted into the officer class. The tables in the Mess were set for four people, and it was a custom that each table was filled before anyone sat at the next. For example, if there were three people at one table when I arrived with another R.A.E.C. sergeant, one of us would join the existing group, and the other sit alone at the next table. This admirable arrangement meant that we were forced to talk to the Signals sergeants, breaking down barriers.

In normal conversation the sergeants never talked about their adventures during the war. Once a fierce sergeant, who was due for demobilization, asked me to help him redraft a letter to an ex-officer, who owned an estate near Nottingham. The sergeant explained to me that he had saved the officer's life by dragging him from a burning house at Dunkirk. The officer had promised him a job on his estate when he retired from the regular army. The draft he presented to me was littered with spelling and punctuation errors. I told him it just needed minor alterations, revised it completely, and wrote out a fair copy for him. When he shook my hand and thanked me, I could see he knew exactly what I had done, and appreciated that I had not wished to humiliate him.

He received a favourable reply, and I hope he was happy in his new work as a handyman.

One day the Regimental Sergeant Major called me to his office, and told me he had selected me to become treasurer of the Sergeants' Mess. He explained to me that though I had no experience of accounts, I would soon learn, and that I was the only man he could trust not to put his fingers in the till. This duty, which I carried out for a year, helped me to acquire prestige. The wily old sergeant who handed the books over gave me good advice about the monthly meetings of the Sergeants' Mess: 'Give them the minimum of information. The more you tell them, the more they want to know.'

Soon I faced my first three-monthly audit. I was nervous, and the night before worked late checking and re-checking the figures. To my annoyance, I discovered a small error of two shillings in my favour in the daily stock account. Next morning I rushed over to the Major's office, and breathlessly explained my error; to put it right would mean changing the final accounts. 'Forget it,' he advised me. 'It doesn't matter. It's too late to retype the accounts.'

When the audit was completed, with no check on the details of the stock account, the visiting officer congratulated me on their presentation, but then asked: 'What about the two shilling error in the stock account?' I felt a fool, and realized that the officers had been joking about the honest young sergeant who was so worried about a minor error. I learnt never to submit accounts with any mistakes, and never to rely on other people's discretion when I am at fault.

The regular monthly Sergeants' Mess dances proved an education for me. The 'ladies' were older than me, so I did not participate, and only gradually realized that several were prostitutes. On these occasions I would help the barman, learning how to serve beer. The ladies were often happy to accept short measures in their gin and lime or orange, for they knew the aim of their escorts was to make them drunk. One night when I was cleaning up in the early hours a sergeant entered the bar, put his head in his hands, and, weeping, confessed: 'I have sinned.'

The sergeant in charge of the bar, called Varley, slept in an adjacent bedroom alongside the safe. Each morning I joined him after breakfast to check the stock and balance the trading account. One day I found him in tears. He had spent the night in Harrogate (with his wife, he told me, and it never occurred to me that he had probably been with a prostitute); on his return he had discovered that the safe had been forced open, and forty pounds removed. This was a large sum in those days, when a sergeant earned only three pounds fifty pence a week. He had no savings, and expected to be court-martialled. That evening was a dance night, so I explained to him how we could make forty pounds profit in one evening. The Mess allocated £100 for half-price drinks, which went back to full price when the money was spent. No one except the treasurer knew when the money had all been expended, so we would announce that the £100 was gone when in fact the total only reached seventy-five pounds. The rest of the forty pounds we could make by serving short measures, particularly of gin to the ladies. We succeeded brilliantly, and Sergeant Varley was saved from disgrace and demotion to the ranks. I am not sure about the morality of this manoeuvre, although it did not worry me at the time. A few sergeants ended the evening less drunk than usual, and some women were in a better position to control their fate. In the army, still only nineteen years old, I had learnt that the main rule is to defeat the authorities.

Army plans for education often verged on the ridiculous. A new order decreed that even sergeants and sergeant-majors should attend one seminar a week on current affairs. On the day of the first seminar I was forced to attend a meeting at the army library in York. I put the seminar in the charge of Sergeant Chalmers, an extremely intelligent public school boy from Winchester. He chose as the topical subject for discussion 'The New Look' – should women wear skirts above the knee – which he mistakenly thought the non-commissioned officers would enjoy. The next day I faced the lieutenant-colonel to answer complaints that the seminar had been an insulting waste of time.

Our masters at the education centre in Darlington were going berserk over new progressive reforms. In autumn 1948 I was ordered to teach according to the project method. We taught four basic subjects: English, maths, history and geography. In the new scheme, for the first twelve weeks every lesson must deal with clothing, the next twelve with food, and the final twelve with shelter. We were teaching a few basics to our men, mainly improving reading and writing skills, and this project plan seemed to me irrelevant to their needs. With only six months to go until demobilization, I decided to ignore the order. Unfortunately, after fifteen weeks I received a letter saying that the following week the colonel from Darlington would visit us to inspect how well the project method was developing. The next day we explained the problem to the men, and then spent the succeeding few days dictating exercises and notes to them on clothing and food. They understood the need to deceive officers, and were most co-operative. The colonel arrived and departed, moderately satisfied.

I organized trips to Ripon Cathedral and Fountains Abbey. At the morning parade for the draftees, the duty sergeant allocated the men to fatigues. He often had difficulty in finding enough for them to do, so I persuaded him to ask for volunteers for an educational visit to Fountains Abbey. To most conscripts this did not appeal, but among the Royal Signals there were always a few men, like me, waiting to go up to University. About ten to twenty would volunteer, and I would march them away into Ripon. As soon as we were on the road to Fountains, I would call them to a halt, explain to them about the monastery, and then suggest that we all forgot army rules and walked at our own pace. They could view the ruins at their leisure, and we would meet at the exit three hours later. I asked them not to draw attention to themselves if any officer appeared, and I was never let down. Several times a volunteer thanked me profusely for the opportunity to escape for one day, and to visit a site so beautiful as Fountains Abbey. After my months at Lincoln and Oswestry I understood their jubilation.

I cycled regularly to Harrogate to attend dances, a distance of twelve miles. Unfortunately, I would almost always cycle back to camp, sometimes in the pouring rain, sometimes under a full moon, without any success in befriending one of the girls. Only once did I manage to persuade a girl to let me take her to the theatre, where she talked to me about her boyfriend in Edinburgh. At last in the summer of 1948 my luck changed. The education sergeants were given free tickets for the final dance at the local teacher training college at Ripon, where I met a girl called Joyce. Only a few days remained before she departed to teach in Sheffield, so we spent the next two years meeting at railway stations, and visiting romantic places such as York, Knaresborough and Lincoln. Joyce had another boyfriend, and our friendship petered out during my first year at Cambridge.

In January 1949 I was promoted to warrant officer, second class. The Royal Signals sergeants, for whom such a promotion was their greatest desire, found it difficult to believe that I would not sign on as a regular soldier, but preferred to study at Cambridge.

At last, in March 1949, demobilization arrived. I was sent with a batch of conscripts to a camp at Pocklington in Yorkshire. On the final day I was allowed to wear civilian clothes, but we had to hang about for three hours waiting for the lorry that would take us to York, where we were to hand in our kit. At last the lorry appeared, and we ran across the parade ground to scramble aboard. After we set off I discovered that in the rush I had dropped the parcel containing my trousers. At York I explained this to the sergeant, who looked at me with contempt, presuming I had stolen them, but he took no action. At the last moment, as I stood before a second lieutenant to sign the final document, I forgot to call him 'sir'. As a sergeant-major I was used to working with officers on familiar terms. The sergeant barked at me: 'What else?' 'Thank you, *sir*,' I replied. It was an appropriate symbolic last moment of humiliation. As I travelled by train from York to Hull, and across the Humber on the ferry to New Holland, the sense of freedom made even the house on Laceby Road seem like paradise.

Between March and October, when I was due to go up to Cambridge, I needed a job. I was fortunate to be taken on as a temporary supply teacher at Immingham Secondary Modern School, where throughout the summer term I taught all ages and abilities. Immingham is a port about seven miles down river from Grimsby. I used to cycle there and back each day, enjoying the flat Lincolnshire landscape. The school was one-storey red-brick, rather like Nunsthorpe; children who had failed the eleven-plus went there, and some of them were illiterate.

I soon discovered I was ill-equipped to teach children. In the army I had learnt that the way to teach adults is to adopt an easy, informal manner, encouraging them to express their own views and to participate in deciding what and how to learn. On my first day at Immingham I took over my classes with complete confidence, but within a week the children were busy exploiting my friendliness. I was shocked by the sergeant-major voices used by the male staff when reproving thirteen-year-old boys for some minor offence. I soon learnt that in this tough school the only way to survive was to impose your authority from the start; only when discipline had been established could you assume a more friendly approach. I discovered I could keep order if I read exciting adventure tales to the children, and I scoured the Grimsby Public Library for appropriate material. One of the roughest boys in the school brought me a comic with the story of the Count of Monte Cristo, which I had been reading to them. This seemed a modest success, but by and large I was a failure. I recognized that professional teacher training is essential. I also learnt that teaching children is one of the hardest tasks in the world. Each day when I returned to Laceby Road I would sink into an armchair for thirty minutes or so, maybe just listening to the radio, exhausted. People who have not worked for a day in a class-room with thirty rumbustious children have no idea of the strain, even for the best teachers.

I was very anxious to see the world, which for me, with only my small savings from my army pay, meant cycling holidays to Youth Hostels. During the Easter vacation, I organized for myself a little trip round England on the racing bike I had bought in Ripon. I knew that my average speed was twelve miles an hour, so I reserved beds at Youth Hostels about seventy miles apart. That meant, I calculated, only about six hours' cycling per day. My first Youth Hostel was near Oakham, in what used to be called Rutland. That morning there were showers of rain and strong blustery winds from the south west. I huffed and puffed, and eventually arrived in Rutland about an hour after the warden had retired to bed. When I knocked on the door he was kind to me, and even heated up some tomato soup, for I was trembling with fatigue. The next day I cycled to Oxford, then to the Malvern Hills and back via Derbyshire, straining away at my ridiculously over-ambitious schedule. In Derbyshire, near Matlock, I slept in a bunk in a little wooden hut, whose roof beams were laid across the walls with gaps through which I could see the stars. In the night it snowed. There was just one other man in the hut, and at about 3 a.m. we dressed ourselves, hugged our blankets round us, and talked away the remaining bitterly cold hours. He was waiting to go up to Oxford, and we had much in common. In spite of the cold, I felt at rest, serene and at peace with myself. Freedom from the army meant so much to me. I was rediscovering my true self, no longer forced to kow-tow to rigid disciplines and meaningless work.

In the summer I determined to cycle to France, my first trip outside the British Isles. I was forced to travel alone, for my friends from Wintringham were all scattered. This time I reduced the miles required each day, and successfully journeyed south, through the centre of London over Tower Bridge, arriving in Dover after five days. The next day I presented myself at the small Townsend ferry (later Townsend-Thoresen). Unfortunately, for the first time since the war car-owners had begun to travel abroad in such large numbers that the ship's complement of passengers was reached before the cyclists – just three of us – could board. We had to wait for the late afternoon sailing. With the two other boys, both sixth-formers who seemed very gauche to me, I spent the day visiting Dover Castle and rowing round the harbour. At last we set off, but by the time we entered Calais harbour it was almost dark. As we approached the jetty we could see that the docks were still covered with piles of rubble from the war. I had booked a Youth Hostel, the nearest one, about thirty miles away. I feared to take a room in a hotel, partly through timidity, partly because I was carrying only a small amount of cash. The two boys were going to camp, so we joined forces. They were starting to bicker with each other under the strain, and welcomed my leadership. We clattered over the cobbles, an unexpected hazard, until about two miles on the road south we saw a lighted doorway of a farm. 'Peut-on camper ici?' I asked, trying out my French for the first time. The farmer was effusively friendly, and found us a dry spot beside his barn. We erected the tent in the dark with some difficulty. I was carrying only a sheet sleeping bag, but I slept soundly on the rough ground, tired out after my days of cycling.

The next day we proceeded to Abbéville, on the Somme, also devastated by battle, with the church tower stuck up crazily above broken walls and roofless houses. As we cycled along we saw bullet holes in sign-posts, damage everywhere. At Abbéville we camped together again, unfortunately on a slope, so that during the night I woke up several times with my legs stuck out beyond the tent flap. My new friends then departed for Paris, whereas I turned towards the coast, as I had originally planned. I spent nights in Youth Hostels at Yport and St Valéry, shocked by their filthiness compared with the spruce cleanliness of their English counterparts. Whereas in England we were assigned cleaning tasks after breakfast, and were not allowed to depart until they were satisfactorily completed, in France it was customary to leave everything dirty, the room unswept and the utensils still greasy. The newcomers in the evening cleaned what they wanted to use, or just contributed their own dirt. At Yport an older English cyclist told me hotels were not too expensive, so I decided to experiment. I found a small hotel in a little village, and as I was the only guest, I was shown, to my surprise, to a huge room overlooking the village square. After a meal of chicken and chips, the hotelier talked to me about his war-time adventures with de Gaulle in London. He was really chuffed to be entertaining a young English boy; I felt that my youth represented for him the new world for which so many of his friends had died. He charged me almost nothing. The next morning I flung open the shutters of my bedroom to see a square full of stalls, red and white awnings, crowds of men in blue denims, chickens running everywhere, but above all the sun, the sun, hotter than I had ever known in England. The stones of the Gothic church opposite absorbed light as if the warmth had entered their very being. I added one more epiphany to my collection.

Flushed with my success, I stopped at a restaurant, instead of buying bread and butter and cheese and fruit from the shops as before. I ordered an omelette and 'vin blanc'. The waiter brought me a full bottle of Loire wine. As I cycled away, I realized I was drunk, and wobbling from side to side. I collapsed under a haystack and slept it off. My school French, after seven years of study, proved quite inadequate. It was four days before I realized why I kept being served black coffee: I had not been taught to ask for café-au-lait. The night before I sailed from Calais I tried to explain to the hotelier, just for conversation, that I might be sick on the crossing. I forgot to use the future tense, and so he began to fuss around anxiously, expecting me to mess up his floor.

On my last day I found a beach, parked my bicycle and rushed into the sea. After a while I noticed that the previously crowded water seemed surprisingly empty. I looked up to see a thunder cloud approaching fast. Before I could return to my bike a heavy downpour soaked my shirt and shorts, which I had left hanging on the handle-bars; I had a second dry shirt, but cycled off in sodden shorts. I caught a heavy cold, which worried my father when at last I arrived back in Grimsby. He thought I was crazy to cycle to France, and, of course, he feared that, like my mother, I might contract tuberculosis.

I was very satisfied with my adventure. With a cheap Kodak camera I had photographed Canterbury Cathedral, the Townsend ferry breasting the waves, the pebbled sea-front at Dieppe. I affixed and carefully labelled my snaps in a new photograph album. The journey became for me a permanent possession, secure and unchanging, like the photographs themselves. At Laceby Road arguments still erupted at regular intervals; my other world, created for myself, must be stable, rich in aesthetic pleasures, ideal.

# 4

# *Cambridge Pastoral*

Courts, cloisters, flocks of churches, gateways, towers:
Migration strange for a stripling of the hills,
A northern villager.

'The Prelude', William Wordsworth

In October 1949 I set off by rail from Grimsby Dock Station on my journey to Cambridge. I had sent in advance my bicycle and a large blue trunk full of books. My father gave me a five pound note as a farewell gift. For a number of years after the war conscripts like me were eligible for grants under a government Further Education and Training Scheme, intended primarily to help those who fought in the war. This grant was higher than the state award for which I had qualified through my Pembroke College exhibition. With my small savings from the army (about seventy pounds) this new grant provided all I needed at Cambridge, including fees and living expenses. In addition to the occasional five pound note, my father charged me no board while I was at home during vacations. Each summer I went up to Cambridge for the long vacation term, for which my army grant also paid. After I married in 1954, my father stopped handing out the five pound notes. I was slightly surprised, a sign of how I took his support for granted.

I changed trains at Spalding, in south Lincolnshire, and so, with two hours to pass, I walked out into the town. It was a beautiful autumn day, and in a little park, close to an aviary with squabbling parrots and canaries and birds I could not name, I sat down on a bench to think things over. I was highly excited, very nervous

74

because my army days had taught me that the unexpected can be unpleasant, and there was no Fred Chamberlain to accompany me. I knew no one who was going up to Cambridge in my year. Yet I was also unbelievably happy. Time seemed to stop; the birds chattered and preened, and five minutes extended itself into an eternity. Once again I was overwhelmed by joy at no longer being a conscript.

I visualize the word 'Pembroke' as a light yellow colour, soft and gentle, reverberating with all those desires which sustained me during my army years. Pembroke is a medium-sized college, down Trumpington Street, separate from the great colleges, King's or Trinity or St John's, with their gardens and lawns running down to the river. In my day Pembroke was private and quiet, its courtyards rarely disturbed by tourists, except at the height of the summer season. On arrival I was allocated a bed-sitting room in the central Victorian building, right at the top; it was an attic room, with wooden beams slanting down in the corners, and a small window overlooking New Court. As I opened the door I felt as if I had lived in the room before, in some previous existence, or perhaps in a dream. The dark corners recalled to me Mrs Clennam's house in Dickens's *Little Dorrit*. I immediately fell in love with its privacy, perched in my eyrie above the college with the nearest wash-basins five floors down below.

I greeted my neighbour eagerly, and found he came from a minor public school. He was polite enough, but we immediately felt alien to each other. Small and neat, he was dressed in a dark suit with yellow gloves, while I was attired in my ex-grammar school uniform: a blue Harris tweed sports coat and grey flannels. We soon separated, and never became friends. I set out alone to wander around Cambridge through the Backs, bemused by their loveliness, and then went down to the dining hall for my first college dinner. About twenty undergraduates sat round a long table. After the pudding was served, I suddenly noticed I was the only one eating it with a spoon. I am proud to recall that I did not change over to my fork. The other young men were all from public schools, assured, with friends they seemed to know well. I felt like a fish out of water, but after my army initiation was not too concerned about my isolation.

After dinner I set off alone to a meeting of the Cambridge Heretics in Trinity College which I had seen advertised during my walk around the colleges. The speaker was Stephen Spender. He explained that readers in our time no longer possess a common body of knowledge, so that if we consider a gasometer, a very different object is seen by a layman, an expert in gas technology and an aircraft pilot. This illustration was used to explain the multiple perspectives of modern art. Afterwards there were many questions whose sophistication astonished me. We discussed Apollinaire, of whom I had never heard, the Dada movement, and the perspectives of Picasso. I reeled back to my attic, having touched no alcohol, but drunk on ideas. It was probably all very pretentious, but I was impressed.

The next afternoon, after reading a notice on the boards outside the Pembroke dining hall, I attended a health clinic for a check-up. Everyone else had completed a form in advance. The doctor provided me with a duplicate, but I realized for the first time that I was not receiving mail. The next morning I made enquiries, and discovered the existence of the Junior Common Room, where my pigeon-hole was chock-full with invitations to society meetings, many by then out-of-date.

Teaching did not commence until the following week, so I had loads of spare time. I sat in my attic taking notes on Matthew Arnold's *Empedocles on Etna*; there seemed nothing else to do. Fortunately I had seen a notice inviting all Pembroke freshers to a football practice. I had brought my kit, and cycled down to Pembroke Sports ground, half-way to Grantchester. Almost all the players were ex-grammar school boys, with whom I had much in common (only a few public schools, such as Bradfield, Eton or Charterhouse, play what they call 'soccer'). I never again lacked friends at Pembroke. One non-grammar school boy, a tall, willowy freshman, immediately endeared himself to me with his gracious manners (I later found out he was from Charterhouse). Everyone took for granted that he would play inside-right, my position, in the first team. This presumption annoyed me until I watched him play, for his ball skills were clearly superior to those of the rest of us. His name was Peter May. He later captained the Cambridge University soccer team, but his real fame, of course, was as a county cricket player and the future captain of England's cricket team. After the practice three of us ex-grammar school boys adjourned to tea in a second year undergraduate's digs. We talked for two hours, and from then on conversations over tea about everything from football to Plato to God became a normal daily activity for me.

My first lecture was given by A.P. Rossiter on 'The Evolution of English Drama to Shakespeare'. The Mill Lane lecture theatre was crowded, almost entirely with men except for a few girls from Newnham and Girton Colleges. The lecture worried me. At one stage Rossiter broke into a long Latin quotation, which he neither translated nor paraphrased. Was I the only one who could not follow? (After a few weeks I realized almost no one could follow.) He ended by reading the famous parable from the sermon in Kafka's *The Trial*.

A man from the country begs for admittance to the Law, but the door-keeper refuses to allow him to enter. The countryman sits waiting at the side of the door, and days and years go by. The door-keeper never allows him to pass. At last when the man is old and about to die he asks the door-keeper a last question: 'Everyone strives to attain the Law . . . how does it come about, then, that in all these years no one has come seeking admittance but me?' The door-keeper perceives that the man is at the end of his strength and his hearing is failing, so he bellows in his ear: 'No one but you could gain admittance through this door, since this door was intended only for you. I am now going to shut it.'

I was not sure how this related to English drama before Shakespeare, but I was sufficiently excited to buy *The Trial* that afternoon from Heffer's bookshop, and to read it through that night in one sitting.

At first I took notes during lectures in pencil, transcribing a fair copy in ink in the evening. I soon realized that this was a ridiculous waste of time. No one advised me on study skills; I learnt by trial and error. Four lectures were scheduled for that first morning; the third was delivered by the great Dr F.R. Leavis. There were no empty seats in the large lecture theatre, and some undergraduates sat sprawled on the floor at his feet. Leavis's lecture turned out to be a long, paranoic ramble through his misfortunes in the 1930s, when his admiration for T.S. Eliot brought him contumely from the Cambridge establishment (for example, F.L. Lucas of King's College commented in the *New Statesman* that a 'poem that has to be explained in notes is not unlike a picture with "This is a dog" inscribed beneath.') After Leavis's performance I abandoned the fourth lecture, and adjourned to Pembroke for lunch, although I continued to attend his lectures. In the middle of his reminiscences and snide remarks ('You can go now and hear the hen cackling,' he said, when T.R. Henn of St Catherine's College was the next lecturer), he would provide me with sudden illuminations worth far more than the conventional, well-organized lectures of Joan Bennett or E.M.W. Tillyard.

Leavis helped me to understand metaphysical wit for the first time, to extend my pleasure in poetry, which had previously been exclusively devoted to the powerful rhythms of Milton, Shelley or Tennyson. When talking about John Donne's 'The Sunne Rising', he explained that when the lover, in bed with his mistress at dawn, tells the sun to 'Call country ants to harvest offices', the word 'ants' conveys both a fact – the labourers are busy like ants – and an attitude of contempt towards them; in contrast to the lovers they are small as ants. I saw for the first time how a poet can use individual words for double effects. In my second year my supervisor, Matthew Hodgart, arranged for me to attend Leavis's seminar at Downing College for one term. We examined passages in prose and verse, and tried to decide by internal evidence when they were written. Leavis's own Downing students sat at the front, while we immigrants from Pembroke hid ourselves in the rear. As in the lectures, Leavis rambled on tediously about the past, throwing in occasional sharp perceptions about individual words or phrases. He was not successful in provoking discussion, though he tried. The Downing students would occasionally throw in a remark, but mostly the seminar became a Leavis monologue. I spoke only once. Leavis handed out a prose passage describing a domestic scene, and asked us to work out the author from the style. 'It's Richardson,' I answered. 'How do you know that?' he asked. 'I read the passage in Richardson's *Clarissa* yesterday evening,' I replied.

Years later, in 1963, I reviewed the complete *Scrutiny* in the *Spectator*. I recalled Leavis's seminar, and how at morning sessions he wore an old dressing gown which revealed his bare chest. Leavis replied to only one of the numerous reviews of *Scrutiny*. In a short letter to the *Spectator*, he insisted that he had never worn a dressing gown at seminars. Presumably he associated dressing gowns with Bloomsbury or Noel Coward farces. Leavis never wore a tie, and I had taken it for granted that his heavy brown woollen overcoat, with his bare neck, was a dressing gown (like those worn by my working-class relatives). Other Cambridge supervisors took their first sessions in dressing gowns after spending the night in their rooms.

In my time Leavis still dominated Cambridge thinking about literature, and I had graduated and left before lecturers such as Donald Davie and John Holloway introduced credible alternative ways of thought. Leavis's contempt for most writers, for Shelley and Tennyson for example, harmed me in ways I now bitterly regret. In my first weeks at Cambridge I abandoned my attempts to write verse and fiction, and did not recover my confidence as a writer until 1960, helped by the experience of working as a poetry editor of *Critical Quarterly*. Leavis's scorn was easy to imitate, and made my own personal writings seem feeble (as they were, but they were beginnings on which I might have built). Years later, my co-professor at Manchester University, John Jump, told me how he was similarly rendered impotent as a writer by Leavis's harsh puritanical criticism, and how it took him almost twenty years to break free.

After my first term I stopped attending lectures, with one notable exception. Ian Watt was giving the lectures on the English novel which he eventually published as his famous *The Rise of the Novel*. I attended regularly, and found my notes of great value. Other lectures I found boring, and my time was better spent reading in the University library. Soon afterwards Cambridge refused to renew Ian Watt's appointment, and he departed for the University of California at Berkeley.

I settled down to one hour of teaching per week, my supervision with Matthew Hodgart, which I shared with one other undergraduate, and for which we both wrote an essay. Matthew Hodgart did not fill in the one-hour slot by making us read our essay (as lazy tutors often did) but tried to converse with us about the authors who were the subject of those essays, which he marked with care. He did not always find it easy to maintain the flow. There were silences, and I was certainly not sufficiently sophisticated to introduce new questions or topics. But I learnt a great deal from Hodgart, who supervised me for two years. Like Leavis, he offered me insights which I still quote in my lectures today, when the piles of notes I accumulated from critical books are forgotten. There were no seminars at Pembroke, but this did not matter. Every meal was a seminar, when those of us reading English would discuss how our essays were progressing, and what we had been reading. While the University lecturers were wasting their time with very small audiences, we taught ourselves.

I joined the Cambridge Union, and attended a first debate at which an undergraduate called Norman St John Stevas, later Minister for the Arts in Mrs Thatcher's government, acted as one of the principal speakers. His public school rhetoric did not appeal to me, and the wit of all the participants seemed to me self-indulgent and cheap. I did not attend any further debates, and after one term allowed my subscription to lapse.

My moral tutor (a normal method of pastoral supervision at universities in those days) was W.A. Camps, a classicist, who invited me regularly to tea with other undergraduates. As soon as we broached a subject, such as the nature of tragedy, he encouraged us to explain things to him, to enlighten his ignorance. Gradually we realized he knew far more than we did. We never objected to this ploy to start conversation; he was genuinely kind to us, and I learnt much from his quiet, urbane wit. The Dean, Meredith Dewey, also invited us to tea, or to drink wine after dinner. I explained to him that I was religious, although preferring not to join one church, but to attend them all. When he discovered I had not yet been to College Chapel, he pulled my leg with great good humour; as a result I attended Evensong regularly for the rest of my time at Pembroke. I enjoyed the formality of the language, and the beauty of the setting and the music in the Wren Chapel.

One evening I had been studying late, and my books were strewn about the room. As I clumped about in heavy, brown shoes, making coffee, I heard a gentle knock on my door. It was Canon Knox, brother of the famous Ronald Knox (best known for his translation of the Bible). He explained that his bedroom was beneath mine, and my walking about was keeping him awake. When he realized I was alone and studying, Knox flushed with embarrassment, and immediately invited me to tea. He was thin and small and pale, and I still dream of this strange old man knocking at my door in the middle of the night. Excessive noise was against the rules, and wild parties would be interrupted by the porter (these were very few; the men who fought in the war worked hard as undergraduates). The gates were locked at 10 p.m. If an undergraduate returned to college after 10 p.m. he paid twopence, and if after eleven fourpence. To ring the gate-bell after midnight was counted a serious offence, involving a compulsory visit the next day to explain your doings to your tutor. The back gate was not difficult to climb; its iron bars ended in sharp points at the top, but you could lift yourself over, perhaps slitting your gown, which was compulsory wear after dark (if caught on the streets without your gown, you were fined six shillings and eightpence). The system was sensibly pragmatic. If you were out late you could climb the gate, and not bother the authorities. But this feat was sufficiently awkward to deter us from staying out regularly after midnight, and there was always the chance a porter would sneak up on you as you dropped to the ground inside the gate. During my time at Pembroke I climbed in only twice, on both occasions after getting carried away by arguments in a friend's room who lived out of college.

The atmosphere at Pembroke was so different from today, when roistering and pop music often break the silence in the early hours. The strict but benevolent regime at Pembroke made grammar school boys like me very happy. The terms lasted only eight weeks, so we spent our time in study and conversation. I felt immensely privileged to be spending three years reading and studying great books. That was the centre of my contentment at Pembroke, and I appreciated the college way of life, so conducive to quiet thought and contemplation. We rarely paid for entertainment, with the exception of the Cambridge Film Theatre, where we enjoyed foreign films in the great days of

Arletty, Jean Gabin and Fernandel. I played football twice a week, and often in the afternoons would join friends such as Tony Dyson or Geoff Roberts, also reading English, on walks down the river to Grantchester. On Saturdays there were occasional away-football games at Oxford, to which we travelled by coach. There might be some drinking on these occasions, but most of us were too poor to buy spirits or even beer in any quantity. At the end of a game we were given a half pint of shandy; it was rare for me to drink on any other occasion.

During the Easter vacation, I went down with jaundice. I hated being ill, but for several days was too weak to climb out of bed. We did not send for a doctor. After my mother's sufferings, my father held doctors in contempt, and encouraged me to get well by my own efforts. When I returned to Cambridge for the summer term, my cheeks were still tinged with yellow, but illness was not going to prevent me from taking the first year preliminary exams.

I did not do well, however. I still did not know how to write successful essays about individual authors, spending too much time either praising or deriding the critics. When I started the first examination I discovered I had lost the fluency I took for granted at school. I laboured away, but found writing in these conditions difficult. For my weekly essays for Matthew Hodgart I had always prepared a rough draft, and now in the exam room I had no time for this. I became flustered and unsure of my style. To make things worse, when I faced the paper on metaphysical poetry, for which I had prepared questions on Crashaw, Traherne and Vaughan, these poets were not mentioned. I was forced to express my personal feelings and ideas about Donne and Herbert, for whom I had few apposite quotations and references to support my argument.

To my disappointment, I was awarded a lower second. If I repeated this performance at the end of the next year I would lose my exhibition. I was given a first class mark for the practical criticism paper, but my other scores were in the low fifties. The exception was the metaphysical paper, on which, in spite of my ill-prepared essays, my personal commitment and enthusiasm were rewarded with fifty-eight per cent. I consoled myself that if I returned to my policy for my exhibition, trusting my own judgment backed up with precise references, I must do better, and score over sixty per cent, the mark needed for an upper second. I did not tell my father about my lack of success. Fortunately he knew nothing about firsts and seconds, and was satisfied that I had passed and would continue into second year. I worked through the long vacation term, took a short break potato-picking on a farm near Durham to make some money, and returned to Pembroke in the autumn to fight again.

Some years everything goes right – halcyon times; my second year at Pembroke proved to be among the happiest in my life. When I first met Tony Dyson, queuing to see Matthew Hodgart in our first freshman week, I felt instinctively that we would never be friends. On this occasion first impressions proved very wrong. Tony was tall, gawky, unathletic, and never stopped talking about books. Even in a crowded bus or tube he discussed literary questions with complete absorption, oblivious of the other passengers. In our second year we met almost every day for walks or tea, discovering that we had much in common. We both loved romantic music – Brahms, of course, but also Mahler – and reacted to aesthetic experience as if it were some form of mystical illumination. Our tastes – and this continued to amaze us for the next forty years – were surprisingly similar. In the 1960s, for example, when editing *Critical Quarterly*, we were both convinced that the most important British poets after the time of Dylan Thomas were Philip Larkin, Ted Hughes, Thom Gunn and R.S. Thomas. Presumably the similarities in our background explain in some way our common tastes; we prefer to say that we think the same because we are right.

Tony came from Paddington in London, and, like me, his family was on the borderline between the working and lower middle classes. In the 1930s his father was often ill and unemployed, while his mother helped the family budget by half-time employment as a shop assistant (half time in the 1930s meant 12 noon to 7 p.m.) and by taking in lodgers. He attended Essendine Road Elementary School – very similar in ethos to Nunsthorpe – from where he won a scholarship to Sloane School, Chelsea. Its head, Guy Boas, was famous for his Shakespeare productions in which all parts were played by boys from the school. After the award of an open exhibition in English at Pembroke College, Tony was deemed physically unfit to serve in the forces because of a heart condition, and so spent two years as a clerk at the Ministry of Food before going up to Cambridge.

My academic success at Cambridge depended largely on what I learnt from Tony. If he had not become my friend I would never have succeeded in the Tripos examinations, nor become a university teacher. In the preliminary examination, although awarded only an upper second, he had gained high marks in the Shakespeare paper. He explained to me that he developed a personal 'theory' about each Shakespeare play (interpretation is a better word), and backed this up with precise references to the text, all taken from his own reading. Tony's 'theory' would be closely related to the central meanings and aesthetic qualities of each play, so that when he faced the actual exam question he could quickly work out how his 'theory' could be adapted to make an appropriate answer.

I followed this advice for all the literature papers in Part One of the Tripos. As I have a bad memory, I made long outline notes with headings and sub-headings for each 'theory', and learnt them off by heart, together with the supporting textual references. Other students used the same method, and an Australian friend of mine stuck his schemes all over his study walls, with coloured headlines in red and green, so he could cast his eye over them while sipping his coffee. My 'theories' were derived from my own personal responses to literature, plus ideas from Tony Dyson and Matthew Hodgart and critical books which I had found stimulating and in tune with my own thinking.

Tony and I sat Tripos in the Cambridge Senate House. All my plans worked out, and on every question I was able to use my prepared theory. Leavis, aggrieved by the lack of success of his own students, once wrote that an undergraduate who is awarded a first must be a walking cliché. I had arranged with Tony that he would send me a telegram on the day the results were posted outside the Senate House. Before the expected time I received two telegrams. The one I opened first read: 'You And Tony Walking Clichés – F.R. Leavis' (it was sent by my friend, Geoff Roberts). With my heart racing as I opened the second telegram, hoping my interpretation of the joke was correct, I read Tony's message:

'Results Early. We Both Have Firsts. Congratulations. A Happy Vac. Letter Following.' But my success in Tripos was not the most important event for me in that halcyon year.

Towards the end of the war my father's increased salary enabled him to buy a second-hand Wolseley car. He took a few driving lessons from an ex-chauffeur, and then drove himself sedately at twenty miles an hour along the uncrowded Grimsby streets. During the war there was no driving test for him to pass. The Wolseley started without much difficulty in third gear, so my father never used first or second. In the flat Lincolnshire countryside he could start in third and only change to fourth for higher speeds. He used to say: 'I don't believe in using all those gears.' I learnt to drive mainly from this example, for driving tests had still not been re-introduced; only years later, when I bought a car of my own, did I discover how primitive were my father's driving techniques.

Just before Christmas in my second year at Pembroke the old pupils of my school (the old Winghams) held a dance at the Gaiety in Grimsby. After the dance I drove home a girl called Jean Willmer, with whom I had been friendly when we were at school; we had both taken part in the annual Shakespeare plays. Jean was two years younger than me, and had already qualified as a teacher after two years at Sheffield Training College. Her father worked as a guard on the railway, and she lived in the end terrace house in Henry Street near the centre of Grimsby. After the evening of the dance we arranged to meet again to go dancing at the Winter Gardens in Cleethorpes; already, I think, we knew this would be a permanent relationship. We were married in 1954, soon after I was appointed assistant lecturer at Hull University, and I really have not much more to say about our relationship: it has been idyllic.

Tony Dyson believes there are no completely happy marriages, and that we are the exception that proves the rule. We have much in common, the same grammar school and Methodist background. Perhaps, above all, our families' lack of money and war-time hardships made us both determined to live to the full, to enjoy everything from travel to books, French cooking and new companions. For both of us the journey into adulthood became a process of discovery of privileges and pleasures denied to our parents. Some grammar school children from working-class homes (the poet Tony Harrison, for example) have never overcome their sense of guilt at the separations inflicted by their education. Jean and I have never felt separated from our many working-class friends and relatives, who have visited us and gone on holiday with us regularly over the years. I have only to think of King's Terrace Mission (and Jean of Lord Street Methodist Church, which she attended for many years) to recall people whose capacities for love were of the deepest, a true aristocracy. Jean's own mother and father also enjoyed an idyllic marriage, and their home was a centre for their neighbours, whose constant comings and goings, when I first became a regular visitor at Henry Street, amazed me.

After Tripos Jean and my cousin Diana joined me for a two-week cycling holiday in France. The total cost was about twenty-two pounds each, all we could afford. We travelled by train to Paris, where I had booked us into a youth camp not far from the Sorbonne. It turned out to be a squalid, filthy place. The beds, in large separate tents for men and women, were placed in long lines only a few feet away from each other. Several men returned at dawn, and my French was good enough to understand what they had been doing. We were thankful to leave and to cycle across the Place de la Concorde, through the Bois de Boulogne, and then to Chartres, where we spent the night in a hotel overlooking the cathedral. I sacrificed the bedroom with a view to the two girls, and slept soundly in a room whose window faced a brick wall. In the morning they were exhausted from lack of sleep because the restaurant clientele had been drinking and laughing under their window until the early hours. We then took our bikes by train to Saumur, and cycled slowly up the Loire to Orleans, staying both at Youth Hostels and hotels. On discovering that hotel beds and food were so cheap we no longer put up with the sleaziness of French Youth Hostels.

Our grammar school French let us down continually, however. One hotelier (they were all extraordinarily friendly) insisted I should play chess with him, and I surprised myself by winning. I was exhausted and the girls had already gone to bed, when in a few remarks after the game ended I once again mixed up my tenses. The hotelier thought I was proposing a second game, to which he assented eagerly, so I had to knuckle down to a further half hour's play. I tried subtly to let him win reasonably quickly, hoping he did not notice.

When we returned to Paris by train we determined to find a hotel. As we paused outside the railway station an old man asked us if we were looking for a hotel. As we were, we allowed him to lead us to the Hotel de France, just round a nearby corner, and sufficiently cheap for our small budget. I presume he was given a small commission. In the narrow lane overlooked by our bedrooms, prostitutes stood strung out at distances of about ten yards, and I began to worry about the real function of the Hotel de France. We found a nearby restaurant with a reasonably-priced menu. Two businessmen from the Far East (perhaps Vietnam) at an adjacent table found our French very amusing, and at the end of the meal bought us each a Benedictine. We had never tasted liqueurs before, and found the drink too sickly sweet; as soon as the men had departed we poured the liqueurs into a plant-pot.

From my point of view my third year at Cambridge, with Jean exchanging letters with me during the term, proved an ideal arrangement. Without any sense of loneliness or need for female company, I settled down to the second part of the English Tripos and to my football. In my second year I had lived above the dining hall, in luxury with a small bedroom and wash-basin, and a separate living room. As an exhibitioner I had the right to stay in college, while other friends were forced to search for digs.

My next-door neighbour was Peter May, who was often criticized for spending so much time playing football and cricket. He was right to feel aggrieved by such criticism. His bedroom was next to mine, and every morning I could hear him getting up promptly at 7 a.m. so he could study for several hours before taking part in games. Because he was famous, already an established cricketer, I treated him warily. I felt I should not impose myself on him, and was naturally a little shy of someone about whom I was reading in the sports pages of the newspapers. In my third year my bedmaker told me she thought he was lonely, and I regretted my restraint.

In my second year I started playing right-half, as I could not hope to replace him in the College side. It was the custom for University players to serve in the University's teams until the match with Oxford before Christmas, and then in the Lent term to join the College side for the annual cup competition. In my second year I gained my College Colours playing behind him, partly because as soon as I got possession of the ball Peter appeared in positions to which I found it easy to pass. He once spent a training session patiently trying to teach me how to kick the ball with my instep, not realizing that my fallen arches made this very difficult.

Tony Dyson had been converted to evangelical Christianity when as a teenager he walked into a church by chance and listened to an emotional sermon. His family never attended church. At Cambridge he was a member of evangelical groups, and he tried to interest me in their services. He lost his faith when, as a third year student, he studied ethics for a paper called 'The English Moralists' (he found and lost his faith again in the 1970s when he edited a journal called *Christian*). I attended the services with good-will, but soon felt grave doubts. A preacher described how he had been conversing with an old lady who was dying. She was a sweet person, he said, and she told him she hoped to go to heaven because she had always tried to be kind to people. He was horrified at her theological innocence, and told us that because she failed to understand that she was a sinner in need of Christ's redeeming powers she was in danger of damnation. I was disgusted by his arrogance and his lack of compassion for an old lady who, like my friends at King's Terrace, held no clear rational theological ideas, but simply tried to do good. I felt I would prefer to share the after-life with the old lady than with the preacher. I stopped attending the evangelical services.

I was converted permanently in my third year, though not to orthodox Christianity. It was an unusual conversion, affecting me deeply, and the resulting beliefs were very influential on my thinking during the Black Paper campaigns. It happened during the Christmas vacation, while I was reading for the first time C.S. Lewis's *The Screwtape Letters*, first published in 1942. In these well-known letters an experienced devil called Screwtape advises his nephew, Wormwood, on how to tempt his human patient, who has been converted to Christianity, to commit mortal sin. In the tenth and eleventh letters we discover that at his office Wormwood's human patient has made some desirable new acquaintances – rich, smart, superficially intellectual, and brightly sceptical about everything in the world. The patient now exists in two different kinds of society – with his church companions, and with this new set of sceptics. Screwtape points out that many human beings live, for quite long periods, two parallel lives. While kneeling with the grocer on Sunday at church, Wormwood's patient will feel superior because the grocer could not possibly understand the urbane and mocking world which the patient inhabits on weekdays. He can enjoy bawdy and blasphemy over coffee with his new friends because he knows he is aware of a 'deeper', 'spiritual' world they cannot understand. 'You see the idea,' Screwtape explains, 'the worldly friends touch him on one side and the grocer on the other, and he is the complete, balanced, complex man who sees round them all.' From this double role the patient will derive great self-satisfaction.

This letter threw a hurtful light on my own vanity. At Pembroke I led two parallel lives, with my football companions and with the literary set reading English. With friends like Tony Dyson I felt superior because I played football for the College team and spent time with extrovert companions who would find him narrow and academic. With my soccer friends I felt superior because I had won first class honours in the Tripos, with tastes in literature which they did not share.

Retrospectively my vanity seems to me by no means exceptional, but that is the point. I was shocked both to discover my own vanities, and to realize that all human beings indulge in such self-deceptions. As I read *The Screwtape Letters* I moved in one hour from the belief that human beings were naturally good to the belief that all of us are naturally selfish and self-deluded. At that time I translated this conversion into a belief in the Christian doctrine of original sin. With regard to education, I understood the need for rewards and discipline if children and adolescents are to be persuaded to obey school rules and to study hard. I did not undervalue the importance of pleasure in learning, but believed, as I still do, that children are innately selfish, flourishing only in a carefully structured environment, with clear goals controlled by adults. In this kind of environment they may discover – as I had done – the joy and self-fulfilment that comes from abandoning yourself to the disciplines of study, to the discovery, for example, of what great writers felt and thought.

I still longed to teach. I decided that if I was awarded a second in Tripos Part Two I would work for the one-year graduate teachers' certificate; if awarded a first I would stay on at Cambridge for postgraduate research and a career in higher education. I applied and was accepted for the graduate course. The professor of education who interviewed me was impressed by my first, and told me that little could be taught about education, and that the extra year would give me the chance to read and reflect. My friends, such as Geoff Roberts who actually took the course, found that the professor was right. Apart from the compulsory term spent in teaching practice in a school, their year's training was almost useless, except for the opportunity it gave for private reading.

During our third year Tony and I worked and argued together almost every day. We were fascinated by the Tragedy paper, which introduced us to the Greek dramatists, to Aeschylus, Sophocles and Euripides. We also translated set texts in French and Italian, including Ariosto's *Orlando Furioso*, which tells the story of the fair Angelica and the madness of Orlando, whose love for her is unrequited. After Tripos I received just one telegram from Tony: 'We Both Have Firsts. Congratulations. My Love To Angelica. Will Write.'

That summer Jean and I decided to hitch-hike to the Mediterranean. We wanted to explore France, but had very little cash. Hitch-hiking was popular in the early 1950s; hundreds of young people, from Germany as well as Britain, France, Belgium and Holland, were beginning to break free from the prison-house of the war, and set off on ambitious explorations. We soon discovered there were too many hitch-hikers on the main roads south of Paris. We had travelled by train to Paris and then to Fontainebleau; when we began our hitch-hiking, though, there were about forty hitch-hikers, of different nationalities, spread out along the first kilometre. We made little progress, often stuck for hours by the road-side. Our first major lift was given by a lorry driver who was excited by the infamous murder of an English tourist called Drummond, whose body had just been discovered in the south of France that morning. He insisted on stopping at a bar, and after buying us a St Raphael (another new experience) found a newspaper so we could read the horrifying details. The account of the murder of a British tourist was not an encouraging start for us. A young car driver took us 100 miles to Chalon-sur-Saône, making a diversion from the main road to visit friends he had not seen since the war, and with whom he had worked in the Maquis. Seven years after the war it still filled our imaginations.

On the road south of Chalon our fortunes changed. We had been standing for over two hours on a hot day without a lift, the black Citroëns of the French middle class sweeping past with disdain, when a man who spoke fluent English stopped and told us he was driving to Annecy in the Alps. Such a huge lift was too tempting, so we abandoned our plan to see the Mediterranean, and travelled with him. His father had worked as a chef at the Savoy Hotel in London, so he had been partly brought up in England, and was pleased to have companions with whom he could use his English. For Jean and me the journey into the Alps was truly miraculous, a revelation no longer possible for children of the television age. We had never watched colour films, never seen mountains and lakes – not even the English lakes. We climbed the narrow, tortuous roads from Bourg-en-Bresse to Nantua and then to Annecy, where he deposited us in the Avenue D'Albigny, where still today a line of mature plane trees borders the lake. Annecy lake, an astonishing glittering green, with the mountains grouped around, seemed straight from a fairy-tale. The word 'awe' has been debased in contemporary usage, but at that moment we both experienced its true meaning.

We abandoned hitch-hiking, stayed ten days, and then caught a train back to Paris. Just before we left we visited Annecy railway station to buy our tickets, and then wished to return to the lake. On a hot day, carrying packs on our backs, we walked over half a mile before we realized we had chosen the wrong direction. We stopped, worn-out and crestfallen. It was a moment of truth. I regard myself as even-tempered, but when Jean laughed first at our predicament I knew my married happiness was assured.

I then returned to Cambridge for postgraduate work. Both Tony Dyson and I regard these years (two in my case, three in his) as a disaster. We were very happy. We both were forced to move into digs, but found suitable accommodation in the area of Grantchester Meadows, and we made new friends. Ted Hughes, now Poet Laureate, came up to Pembroke in 1951 to read English, and though he was never a close friend of mine I saw him often. He and a Frenchman called Tavera invited me to a wine party. I had never been to such a function before; as the invitation card said 8 p.m., I typically arrived on time, to the embarrassment of Ted who was still preparing the room. The next guest turned up forty-five minutes later. As a postgraduate I continued to play football; the arrival of two excellent half-backs among the freshers relegated me to the second team, but I was not bothered. Jean and I were preparing to be married, and in 1953 managed to afford a cheap package holiday to Krumsee in the Tyrol.

What was disastrous was the postgraduate course. Tony and I now both agree that we learnt little from our studies, and that our abilities in written English declined. The problem still exists today, when large numbers of graduates in English, with first degrees of high quality, spend two, three or more years trying to write a thesis.

For the Tripos I submitted 5,000-word voluntary essays on George Eliot and Henry James which could be taken into account in the assessment if of sufficiently high quality. Strongly influenced by Leavis, I wanted to write literary criticism, and I had comparatively little interest in scholarship. My thesis for a Master of Letters degree was pompously entitled 'Moral Implications in the Fiction of Henry James'. I wanted to write a critical evaluation of James's values as exemplified in his fiction. My supervisor was Joan Bennett, a little old lady with an enormous head. We met about once a month for pleasant chats over tea, and I submitted some essays on individual novels; otherwise I was on my own. Joan Bennett was kind to me, but had her own uncertainties about the usefulness of postgraduate research. Neither of us had any clear idea of how to proceed. With characteristic thoroughness I determined to read everything James had ever written, plus all the secondary material. This took me most of my two years, during which I could discuss my views with no one, except Joan Bennett. Tony had read little James, and after ploughing his way through the first chapter of *The Golden Bowl* six times declared himself still baffled. I became obsessed with minor issues (the use of water imagery by James, for example).

My Cambridge training in practical criticism meant that I had little competence in the disciplines of philosophy or history or linguistics. In my second year as a postgraduate I heard of Wittgenstein for the first time from a student I was supervising. I had never studied Marx or Freud, except in the most casual manner; I urgently needed the American seminar system, so that with other postgraduates and under careful supervision from a specialist I could have studied literary theory and the history of ideas. Steven Marcus, from Columbia University in New York, later famous for his books on Dickens and Freud, was at Pembroke at that time, also working under Joan Bennett. We met informally a few times, but what I really needed were regular seminars with students of his sharp intellect who could assess and criticize my developing ideas. I was in no way ready to prepare a major work on Henry James, about whom so many books had been published in previous years. I worked very hard on an almost useless project. Tony was writing a thesis on ethical ideas in eighteenth-century poetry, and he too began to detest the demands of this sterile occupation. During these postgraduate years at Pembroke I was desperate to find a job, which meant I had to do well with my thesis, although deep down I knew my real interests were elsewhere.

These two years were to some degree saved for me because I undertook a great deal of teaching (more than the regulations allowed). Tony and I wrote a joint letter to various colleges, asking for work in supervising undergraduates. A.P. Rossiter responded positively, referring to us as Clennam and Doyce (from Dickens's *Little Dorrit*), a nickname we have used together in our correspondence ever since (and also Pox and Byson, invented by the *Review* in the 1960s in its satirical pieces on us).

My main teaching commitment, however, was to the Workers' Education Association, for whom I allocated about two days per week, including preparation and travel, during my two postgraduate years at Pembroke. In the summer of 1952, after I graduated, I attended a two-week W.E.A. course in Cambridge for prospective tutors. Real W.E.A. students, on a separate course, were invited to volunteer to attend. Each trainee gave a twenty-minute talk on a subject of his or her choice, and then organized a discussion for twenty minutes; the session ended with criticisms of the trainee, first from the W.E.A. organizer, and then from the real W.E.A. students. After my R.A.E.C. training this proved a second short but invaluable introduction to the teaching of adults. It astonishes me that university teachers may still receive no training. The other trainees on the W.E.A. course made all the classic errors. Nervous and twitchy, one young man actually threw the chalk up in the air repeatedly while, as we lost track of his argument, we watched anxiously to see if he would drop it on the floor. Another buried himself behind the lectern and read a prepared script so badly we missed key words. Later, as a university teacher, I heard similar accounts of incompetent teaching. One lecturer prepared her material with great care, but to her consternation her class rapidly shrank in size until by the sixth session there remained only three or four students in the front row. She approached one of them nervously, and asked why the others had stopped coming. The student told her: 'They can't hear you.'

My first assignment was to teach a ten-week course entitled 'The Countryside in Literature' at a village called Methwold in Norfolk. The title sounds quaint today, but I was told it would attract good numbers from village groups. I spent a week preparing for the first session, choosing passages of different levels of difficulty to cater for the variety of people expected to attend. Village classes rarely included more than one or two real 'workers' (such as farm labourers), and were mainly middle-class housewives, with perhaps the vicar's wife or the local school-teacher. I chose popular passages from books such as A.G. Street's *Farmer's Glory*, for example, together with some Thomas Hardy and Wordsworth. I had learnt to type with two fingers in the army, and owned a cheap Olivetti typewriter. I hammered out eight passages, using carbons so that everyone could read a copy. I had been told by the Methwold secretary that twenty to thirty people might attend, so this meant I typed my passages five times, with six carbons. I had no duplicator, and no idea where such a resource could be found.

The first ninety-minute session was scheduled to take place before I returned to Cambridge, so I drove down from Grimsby to Methwold (over 100 miles) often down winding country roads, in my father's Wolseley. As I arrived over an hour early, I parked a mile short of the village and checked through my notes. I was nervous and, after taking some deep breaths, drove down to Methwold to arrive about fifteen minutes early. At 7.30 p.m., the due time to start, there were three people present; by 7.45 p.m., there were seven, and one more arrived half an hour late. Before the evening was over I would have driven about 250 miles to teach eight people. The pay was twenty-five shillings a session, plus a small allowance for petrol. As I returned home up moonlit Lincolnshire roads I felt chagrined, with most of my typed sheets unused, yet also mildly pleased, for the evening had been successful. At the end an old countryman shook me by the hand, and promised me he would bring along two friends next week. In subsequent weeks my numbers at Methwold increased to fifteen, and remained steady. For the next two years I travelled from Cambridge twice a week to small villages, spending hours in preparation. The people I met, the teaching challenges, felt so much more real to me than my so-called 'research' on Henry James.

In my second year I was invited to Harlow, on my map a small village south of Cambridge. The class had agreed to take my course 'The Countryside in Literature', which by now was tried and tested and very well prepared for village groups. When the secretary picked me up at the railway station I was a little surprised to be met by a sophisticated, highly articulate young architect; often the W.E.A. secretary was not typical of the group, however. But when we turned into an area of new buildings, arriving at a huge, brand-new school, I realized this would be no ordinary village group. When the class assembled I was confronted by almost all young professionals, busy creating the early stages of Harlow New Town. I immediately jettisoned most of my prepared notes and passages, and gave them an impromptu talk on D.H. Lawrence, on the links between his concepts of Nature and sex and society. It went down very well, and eventually I was invited to give a second course there.

In those days after the war the W.E.A. performed miracles in keeping alive literary and cultural debate. Some tutors became famous (Raymond Williams and Richard Hoggart, for example); others taught with passion and an eccentricity untrammelled by examination requirements. When I taught a class near Peter-borough I was given a lift back to Cambridge by a middle-aged history tutor who insisted, even in January and February, on driving an open car. I borrowed a heavy woollen overcoat from my landlord, and sat slumped in the passenger-seat as the bitter winter air rushed over the windscreen. If our headlights picked up a rabbit my driver chased it down the road, often careering wildly onto the grass verge. We would stop and hope to find a dead rabbit, which he would sling into the boot to be cooked the next day.

A Cambridge organizer, a woman in her thirties, visited my class at Harlow, and gave me a lift back in her car which had a broken sunshine roof. On the way home we drove through a thunderstorm, so I had to hold the roof closed with both hands, while she gripped her side with one hand and steered with the other. At a narrow stone bridge she took her hand off the wheel to change gear, and we leapt up onto the pavement and scraped against the bridge parapet. But we survived, and I was proud to continue to teach for the W.E.A. for many years after I was married.

In my second postgraduate year I started applying for university assistant lectureships. Jean and I agreed we would go to any university except Aberdeen (too far north) and Hull (we had found it boring when we were children). After twelve unsuccessful applications (never once short-listed), Hull offered an assistant lectureship in English. Desperate, I applied, together with another application for an extra-mural teaching position at Liverpool. I was short-listed for both jobs.

Professor Basil Willey, a Fellow of Pembroke College, told me that the Hull position was destined for Richard Hoggart, who wanted to move from extra-mural to an internal teaching lectureship at Hull. During the Easter vacation I travelled by train and across the Humber by the New Holland ferry to Hull for the interview. I was not nervous, because I knew I had no chance, and looked forward to practising my interview techniques in preparation for Liverpool a few days later. There were four candidates, and I was astonished to be called back at the end of the afternoon to be offered the position. Apparently there had been some hitch in the arrangement with Richard Hoggart. The Vice-Chancellor seemed very pleased to hear that I had taught at

Immingham, and intended to marry a Grimsby girl. At the end of a railway line, Hull University had problems with lecturers who spent all available time applying for jobs elsewhere and leaving the neighbourhood as often as possible. That day my father was at the Savoy Hotel in London attending the annual shareholders' meeting of E.W. Nickerson and Co. Ltd. I sent him a telegram whose simplicity amused him for years to come: 'Got the job. Brian.'

# 5
# *A Literary Life in Hull*

I have my children. I am a millionaire.

Gagik Beidzyan, survivor of the Armenian earthquake
on its first anniversary, 1989

Jean and I were married on 7 August, 1954. On the way to Lord Street Methodist chapel, riding in a Rolls Royce loaned by one of my father's business colleagues, wearing my new dark-grey suit with a button-hole carnation, I felt a fool. I dislike taking part in ceremonies. In the last four years I have presided as Pro-Vice-Chancellor at many crowded degree congregations, pacing slowly down the aisle in Manchester University's magnificent Whitworth Hall in my cap, hood and gown, always feeling ridiculous. But in principle I believe ceremonies perform a valuable social function: they witness to the dignity of man. At my wedding, as we stood at the front in the small, dark, ugly chapel, like a Victorian school-room, I was deeply moved by the enthusiastic singing of hymns and the traditional words of dedication. For both Jean and me marriage is a privilege and a source of unbelievable happiness, the coming together of two human beings who, if they are fortunate, join together to create new life. On that wedding day in 1954 and still today thirty-eight years later, we believe that the greatest joy is to be found in loyalty, friendship and love in a permanent relationship, a true marriage.

After the ceremony, the reception proved an anti-climax. To save money we had ordered a buffet, for we had invited many guests from our two large families. Our relatives were not accustomed to this kind of function, however, and sat down on the uncomfortable, plain wooden chairs, waiting to be served. I spent the early part of the reception dashing around with plates of ham and cheese sandwiches. As in Philip Larkin's poem, 'The Whitsun Weddings', we left by train on the conventional honeymoon trip to London, where we spent the night in the Strand Palace Hotel. But we changed the routine by proceeding the next day to Krumsee in the Tyrol, where we had booked a room in a farmhouse we had discovered the previous year. On the farmhouse lady's kitchen wall there was a plaque with photographs of members of her family killed during the two world wars. We felt grateful to have survived, to be enjoying peace-time security.

The weather was perfect, and we spent our time walking through the meadows, savouring each bird call and flower and ray of sunlight through the trees. For both of us a huge pleasure is to swim in a placid, sun-lit Alpine lake, gazing up at wooded slopes and mountain peaks. At the end of one trail we discovered Berglsteiner Lake, only accessible by forest paths. We swam round its small rocky island, feeling we had entered a secret paradise. Years later we returned with our three teenage children to discover that a road and car-park had opened up the lake to tourists, with a warden demanding a small fee from the swimmers. The lake surroundings were still well cared for, and I do not really mind when I find that new people are enjoying what I was fortunate to discover so many years ago. On our return journey we arrived at Innsbruck railway station in need of a room for the night before taking up our couchette reservations for Calais. As in Paris in 1951 an old man asked us if we wanted a room, and took us by bus to an apartment block. We slept in the bedroom of a woman who lived alone with a child, and who seemed very pleased to let her room for a very small sum of money. I presumed she was a war widow, trying to make ends meet.

Back in Hull we rented a little terrace house in King Street, Cottingham, for two guineas a week. Cottingham, a large village west of Hull, is the site for the University halls of residence, standing only a mile or so from the University itself. Heavily bombed during the war, Hull in the 1950s was still blighted by vacant lots covered with weeds and rubble. Philip Larkin evoked the atmosphere of Hull, its docks and streets intermingled, in his poem 'Here': 'grim head-scarfed wives', 'A cut-price crowd, urban yet simple,' 'a fishy-smelling pastoral of ships up streets'.

Hull University had just been granted university status, after many years as a college attached to London University. It could now determine its own courses and grant its own degrees. When I arrived in 1954 it was a very small institution, with only about eighty staff and 800 students. Soon I knew every member of staff; it was common for me, the most junior, to chat over lunch with the most senior, including the Vice-Chancellor, Brynmor Jones, himself. During those early years, Hull was a lively community, with many young lecturers poised to make their reputations – Richard Hoggart, about to publish *The Uses of Literacy*, George Hunter, now teaching at Yale, Malcolm Bradbury the novelist, Barbara Everett, now at Oxford, who delivered the Clark lectures at Cambridge in 1989, and Peter Worsley, the sociologist. Above all, there was Philip Larkin, appointed librarian in 1955. I once heard him tell a revealing story about his interview at Hull for the position of librarian. In the previous week he had published his poem, 'Toads', with its famous lines:

> Why should I let the toad *work*
> Squat on my life?

As his train looped eastwards alongside the Humber, he reflected wanly that it was not exactly the right poem to print just before an important job interview. 'I needn't have worried,' he continued in mock-lugubrious tones, 'the committee hadn't read the poem. They didn't even know I wrote poetry.' I certainly had never heard of him before he arrived at Hull, and only through him made contact with George and Jean Hartley, who edited *Listen*, and whose Marvell Press was about to publish Philip's *The Less Deceived*. They lived in poverty in a small house in Hessle Road, and later Jean and I went with Philip to have dinner with them a couple of times. I now think that it is a disgrace both to me and to my Cambridge training that I had not met them during my first year at Hull, and that I knew almost nothing about new contemporary poets.

Although in the 1950s Hull University was an exciting small community, I felt very cut off from the rest of England. Once I was invited to Leeds to hear T.S. Eliot lecture. Before motorways the journey by car was tiresome, so I did not take the trouble, and I now much regret the missed opportunity. But I feared I might vegetate at Hull, so I undertook some spectacular journeys. I once travelled five hours by train to Exeter to speak to the English Society, only to be confronted by an audience of eight students.

Malcolm Bradbury provided a considerable stimulus. In 1960 we were both invited with our wives to meet Saul Bellow at the Midland Hotel in Manchester, at a dinner organized by the American Embassy. Malcolm had bought a new Volkswagen Beetle, so he drove us, taking over three hours on roads that led through one Northern industrial town after the next. In those days drivers of Beetles, a new phenomenon, flashed their lights at each other; we drove to Manchester in high spirits, flashing away at kindred spirits. Saul Bellow paid particular attention to us, perhaps because we were among the youngest there. I was deeply impressed by him. He spoke with great vivacity and with an integrity of language as if his words had been newly minted by himself. He joked that at first he had been surprised that the American government had wanted to pay for a trip which included countries behind the Iron Curtain, but then he realized his paymasters were clever. His Communist hosts would be impressed that the United States was willing to be represented by such a notorious iconoclast. When we were about to leave, he waved his arm towards Jean, who was heavily pregnant, and wished all might go well. Celia, our third child, was born in June; she now has three children of her own, so his salutation proved a good omen.

When I was appointed at Hull University Professor R.L. Brett had been in charge of the English department for two years. He and his wife (Ray and Kitty) were practising Christians in the best sense, and during my early career I was very fortunate to work for such a generous man. When he came to Hull he introduced tutorials; previously all the teaching had been by way of lectures. There were only six members of staff, three teaching Old English and medieval literature (Margaret Espinasse, Rosemary Woolf and Alan Binns) and three teaching literature since the Renaissance

(Ray Brett, George Hunter and me). In order to cut our teaching time the literature group taught one period to all three years of undergraduates, thus reducing the necessary number of lectures. Before I arrived I had to prepare a course of lectures on the English novel from Defoe to Thomas Hardy, a gargantuan task which kept me very busy in the weeks after Jean and I arrived in Cottingham.

Once term started my teaching load was light, only eight or nine hours a week, and life at Hull University proved very easy. On my first day Donald Charlton (later professor of French at Warwick) kindly told me that no one was ever sacked (except for real crimes), and that I had a safe job for life (until I was sixty-seven). When I had prepared my lectures, I had only to make minor revisions each year, and perhaps completely rewrite one or two that had been unsuccessful. We had few tutorials, so that often I would take one before coffee, and then chat with friends right through to lunch. As the babies began to arrive (three between 1955 and 1960) I usually cycled home by 4 p.m. to help Jean with the chores.

Young lecturers were granted tenure to allow time for research, so that they could develop their ideas independently without pressure for quick publication; for most of us, though, the temptation to relax became irresistible. I submitted my thesis in 1956, the regulations allowing it to be considered for a PhD, even though I had spent only two years full-time at Cambridge. My examiner, Dorothea Krook, insisted that it was not a contribution to knowledge, but a piece of literary criticism; she therefore awarded it the MLitt. My own view now is that it was not even worth that award. My Cambridge training provided me merely with a facility in practical criticism, useful for teaching and textbooks, but for most postgraduates not a sufficient basis for a major thesis or book.

As at Cambridge I found stimulus in W.E.A. teaching. My classes met in outlying parts of Yorkshire, such as Withernsea on the coast. Through winter cold, pushing my way against sharp winds from the North Sea, I rode my new Vespa across the flat East Riding roads to a class often only eight or nine in number. After three years at Withernsea, teaching a course on the English novel, I told the class I thought it was time for another tutor to take over. 'I've told you all I know about the English novel,' I said. The secretary replied:

'But we've forgotten what you told us a couple of years ago. You must come back.'

Much as I enjoyed the enthusiasm of W.E.A. students, as the years went by I worried that this kind of teaching made me too anxious to please, too tactful when responding to naive opinions because I feared that unintentional rudeness might turn someone against me and reduce the numbers in the class. I felt more at home teaching undergraduates, and was very happy in this work. I enjoyed the interplay of ideas and personalities in tutorials and seminars, the joy of expressing enthusiasms and of succeeding in drawing out the shy and the diffident. As a teacher I am in the liberal tradition, anxious that students should develop their own views, and wary of imposing my own too pugnaciously. I have never fully solved the problems created by my open approach.

At Hull I was worried by the number of students who imitated received opinion, and never honestly expressed their own views. I was very conscious of my own diffidence when I was in the sixth form at Wintringham, and so tried to draw my students out. When interviewing students for admission at Hull University I noticed how many of them, when asked for their opinion about a book or a poem, would reply 'we thought' or 'we decided'; they submitted themselves to the class view, prompted by the teacher, rather than developing their own ideas. George Hunter and I arranged a seminar on *Twelfth Night* in which we adopted diametrically opposed interpretations of the function of Malvolio. Should we sympathize with him or not? We thought students would be encouraged to join the debate in the knowledge that they would be supported by a member of staff. At the end of the seminar a student came up to us and asked: 'But who was right?' So many students wanted us to tell them what to think.

I printed this anecdote in an article in a national student magazine. In a reply Arnold Kettle, a member of the Communist Party and later professor of English at the Open University, argued that the student's question was very proper. The danger of liberal tolerance, he said, is that it allows credence to all views, and becomes ineffective and impotent by refusing to commit itself to a firm line (he would have detested the relativism implicit in much post-structuralist writing). In my teaching I have found it difficult to hold the balance between clear statements of my own beliefs and open-minded encouragement of dissent. At times I feel I am too friendly, too considerate towards views I hold to be wrong. Because I consider I am over-tolerant, I was shocked and dismayed during the Black Paper years to find myself portrayed in the media as the authoritarian Enoch Powell of education.

In the late 1950s I started trying to express my liberal values through active political commitment, and to clarify them for myself by examining relevant works of literature. I wrote a series of essays which eventually became my first book, *The Free Spirit*, published in 1963 by Oxford University Press. The role of a free spirit (a phrase used by Henry James in his Prefaces to describe characters such as Fleda Vetch in *The Spoils of Poynton*) was my ideal. I have described how in my adolescence in Grimsby I was creating my own identity, sloughing off the puritanism of my family background. The fictional free spirits whose careers I examined in my book included Isabel Archer and Ralph Touchett in James's *The Portrait of a Lady*, Fielding in E.M. Forster's *A Passage to India*, and Bernard Sands in Angus Wilson's *Hemlock and After*. These are men and women who break away from established moral, social and religious traditions, and try to put their humanist ideals into practice. The outlook of the free spirits owed much to John Stuart Mill and the liberal middle-class culture of the late nineteenth century, with its faith in historical progress, individual freedom, tolerance and the power of reason. The free spirits were people of courage and honour, like James and Forster and Wilson themselves, caring deeply for individual liberty and responding sensibly and flexibly to particular moral or social problems. Their anti-dogmatism, their tolerance and their passion for justice had an important and healthy influence on our national life, in the struggle for women's rights, for racial equality or the extension of educational opportunities to all classes. Tony Dyson and I both like to think that we have been working in that tradition.

The novelists I discussed in my book were very much aware that the free spirits found it difficult to put their ideals into practice, often withdrawing into quietism and pessimism. In many novels, such as Lionel Trilling's *The Middle of the Journey*, the free spirit (Laskell in this novel) is associated with sickness, with debility. The moral tensions of writers in the liberal tradition are reflected in structural weaknesses in their novels, in the sentimental ending of Forster's *Howards End*, for example. I felt caught in similar tensions in my own teaching, in the conflict between my desire to be tolerant, to welcome dissent, and my determination that as many people as possible should be enriched by culture, by the Arts.

In wider social and political issues how could liberalism influence government policy? Tony and I both voted Labour, and held Clement Attlee in high esteem. I canvassed for Labour at the Hull by-election of 27 January 1966, when the seat was won by Kevin McNamara with a majority for Labour more than four times greater than at the last General Election. This success helped to persuade Harold Wilson, the Prime Minister, to call a General Election on 31 March, when I once again canvassed for Labour. In the late 1950s Tony and I were both supporters of the Campaign for Nuclear Disarmament and took part in the Aldermaston March. At the end of the march, in Trafalgar Square, I was interviewed by BBC radio about my reasons for supporting unilateral nuclear disarmament. I was then convinced that there should be an international movement to ensure that Russia and the United States became the only countries with the nuclear deterrent. At Scarborough, during a Labour Party Conference, Jean and I pushed a pram with our first baby on a CND march. At Hull University I paraded about wearing a CND badge in my lapel. Tony and I both resigned from CND when the Committee of 100 started attracting attention by sitting on roads and pavements and inviting arrest. I thought this policy would alienate moderate opinion, and I have always believed strongly in the rule of law. We wanted effective policies, not gestures of dissent.

In the 1950s Tony founded the Homosexual Reform Society; he played a leading role in changing public opinion so that the recommendation of the Wolfenden Report of 1957, that private adult relationships be removed from the domain of the criminal law, was eventually implemented. His genius in organizing pressure groups, so important during the Black Paper campaigns, was developed during these courageous pioneering days, so crucial for homosexual reform. At that time homosexuality was still a crime, with offenders sent to gaol, and Tony showed great moral courage in coming out so publicly on this issue. It seems hilariously inappropriate that later during the Black Paper furore he should have been accused of conformism and conventionality.

My uncertainties about liberalism and Christianity were to some extent resolved by my reading of the American Protestant theologian, Reinhold Niebuhr. I remained sceptical about the Resurrection, and could find no moral explanation for the existence of pain, but Niebuhr helped me to understand how my liberal ideas could overcome passivity and despair. Niebuhr admits, with some qualifications, that Christianity has been more frequently a source of confusion in political and social ethics than a source of insight and constructive guidance. Christian orthodoxy has often been excessively conservative, sacrificing time and history to eternity, and making the doctrine of original sin into an excuse for believing that progressive action is impossible. In contrast, Christian liberals have behaved as if the law of love could be actualized in the present, and have easily been thrown into uncertainty and despair by the pressure of events. Niebuhr finds the answer to the liberal dilemma in what he call prophetic Christianity. Like liberalism, Christianity tries to bring the whole of reality and existence into some form of coherence; but it escapes from the frustrations of liberalism because it has a sense of a transcendental source of meaning by which alone confidence in the meaningfulness of action can be maintained.

Through all our anxieties and uncertainties, Tony and I have both held fast to this belief that our actions have ultimate meaning. We both think that music is the greatest of the Arts; for us it is impossible to believe that the exquisite beauty of the adagio in Mahler's Fifth Symphony or of Schubert's 'Trout' piano quintet, for example, came into being through some kind of cosmic accident. Like Wordsworth, Coleridge and T.S. Eliot, we have held fast to Plato's belief in absolutes of truth, goodness and beauty, towards which all human action should aspire.

I have found such beliefs, outlined in *The Free Spirit*, sustaining, and felt no need to change them since I first read Niebuhr in the early 1960s. I remain agnostic about an after-life. Like most of us, I am bewildered by time and space, by the apparent contradiction between the incomprehensible size of the universe and the unique richness of the individual consciousness. However, I have never lost my belief in the possibility of improving society, in the ideal of love revealed in the New Testament.

*The Free Spirit* received some favourable reviews, but I know that it is deeply flawed. I am proud of the book's literary criticism, and that some chapters, such as those on E.M. Forster and Angus Wilson, have been reprinted in anthologies; but partly through lack of natural ability and partly through lack of training I am not adroit at handling abstract ideas. I simply had not read enough about ethics. I was also too concerned with English literature; I had not then read Thomas Mann's *The Magic Mountain*, so relevant to my theme, and my book badly lacked a European dimension.

After four years at Hull I felt unused, as if my abilities were dwindling away into the pastoral security of the mild East Riding countryside and the relaxed way of life at Hull University. I therefore welcomed the challenge of starting a new literary journal, *Critical Quarterly*, and of trying to put my humanist ideals into practice by organizing various kinds of literary events.

Because editing *Critical Quarterly* involved me in running a little business, my left-wing utopian ideals of the 1950s were soon tempered by a realistic understanding of the mechanisms of profit and loss, and the need to compromise if an organization is to work efficiently. I learnt, for example, that I must budget for a larger profit than I actually needed. If I tried to operate on small profit margins and misjudged my expenses or sales I might lose sums of money I did not possess. This is very simple economics, but such experiences changed me fundamentally. I grew accustomed to thinking hard about the consequences in real terms of my administrative decisions. This attitude was later of crucial importance in Black Paper critiques of Labour Party policies, for example the left-wing faith in neighbourhood schools.

In August 1958 Tony and I were teaching in Cambridge at a British Council Summer School for foreign students. A morning lecture, which relied mainly on literary anecdotes, was given by G.S. Fraser. In the afternoon Tony and I walked to Grantchester, enraged in a Leavis-like manner by this betrayal of our ideals about the moral importance of literature. We contemplated a book to be written jointly on literary criticism, and then later that afternoon we considered starting a new journal.

F.R. Leavis's *Scrutiny* had ceased publication in 1953, and since then the need for a replacement had become a common topic of university conversation. There was no hope of financial backing, and from our own money we knew we would have difficulty raising even fifty pounds to launch the project. Our discussions moved forwards and backwards between our literary values and questions of administration and finance. At the end of the day we had a scheme for promotion of the new journal fully worked out. We never told George Fraser that he was 'the only begetter' of *C.Q.*, and indeed over the years we learnt to admire his sharp intelligence and generosity of spirit. *Critical Quarterly* later published articles by him on Conrad, Yeats and Thom Gunn.

Tony and I thought of ourselves as teachers rather than as innovators of some new critical theory. Many young writers who start journals give little thought to money or their readership. We were determined to reach a large audience, and this aim influenced the characteristic values of our journal. For the next fifteen years we spent much time at editorial meetings discussing money. The incentive to find subscribers, to be aware of the needs of our readers, and to balance the books contributed significantly to the early success of *Critical Quarterly*. To lie in bed at dawn thinking of an unpaid printer's bill for £300 forces an editor to reflect carefully on the realities of communication, on how the journal can create a style which will attract a specific type of reader. When in 1973 Manchester University Press took over our finances the journal gradually declined in quality because this fierce economic pressure was removed from the editorial team.

Our plan was to move forward in stages, and to leave ourselves the possibility of withdrawal if anything went wrong. Because no one would recognize our names, we decided that we had to associate with ourselves a number of writers whose work we admired. This would provide a group of useful contributors; it would also persuade prospective buyers that this was not to be a young man's folly, but a major new literary magazine. We started by asking two friends to work as editorial advisers. These were John Danby, author of *Shakespeare's Doctrine of Nature*, and Richard

Hoggart, by this time well-known for his *The Uses of Literacy*. Both were generous and warm-hearted, willing to offer assistance while leaving final decisions to Tony and me. Danby was Tony's professor at Bangor, and Hoggart was at that time still teaching in the Extra-Mural Department at my University at Hull, so consultation was easy. Tony had the use of a flat in London, where we met for editorial meetings, and there were many long telephone calls. We had a simple agreement that in selection of material both of us had the right of veto. At that time Professor Brett was in the United States, but when he returned he too gave invaluable assistance.

What name should we choose for our journal? Should it be 'Bastion' (too pompous), 'Horizon' (used before), 'Ariel' (not distinctive enough), 'Bridge' (a card game) or 'Communication' (sounds dull)? In the end Danby proposed *Critical Quarterly*. 'It sounds as if it has existed for a hundred years,' he argued. The next stage in our plan was to write to several friends to invite them to join an honorary committee. These included the poets Philip Larkin and R.S. Thomas, the novelist Angus Wilson, and university teachers such as John Jump, David Daiches and Graham Hough. We sent out sixteen invitations, hoping for five or six favourable replies. Within a few days we received acceptances from all sixteen. We found ourselves in an embarrassing position, for our list now looked distinctly odd. If all these people had been selected, why had others not been asked? We decided to invite every Professor of English in Britain. Again the response was good, with this time just a few refusals. We ended up with an honorary committee of thirty-five. After our first issue was published we were assisted by an American associate editor, R.J. Kaufmann, and he added eleven American names to the list, including Saul Bellow and Richard Wilbur.

Meanwhile we had been obtaining estimates from printers for an eighty- or ninety-six-page, octavo size, quarterly journal. The best estimate came from Hull Printers Ltd., just a couple of miles from my home; the opportunity to drop in regularly to discuss problems proved very useful. Our next step was to print stationery with a large letter-head listing ourselves, our advisers, and our honorary committee. The time had come to risk our fifty pounds. We could not afford to advertise in literary journals, and this was fortunate. In later years, when we were more affluent, we discovered that such advertisements do not bring in many subscriptions. Our plan was to duplicate descriptions of our journal on our printed notepaper and to send these through the post to selected groups of people. Our market would be teachers of English in universities, colleges of education and schools. In addition to our circulars we enclosed a business reply card, which could be returned free of charge. On this the subscriber promised either to buy the first issue at three shillings, including postage, or to pay an annual subscription of twelve shillings. We trusted that a policy of 'order now pay later' would be attractive, and that our readership of professional teachers would not produce many bad debts.

By October we were ready to send out the circulars. In 1958 postage for advertisements cost only twopence, and so for thirty pounds it was possible to dispatch our material to 3,600 people (there were, of course, 240 pence to the pound). The only additional costs were for paper and envelopes. Parties were held at my home, with neighbours enlisted with bribes of wine to write addresses and put circulars in envelopes. Eventually the posting was completed, and we awaited results. The first day seven cards were returned. The next day we were jubilant when a pile of thirty-two arrived. Although we did not realize it, our success was assured. Over the years, during which we repeated these circularizations regularly, we discovered that a good initial response inevitably continues for several weeks. Many subscribers ordered for the year, and we were encouraged to send out further circulars, particularly to libraries all over the world. We were also bullying our friends to subscribe, and soon we had enough money promised to cover our first printing bill, with a good deal left over for the second. We had obtained only three and a half pages of advertising, at ten pounds a page, but this was to improve after our first issue when our circulation figures became known.

The stages we had planned in Cambridge in August were complete. By Christmas 1958 we were editors of a non-existent journal with an impressive honorary committee and over a thousand subscribers. The total cost to our own pockets was not much more than our original allocation of fifty pounds. The first issue was due out in spring 1959.

Since his arrival in Hull in 1955 Philip Larkin had an important influence on my literary values, and so on the policy of *Critical Quarterly*. In our early days he allowed me to use space in his Library as an office. An admirer of Thomas Hardy, he disliked both the obscurity of modern verse and the aridity of much professional literary criticism. He felt that 'poetry, like all art, is inextricably bound up with giving pleasure, and if a poet loses his pleasure-seeking audience he has lost the only audience worth having'. Philip probably had reservations about some of the literary criticism we published in our journal; but he was a good man, willing to support my plans, and to supply us with new poems and a famous article entitled 'Wanted: Good Hardy Critic'. In those days he was not as gloomy as the man Andrew Motion met and wrote about during the period he spent in Hull in the 1970s. We all took Philip's pessimism to be in part a kind of pose, an occasion for his wit. When dealt a poor hand at bridge he once said: 'They used to have pictures on them when I was a child.' At that time we thought he would probably marry, and eventually become librarian at Oxford or Cambridge. Philip thrived on the success of *The Less Deceived*, discussed rhymes with us over lunch, and was publishing the remarkable poems which he eventually gathered together as *The Whitsun Weddings*. *Critical Quarterly* included an article on Larkin in its first issue, and was particularly influential in publishing Movement poetry.

Our journal was to publish new poetry as well as literary criticism, and perhaps its principal success was that so many well-known poems first appeared in its pages – Larkin's 'Love Songs in Age', Ted Hughes's 'Hawk Roosting', Thom Gunn's 'Back to Life', R.S. Thomas's 'Here', Sylvia Plath's 'A Birthday Present', Louis Simpson's 'On the Eve'.

This policy immediately brought a split between the editors and some of our *Scrutiny* supporters. During our years at Cambridge Tony and I were typical of many other undergraduates reading English in taking almost no interest in contemporary verse. We read Dylan Thomas, of course, but our attitude toward new poets tended to be one of contempt. When Dylan Thomas read his poetry at Cambridge we did not even make the effort to attend. The puritanism of the Cambridge English school left us unresponsive to the pleasures of games with words, or to the small felicities of diction which grace even minor poems. Ted Hughes wisely abandoned the English Tripos after Part One and transferred his attention to archaeology and anthropology. It is a sign of the Cambridge ambience that during the three years I saw him regularly I never discovered he was writing poetry.

During the 1950s Tony and I had become increasingly critical of our Cambridge training. As editors we were in tune with George Steiner's views as expressed in 1974 in an open letter to the first issue of *The New Review*: 'One trusts critical ferocity when it has behind it either a manifest creative achievement or a parallel impulse to advocacy . . . It is an open question whether it is *ever* productive to discard courtesy, humaneness, a complete alertness to the vulnerabilities involved, when one is writing criticism.' Tony and I felt that the *Scrutiny* tradition, so full of vitality in the 1930s, had lost this impulse to advocacy. We wanted to turn literary criticism away from puritanism towards intelligent celebration of creative achievements. As editors we committed ourselves to advocacy by printing new poems in each issue, often by unknowns, and by our choice of recent writers to be featured.

In 1958 we felt optimistically confident that we could assist the development of an expanding élite. We believed that it is worth devoting a life to presenting, teaching, and celebrating great art, of both past and present, and that academic criticism can be of benefit to the general reader. Donald Davie contributed a poem to our first issue and became a regular contributor. Our ideas as editors were influenced by his books, *Purity of Diction in English Verse* (1952) and *Articulate Energy* (1957). His emphasis on orthodox syntax and clarity of meaning was a strong influence on the idea of an educated community which inspired the early years of *Critical Quarterly*. Our aim was to ensure that high standards of lucid English and a wide appreciation of great literature remained powerful elements of our common culture.

Each issue of *Critical Quarterly* was to include regular features, with emphasis on recent literature. We were also determined to print only short articles of up to 4,000 words, but under pressure from our contributors this policy had to be abandoned. We always tried, however, to include short articles, as a help to the reader and because a good argument often needs only 2,000 to 3,000 words for clear elucidation. In our opening year we had articles on living authors (myself on Larkin, Tony Dyson on Hughes, Danby on Empson), on recent literature (Tony Dyson on *Look Back in Anger*, Raymond Williams on *Under Milk Wood*). There were also analyses of poems, symposia on the teaching of English, 'Our Debt to Dr Leavis' and on Dickens, reviews of new books, and surveys of recent literary criticism on major works or writers (G.K. Hunter on *Hamlet*, Rosemary Woolf on Chaucer).

In our third year we published a symposium on the trial of *Lady Chatterley's Lover* with contributions from Norman St John Stevas, Martin Jarrett Kerr, Donald Davie and C.S. Lewis. C.S. Lewis argued that in Greek, Latin and Middle English obscene four-letter words were never used for reverential treatment of sex, that no nation, age or class has commonly used such words 'to move desire, for they are the vocabulary of farce or of vituperation'. Lawrence's usage is not to be reckoned a return to nature; instead it is a rebellion against language. To support this thesis Lewis quoted all the Greek four-letter words with definitions. My Hull printer didn't possess Greek type, so he wrote to a specialist printer in the south of England to order the necessary letters. I delight to think of the face of the Greek expert confronted by a business letter asking for delivery of type for all the main Greek obscene words.

This was not the last time we had trouble with four-letter words. Mr Mills, the manager at Hull Printers, was a man of old-fashioned integrity. One day in 1968 he complained to me that he'd discovered his girls shouting and laughing over Philip Larkin's poem 'High Windows', which was first published in the special issue commemorating our tenth year. Mr Mills told me he would deal with the printing of that page entirely by himself. I felt duly chastened.

A notable event in our early years was Barbara Everett's article on *King Lear*, which occasioned replies from William Empson, Kenneth Muir, John Danby, Emrys Jones and John Holloway. Equally controversial was Empson's review of Helen Gardner's 1966 edition of Donne, which accused her of underplaying the erotic in his poetry. Perhaps the oddest event was the publication of Robert Conquest's spoof article, 'Christian Symbolism in *Lucky Jim*'. Dixon was said to be a Christ figure, with the Cross at the centre of his name for him to Di(e)on. Several letters arrived complaining that the articles and books mentioned by Conquest could not be found in libraries. We heard of students at university interviews who seriously argued that *Lucky Jim* was a religious fable. Spoofs can be a dangerous indulgence.

In our first ten years our regular contributors included an excellent younger group (Bernard Bergonzi, Malcolm Bradbury, David Lodge, Barbara Everett, D.J. Palmer, Tony Tanner, G.D. Josipovici). We also had established writers such as Helen Gardner, John Wain, Graham Hough, Richard Hoggart and William Empson.

We printed 2,000 copies of the first issue. It sold out quickly, and we had to order a reprint of 1,000. The circulation crept up steadily towards 5,000, where it stuck for the next twelve years. Since then it has drifted downwards as inflation forced our costs up. We discovered that we could derive little financial benefit from sales through bookshops. Famous shops such as Dillon's in London or Blackwell's in Oxford might sell ten or twenty over the counter, but all shops demanded a twenty-five per cent or thirty-three and a third per cent or even fifty per cent discount, which we could not afford. W.H. Smith took twelve copies of the first issue at their Hull bookshop and put them on display for three days. They sold one, and according to their custom, they then tore the covers off the remaining eleven for return to us to prove they had been unsold. We received one shilling and threepence from the deal. Although advertisements increased to about ten or twelve pages per issue, our income came largely from direct subscriptions through the post. At the beginning of our second year, Oxford University Press agreed to administer our subscriptions for a payment of ten per cent of the money collected. This removed a major burden of work, but until 1973, when Manchester University Press took over, Tony and I retained final responsibility for balancing the books and paying the bills. In 1962 the Calouste Gulbenkian Foundation provided a grant for a full-time secretary for three years, but previously almost all the work was done by the editors. It is not too difficult to bring out a quarterly journal once, but when the thirteen-week cycle is completed it starts again immediately, and there is no rest period. Yet I always found the work exciting, and never lost the thrill of satisfaction when copies of a new issue arrived from the printer. I felt the same about *PN Review*, which I later edited with Michael Schmidt. Writers need encouragement, and without such little magazines to publish unknowns many would fall by the wayside.

In the early 1970s we received a small Arts Council grant to pay contributors, but for most of our thirty years we balanced our books and achieved a small surplus. I had always imagined that material of high quality would come through the post from unknown writers. This is not so. Very soon we were receiving an average of twenty manuscripts per week; in the 1980s the number was sometimes as high as forty, but unfortunately almost all were useless to us. Most of the verse was childlike in technique; it is an interesting phenomenon that so many people write and try to publish bad verse. Many critical articles were from the United States, and presumably had already been rejected by major American journals.

We very rarely referred manuscripts to experts. We believed we ourselves must determine the identity of the journal. Most material had to be specially solicited. At our editorial meetings a regular feature was the compilation of lists of people to whom we might write for an article or poems. What does an editor do if the solicited material proves poor? Our view was that the editor's duty must always be to his audience, and that in no circumstances must he publish material of unsatisfactory quality. A commercial journal can pay the fee and not publish: we could not afford to. The results may be unfortunate; editing a literary magazine is an effective way of making enemies.

Our success persuaded us to bring out further publications. In 1960 we edited a twenty-four-page poetry supplement, intended as a selection of the best recent poems, and sold this for a shilling. It included Larkin's 'Love Songs in Age'. We also organized a poetry competition, printing the two winning poems in the supplement. The *Observer* was willing to print free of charge a brief letter announcing our poetry competitions, and this brought in hundreds of entries. Philip Larkin assisted us with the judging, and the prize was shared between Alan Brownjohn and Sylvia Plath. We sold 12,000 copies, and so began an annual series. We tried various novel ways of increasing sales. Two of my students were allowed to sell the pamphlet in the foyer of the Old Vic before a poetry reading. They sold over 100. When I expressed surprise at their success they told me that many people clearly thought they were buying the programme.

In our second year we published 'The Sediment' by Thomas Blackburn, which won the Guinness prize of £300 for the best poem of the year. At the Guinness party to celebrate the awards I first met Sylvia Plath. She was gratified to hear that our prize had been awarded to her before we knew she was married to Ted Hughes. During the next two years Tony and I had dinner on various occasions with Ted and Sylvia, and we persuaded her to edit our second anthology, *American Poetry Now*, a collection of new writing. This too sold thousands of copies.

I found Sylvia Plath balanced, mature, and full of *joie de vivre*. Once, on entering an Angus Steak restaurant in central London, she walked straight over to discuss the meat with the cook. I could never rival that kind of self-confidence. In the early 1960s I had met hardly any American women, and I took Sylvia's American eloquence and vivacity at face value. As an editor she was most efficient, ringing me up regularly to discuss her selection of poets and the various printing problems. The technical skill of her early poems in *The Colossus*, with their formal control of her personal anguish, reflects the persona she created for herself after her early attempt at suicide. I only met her in the company of Ted, and like many acquaintances was thoroughly taken in by her bright manners. Ted and Sylvia published many poems in *Critical Quarterly*; Ted was always loyal and benevolent, full of constructive advice about new *C.Q.* ventures.

In 1962 Sylvia and Ted agreed to read their poems at our Bangor summer conference for teachers. We understood that they would take over Tony's Bangor flat for a few days' holiday, while Sylvia's mother looked after the children. As late July approached, Tony and I became worried because our letters were not answered; at the last minute they got in touch, but only stayed one night in Tony's flat. Before the reading we took them to Beaumarais in

Anglesey for dinner. At first they seemed a little strained, but as the red wine flowed we all relaxed, and the laughter and conviviality of our earlier dinners were restored. They must have separated permanently only a few weeks later. When in 1963 Tony rang me up during a tutorial at Hull to tell me that Sylvia had committed suicide I found it unbelievable. I asked the students to leave, and sat there very still, too conscious of the silence. I kept thinking of Judge Brack's absurd remark after Hedda Gabler had shot herself: 'People don't do such things'.

The first of the conferences for teachers at which Ted and Sylvia read their poems took place at Bangor in 1961, with an attendance of 160 for six days. Our main speakers were to be John Wain, the poet and novelist, and Huw Wheldon, famous as a television presenter of Arts programmes. Just before the conference Wheldon fell ill, so I had to announce at the first meeting that Stephen Spender had agreed to act as a substitute. 'Better' said a loud voice from the front row. The teachers proceeded to grill Spender about his attitudes to Marxism. Spender seemed a sad figure, too intelligent not to realize that since the 1930s his writings had lacked vitality.

To persuade Spender to accept our last-minute invitation I offered him a fee of thirty pounds plus expenses, very high for 1962. I was worried that our teachers would feel cheated if one of our guest speakers failed to materialize. This ability to use our money as we pleased was crucial to the early success of *C.Q.* We behaved like entrepreneurs, offering poets money, but rarely paying academic contributors who were pleased enough to enhance their reputations by publication in our journal. If we had worked through the bureaucratic machinery of a university, we would have lost this freedom. In January 1962, for example, Tony wrote to Sylvia Plath offering her three to five pounds for any poem she cared to submit. This was typical of our use of money to attract good material. Our income was not sufficient to pay a standard rate to all the poets and essayists, so we paid according to our needs, according to the market.

At first Tony and I were very green at organizing conferences. We tried out many new ideas. Instead of one-hour lectures we substituted three twenty-minute sessions; this was a good idea, but we started at 9 a.m. and gave our members too exhausting a schedule. Some of our university lecturers found it impossible to stop after twenty minutes, and I was continually waving my watch at them. Until the early 1970s, when the pressure of the Black Paper campaign forced us to cut back our literary activities, we organized one or two conferences every year. These took place at Scarborough (where Norman Nicholson was our guest speaker), Matlock (the principal lecturer was a young ebullient Stanley Fish), Hull (William Empson insisted we drank whisky with him during the morning coffee break) and London (as he left the rostrum Angus Wilson overheard a lady telling her friend she had not been able to hear him).

I needed considerable charm to keep the good-will of our speakers. Empson insisted that in the afternoon I took him for a walk in the East Yorkshire wolds. With Malcolm Bradbury and David Palmer I drove him to Brantingham, so we could walk down an adjacent, sheltered valley. After a couple of miles the East wind was driving in our faces, so I suggested we should return. 'Can't we go back by a different route?' Empson demanded. I should have lied. Instead I admitted that a much longer path wound up the valley side and back by an exposed country lane. Empson, already in his late sixties, marched on relentlessly, with me trotting beside him trying to respond to his conversation, while Malcolm and David disappeared in the rear. I was fit from regular squash playing, but still out of breath when at last we arrived back at the car. We waited ten minutes before the other two appeared.

We discovered that conference organizers are under constant pressure, when a student falls ill, or the coffee fails to turn up, or a lecturer talks too much in a discussion. After these conferences I usually needed two or three days of complete rest. There were many hilarious incidents. At Bangor in 1961 our conference included twenty nuns. They were tolerant and accommodating, but at 7 a.m. on the first morning they met together in their hall of residence so that they could troop off to Mass at a local Catholic church. The front door was locked, and no porter was yet in sight. They climbed out of a front window, one by one, much to the amazement of a passing milkman.

We soon learnt we had to impose a less rigorous regime, starting at 9.45 a.m. and, sadly, returning to longer lectures. Our evening sessions when all the tutors and conference members took part in general discussion of literary questions were always popular, but our liveliest evening was always the one when we played our practical criticism dating game. A university teacher not attending the conference chose about twenty passages of prose and verse of the kind set for unseen dating in the Cambridge Tripos. These were duplicated for every member of the conference, and handed out at the beginning of the session. A secretary would be the only person present with a list of the authors and dates of each passage. The lecturers on the platform discussed each extract, trying to work out from the language and themes its approximate historical period. I always started these sessions by telling the audience that we would soon prove to them by our mistakes that we were not cheating. After the panel had discussed the passage for four or five minutes I would invite contributions from the audience. When the arguments began to flag, I would ask the secretary to tell us who wrote the extract and when. I like to think we did not make fools of ourselves too often, and I particularly recall the brilliance of Barbara Everett in her instant reactions to a difficult passage. This 'game' annoyed some of Leavis's followers, who thought we were frivolous. I regard it as a stimulating teaching occasion at which tutors put their own reputations on the line.

In the 1960s *Critical Quarterly's* circulation of 5,300 included teachers of English from about half the grammar schools in Britain. They formed the main clientele for our conferences; I claim we achieved some success in overcoming the isolation of the sixth-form teacher whose heavy work schedules made keeping up-to-date so difficult. In 1963 we transformed ourselves into a Society and started *Critical Survey*, with special emphasis on the educational needs of the schools. This soon had a membership of 2,500. In 1966 I moved to a Chair at Manchester University, and Tony decided to work part-time at Norwich so he could edit *C.Q.* from an office in London. This arrangement worked until 1969 when we published the first Black Paper.

In 1963 we began to organize four-day conferences for sixth-formers, and these continue to the present day. The attendance is usually over 400. Tony and I worked out recently that over

16,000 sixth-formers have attended since we started this event. Strangers sometimes stop us in the street to say how much they enjoyed them. These conferences include not only lectures and seminars but also evening debates on literary issues, and practical criticism sessions to which the students contribute.

The most worrying problem with sixth-form conferences is how to keep order, particularly at night. At our first conference at Ashburne Hall, Manchester, I was awoken in the early hours by a female warden-dragon who hauled in two sheepish boys she had found at a party in a girl's room. In my pyjamas I found myself at a disadvantage trying to calm her down. The next night we recorded interviews with the sixth-formers for a television discussion programme. After filming the television crew parked their gear in their cars and returned inside for coffee. An argument about the value of academic qualifications developed between the director, an Oxford graduate, and a belligerent chief cameraman. They went on and on, and it was past midnight before I finally managed to shepherd them back to the front door. It was locked. Across the garden the Warden had turned out her lights and presumably retreated to bed. I tried the windows that faced the parked cars, but these had special locks to prevent girls climbing in or out. My ground-floor bedroom overlooked the rear garden, so at my suggestion we all climbed out (six of us) so we could walk round to the front. This is what the students had been doing the night before. In spite of my attempts to hush them up, the television team were laughing and cursing as they stumbled across flower beds towards the Warden's house. When we reached there, the door in the wall was locked, and there was no way round. We retraced our steps to my room, whose lights I had left on. I heaved myself up over the sill, and was perched there when two girls came through the door. I had chosen the wrong room. They screamed. 'I'm just climbing in,' I informed them. I pushed through the door to find a matron standing in the corridor; she produced keys and let the television crew escape.

For several years we held summer conferences for sixth-formers at Nottingham University. One warm summer night the students gathered on a knoll to play guitars and sing and cuddle until the early hours. The next morning, the Vice-Chancellor, whose house was nearby, asked what was happening. 'It's the *Critical Quarterly*,' he was told. He replied: 'I've never heard it called that before.'

These incidents seem trivial, but such farcical events persuade many university teachers not to organize conferences for sixth-formers. Gradually we have learnt how to manage these events. For almost twenty years we held them at Hulme Hall, Manchester, assisted by a warden and a manager, Ron Wilson, who were tolerant towards our difficulties, and adept at keeping good order and sobriety during the night.

Our experience in organizing conferences and publishing pamphlets was of great value during the Black Paper campaign, and in the work of the National Council for Educational Standards, founded in 1972. Tony and I applied techniques learnt from our *C.Q.* activities to promote our educational ideals. As university lecturers we had created a life-style in contrast to that of most of our colleagues. We always believed teaching was more important than research, while recognizing that, like scientists, university lecturers in the Arts must publish and keep abreast of their subjects. A friend of mine who is now a professor at Oxbridge once told me that when faced with conflicting demands upon his time between teaching and his own research he puts his research first. I was shocked, and like to think I have done the opposite. Tony and I published two influential text-books, *Modern Poetry: Studies in Practical Criticism* (1963) and *The Practical Criticism of Poetry: A Textbook* (1965) in which we described our teaching methods based on seminar discussion. We also provided criticisms of poems in a manner which reflected our Cambridge training. These two books sold well for over twenty years, and many undergraduates recall how in their sixth form they were first introduced to practical criticism through their 'Cox and Dyson'.

What were the social and political implications of all this activity? How did our work relate to Black Paper ideals?

After 1969 we were often accused of élitism, and this epithet is now often directed towards the followers of Leavis. It is said that journals such as *The Use of English* (1949) and *Critical Quarterly* (1959) were founded on Leavisite principles, and that the same is true of *Universities Quarterly*, edited by Boris Ford from 1955. *The Pelican Guide to English Literature* was published between

1954 and 1961, and this certainly reflected a fundamentally Leavisite canon.

According to Terry Eagleton (now professor at Oxford) and his followers, the teaching of practical criticism by Leavisites existed in a liberal bourgeois capitalist ethos which concerned itself with the unique individuality of works of art (seen as products of genius), the great tradition. We are said to have undervalued and misunderstood the ways in which literature expresses the cultural, social, historical and linguistic forces at work in its period. On many occasions Eagleton has argued that traditional study of literature necessarily underpins a conservative philosophy. The tragic view of art, dominant in Leavis's work and in the schools and universities of the 1950s, is said to promote quietism, passivity, conservatism and a sense of impotence before social problems. Left-wing critics of this persuasion attack the privileged status of literature, the conservative practice of trying to get behind the flux of things to the universal and essential nature of the real, an activity which they say creates an ethos of acceptance, a distrust of radical socialist alternatives.

The conservatism of critics in the Leavis tradition during the 1950s has been linked with the dominance of Movement poetry. *Critical Quarterly* helped to increase the sales of Movement poets, and, as I have already suggested, Tony and I felt very much in tune with the critical values of Donald Davie and the poetry of Philip Larkin. In his book, *The Movement: English Poetry and Fiction of the 1950s*, Blake Morrison ascribes the sense of impotence in poets such as Larkin or John Wain to the post-imperial mood, the loss of international power in Britain after 1945. As Britain declined as a world force, the new writers, mainly of lower-middle-class, grammar-school background, expressed nostalgia for the lost days of Empire; Morrison maintains this is exemplified in Larkin's poem 'At Grass', about old racehorses recalling their past triumphs. Most of the Movement writers, Morrison says, were distrustful of ideals and fearful of radical change: 'They had been trained by teachers, and looked up to writers, who laid emphasis on stability, tradition, continuity, whose influence was to encourage not adjustment *of* society, but adjustment *to* it.'

After the war there was a great longing in England for a return to tranquillity. We had spent six years either fighting or being bombed, and longed for the untroubled world which in our fantasies we thought typical of Edwardian England. During my years as a conscript and as an undergraduate at Cambridge, my main ambition was to marry and settle down in a village with wife and children and no more violence. We feared the great ideological movements of the 1930s – Fascism and Communism – and preferred a quieter style of politics, an easy-going liberal tolerance. In the 1960s the poems we received through the post at the *Critical Quarterly* office were often about such domesticity, what Anthony Thwaite once called 'nappy-and-bottle poetry'.

Although there is some truth in left-wing criticisms of our work, and Tony and I certainly believe in universal values, this linking of the teachers of the 1950s with conservatism and quietism undervalues our evangelical zeal. Our symposium 'Why Teach Literature?' in the first issue of *C.Q.* included D.J. Enright, G.H. Bantock, Douglas Hewitt, Douglas Brown and David Holbrook, all in many respects in the Leavis tradition. In our third issue we continued the debate with the symposium, 'Our Debt to Dr Leavis', with articles by Raymond Williams, Alun Jones and R.J. Kaufmann.

None of these writers would have accepted that our faith in the moral value of great literature could be demystified into passive acceptance of bourgeois ideology. We believed that literature changes people's lives, and works particularly against the commercial values of industrial society. As a liberal, I held that study of literature helps readers to free themselves from repressive ideologies. At the end of his article D.J. Enright reiterates the Leavis belief that the purpose of teaching literature is 'to do good to people'. For G.H. Bantock literature 'awakens and refines sensitivities', while for Douglas Brown literature 'has been continually an instrument of discovery in areas where nothing except the creative use of language had enough delicacy or subtlety or fidelity', and this justifies the teacher's role. David Holbrook, in an article on secondary modern schools, advocates the development of sensibility through literature as possible for all pupils, as 'a really civilized democratic education policy'.

For all of us in the tradition of Matthew Arnold, T.S. Eliot, I.A. Richards and F.R. Leavis, great books possessed an absolute and inalienable value, and we believed that any culture or class of society to which they were irrelevant must be miserably impoverished. Our intent was to make even the rarest of literary artefacts accessible to as wide a readership as possible; we saw this as a truly democratic ideal, as relevant to the secondary modern pupil as to those selected for grammar school.

With this background it is not surprising that Tony and I resented the claims made during the Black Paper campaign that we were élitist. We were particularly incensed because we felt that *Critical Quarterly* had distanced itself from aspects of *Scrutiny* to which this label might be deemed more appropriate. Leavis found much literature published after 1930 repugnant, not in tune with the myth of the decline of the West, with his belief that the vitality of language was being destroyed by the Machine Age and his nostalgia for a lost 'organic' society. Tony and I had committed ourselves to publishing a large amount of poetry by unknowns (such as Sylvia Plath), and to drawing attention to the virtues of new poets such as Philip Larkin, Thom Gunn, Ted Hughes and R.S. Thomas. We also reflected a cosmopolitan attitude to literature very different from the ethos of *Scrutiny*. Tony published on Thomas Mann, Malcolm Bradbury on Saul Bellow, Raymond Williams on Brecht.

I agree that we marginalized the more anarchic and nihilistic qualities of modern literature. We believed that even the darkest imaginative works (Kafka, Samuel Beckett, Ted Hughes and Sylvia Plath, for example) reflect a desire to communicate, to make sense in words of our tragic predicament. But we did not see ourselves, to use the jargon of the 1950s, as an Elect or saving remnant maintaining a great tradition against the barbarism of a mass civilization. Like David Holbrook we advocated a kind of teaching which would be helpful to all children, and believed in progress through education. As I look back on our activities, from our early conferences to the Black Papers, I can claim with confidence that Tony and I were not quietistic or impotent in our influence on education and politics.

# 6
# *Californian Frontier*

On fogless days by the Pacific,
there is a cold hard light without break

that reveals merely what is – no more
and no less. That limiting candour,

that accuracy of the beaches,
is part of the ultimate richness.

'Flying Above California', Thom Gunn

I first felt that my educational ideals were under threat during my year as Associate Professor of English in the United States. On 2 December 1964, I was standing outside the Students' Union at the entry to the University of California at Berkeley. The scene I was watching, of course, has become famous. The plaza was crowded with students packed together as at a football match. In the centre, about 1,000 students, with the Stars and Stripes at their head, were filing into the administrative building, Sproul Hall, to begin their controversial sit-in. Over the microphone Joan Baez was singing 'We shall overcome', 'We'll walk hand in hand', in tones whose nostalgia recalled for me Methodist hymns learnt at Sunday School. I had never heard the singer or the song before, and it made a deep impression.

The crowd drifted slowly forwards, their faces serious and anxious. The sit-in might well have unfortunate consequences for the future careers of the students. The issues were important. They thought they were defending the civil rights campaign, and also freedom of political action on the Bancroft Strip, the Hyde

Park area just outside the University, which had been shut down because of right-wing pressure. We had already heard Mario Savio, the student leader of the Free Speech Movement (F.S.M.) give an impassioned justification for civil disobedience:

> There's a time when the operation of the machine becomes so odious, makes your heart so sick, that you can't take part ... you've got to put your bodies upon the gears, and upon the wheels, upon the levers, tie up all the apparatus and make it stop, and you've got to indicate to the people who run the machine ... that unless you're free, the machine will be prevented from working at all.

The next morning the police arrested about 800 students, and a two-day strike stopped much of the teaching at the University.

Jean and I set off for California with our three children (Richard, Sally and Celia, then eight, six and four) in late summer, 1964. In the 1960s it was not difficult to obtain an invitation to teach for a year in the States. As American professors disappeared regularly for sabbaticals or grant-aided research trips to Europe, it was usual to ask a British academic to act as a temporary replacement. I looked forward at Berkeley to spending a year getting to know the poet, Thom Gunn, who taught in the English department; unfortunately when I arrived I discovered that he was away on leave, and that to some extent I was replacing him. I was recommended to Henry Nash Smith, the chairman at Berkeley, by Ian Watt, now Tony's professor at Norwich, and an admirer of *Critical Quarterly*. I was paid 12,000 dollars for the year, on which no tax was due, so we were moderately affluent.

Jean and I had never flown, and chose to travel by sea to New York, and then by plane to San Francisco. We thought we would enjoy the Atlantic crossing on the S.S. *America*, but we were soon disillusioned. There was little for the children to do, and entertaining them proved burdensome. After thirty minutes in the ship's small play area, forty minutes in the swimming pool, and maybe two hours watching a film, there were still large chunks of time to spend in our cabin. We dared not let them run loose in case they fell overboard.

On our arrival in New York I was initiated into the American way of life. As we left the customs shed, a large sign in bold print told us not to tip the porters. A huge unsmiling gorilla of a man carried our heavy luggage to the taxi-rank, and then shoved out a black, hairy hand demanding a tip. With three children in tow I was hardly in the mood for argument, so I tipped him, thankful to leave the dockside en route for John F. Kennedy airport. On the journey the taxi-driver was most affable, telling us how much he admired the English, particularly the Queen. As he chatted away I was trying to work out the instructions about how much a journey to the airport was supposed to cost. At the airport he asked me for three times the amount I had calculated. I was not sure I was right, so paid him (a year later in New York I checked carefully and discovered he had indeed swindled me). When we checked in for our flight, the clerk at the counter told me I must pay seventy dollars more in tax. By this time I had learnt that politeness and flexibility were not sensible options in New York. I insisted vehemently that I was in receipt of a Fulbright travel grant, and as the American government was paying my fare they should pay the tax. After a wait of ten minutes the clerk returned and issued us all with our boarding cards. I did not bother to point out to him that my wife and children were not being paid for by the Fulbright award. I had learnt the American way of life, and was quietly satisfied that my profit on the family's tickets balanced my loss to the porter and the taxi-driver.

We faced a six-hour wait at the airport, so, euphoric at being in America, we took up an offer of a cheap helicopter ride to the New York State Fair. On the helicopter flight I was astonished by the strangeness of the city from the air, the land so parched, the numerous grey and brown apartment blocks, and the lack of red-brick homes; it was all so different from my fantasies taken from books. When we landed we discovered the reality of August humidity and heat in New York. The children were in clean clothes ready for the flight. After only a few yards walking towards the pavilions we were dripping with perspiration, so we bought them ice-creams. These disintegrated, leaking onto their clothes and hands as we dabbed away with white linen handkerchiefs. We returned early, which was fortunate as afternoon fog led to cancellation of later helicopter flights; we might have missed our flight to San Francisco.

Henry Nash Smith (author of a famous book about the American West, *Virgin Land*) met us at San Francisco airport, and drove us to his home for a brief repast, for we were all very tired. His charm and courtesy were typical of my Californian hosts, and Jean and I soon realized our good fortune in being invited to Berkeley. The difference between American and English conventions fascinated us, as if we were in a foreign country where we spoke the language fluently. We spent the night in a hotel, and the next morning, as arranged, I rang the English departmental secretary for instructions on how to find my way to the University. 'You're on Telegraph,' she informed me. I was bewildered; was she recording my voice? I soon realized, of course, that in American English her words meant our hotel was on Telegraph Avenue. During our first days my normal English politeness provoked strange looks from shop assistants, but I soon learnt to adopt American expressions. I also discovered that to comment on fine weather was absurd in a country where the skies are blue every day from April to October.

When I started teaching I came to know the famous Pope scholar, Maynard Mack of Yale, who was giving a series of prestigious lectures at Berkeley, and who knew England well. Once we passed each other on the campus, and both spoke at the same time. He said 'Good morning' and I said 'Hi'. Mack embodied for me all that was best among American scholars, and was very generous. He invited us to dinner, and arranged for me to edit a collection of essays on Dylan Thomas for his Prentice-Hall *Twentieth-Century Views* series. Drawing on a fund of anecdotes about disastrous productions of *King Lear*, he talked fascinatingly about his Berkeley lectures on Shakespeare.

During our first days at Berkeley Jean and I strolled near the campus looking for an off-licence or similar shop where we could buy Californian wine. Surprised by the lack of any sign of such a place we made enquiries, and were told that no alcohol, except light beer, could be sold within a mile of the university campus. When we took the children to paddle at Stinson beach, we discovered that the Pacific along the Californian coast is bitterly cold, and few people swim without a wet suit. Even further south at Los Angeles the sun-worshipping crowds swim in their pools, not in the ocean. Again and again presuppositions about California proved wrong.

Henry Nash Smith arranged for us to rent an expensive house on Parnassus, in the hills above the campus, just for a few days; we were then to take up permanent residence in a large, ramshackle clap-board house on McGee, between the campus and the Bay. Our monthly rent was only 160 dollars, so we had lots of money left over to pay the necessary bills and entertain ourselves out of my monthly pay cheque of 1,000 dollars. One of the English department's graduate students was married to a car salesman, so Henry Nash Smith arranged a deal for us to buy a second-hand red Rambler car for 720 dollars. I reckoned that as the wife depended on Professor Smith for her grades as a PhD student she would not allow her husband to sell us a banger. This calculation proved correct, and we had driven several thousand miles without serious trouble when a year later I sold the car in New Haven, Connecticut, for 300 dollars. McGee proved a good place to live, and we made many friends. Most of our neighbours had young children, and our house became a play area for the locals. What impressed me was that so many husbands and wives were taking courses at the University, either undergraduate or postgraduate. I saw at first hand the advantages of the American modular system, which allows students to build degrees slowly, brick by brick, taking a year out if circumstances necessitate. The young parents were stimulating company, and this continuing education became my ideal. Many years later at Manchester my friends on McGee were very much in my mind when, with Jim Reason and Sam Moore, I helped to lay the foundation for our successful part-time modular degree.

The student protests over the closing of their Hyde Park area broke out only a few weeks after we settled down in our new house on McGee. At first I was completely in sympathy with them, but as the months passed I learnt by direct experience that the demonstrations might achieve the opposite of what was intended. During the wrangles at Berkeley, I was surprised that many Jewish refugees from Europe during the 1930s, now senior professors, were antagonistic towards Mario Savio and the F.S.M. They feared that civil disobedience might lead to anarchy, and that anarchy would be the seed-bed for a more authoritarian style of government. They feared, and I think they were proved right, that the demonstrations would provoke a popular distrust of the University which would damage both its finances and the strength of its advocacy of liberal values.

Soon after Christmas the F.S.M. began to spawn strange freakish movements which further harmed the image of the University in the public eye. The Free Speech Movement was followed by the Filthy Speech Movement, supported by very few students but of considerable influence on future political development. At an open-air meeting to discuss obscenity, some students and outsiders carried banners displaying a four-letter word. Their argument was that this word was less obscene than 'nigger', 'war', or 'napalm bombing', for example, and that blacks who used the word automatically because they had heard it all their lives were debarred from jobs. They claimed that the laws against public use of the word were largely a class matter, a means of discriminating against the under-privileged. One of my students was arrested for reading aloud *Lady Chatterley's Lover* in a public place. Such events aroused considerable hostility towards the student cause.

One American professor told me that over the next five years the student protests at Berkeley would be imitated all over the States. He was a good prophet, but underestimated the world-wide repercussions. At Berkeley the situation went from bad to worse. I had been impressed by the intellectual vitality of the Berkeley community, both among staff and students. After my departure in the summer of 1965, I was the more saddened to read how disruption, arson and violence became almost commonplace.

Soon after the dispute at Berkeley started, the student committees began to pay less attention to local issues such as the Bancroft Strip, or the use of megaphones in public places, choosing to widen their terms of reference. They discussed reform of the whole university, and eventually of the entire United States. Their talks were endless, and their hopes global in scope. As in Savio's famous speech, the students condemned the impersonality of the multi-university. They moved on to demand a revolution against capitalism itself.

The demonstrations provoked numerous debates. At one meeting between staff and students an early speaker from the professors addressed himself to the issues raised by the use of the four-letter word. In those days, when most middle-class people never used the word, even in anger, he felt embarrassed, and so announced that when he needed the word he would use 'confront' instead. Later in the meeting, another professor, carried away by his rhetoric, argued that the staff must not shilly-shally in their opposition to student breaches of the law: 'We must confront the students,' he cried. The meeting broke down in uncontrollable laughter.

Henry F. May, a senior professor of history at Berkeley, commented in an article of 1965:

> In the person of Savio, the movement speaks with a voice that has been heard in America since the beginning, the voice of an exalted, quasi-religious romantic anarchism. For all of their toughness, some of the F.S.M. are crypto-transcendentalists and neo-antinomians.
>
> (*American Scholar*, Vol 34, No 3)

May quotes Whitman to show how the F.S.M. existed in a well-known American tradition in its hatred of institutions:

> I hear it was charged against me that I sought to destroy institutions.
> But really I am neither for nor against institutions,
> (What indeed have I in common with them? Or what with the destruction of them?)
> Only I will establish . . .
> Without edifices or rules or trustees or any argument,
> The institution of the dear love of comrades.

This reaction to institutions and administrators is common to many student protests. They long for what one F.S.M. leaflet described as 'the loving university'. The invitation is to abandon your stagnant life, and join the new community. To sit-in, or to step off the conventional pavement on the road to join a march, brings a release of frustrated energy, a euphoria that at last the problems of inaction are being solved.

It is perhaps too easy to sneer at the unworldly quality of this idealism. As I listened to Joan Baez, I felt the typical romantic yearning for the better life, a strong social urge which has been the well-spring for so much political reform in the nineteenth and twentieth centuries. One recalls the members of the Labour Party singing, inappropriately, Blake's 'Jerusalem' at Transport House after winning the election in 1945.

At Berkeley, however, I began to realize that in some circumstances this romantic impulse in students can be dangerous. Professor May points out that the F.S.M. was absolutist, utopian, and that no statement could better summarize its methods than 'In Defence of Liberty Extremism is No Vice'. A Czech student, after visiting Western student militants, said: 'You simply haven't faced up to the fact that you can't build Utopia without terror, and that before long terror is all that's left.'

Much student idealism is very difficult to fit into the habits and structures of universities, based, like all institutions, on consensus and compromise. The students were often not so much concerned with practical social reforms as with the making of satisfying gestures. The 'demo', Professor May suggests, was something like an existential *acte gratuit*, a gesture of self-identification. One danger of these gestures is that they take little account of social consequences. In California they produced a swing of opinion against liberal policies.

While the demonstrations turned the University into an area of dramatic confrontations, teaching was rarely interrupted, and by and large classes proceeded as normal. At that time at Berkeley the year was divided into two semesters of fourteen weeks. For each semester I taught three courses, each involving three hours of formal teaching per week, plus one hour per course in my office answering student queries and returning essays. I taught a graduate class in literary theory, a freshman composition class and a course for third- and fourth-year students on E.M. Forster. The graduate class was among the most successful I ever taught in my career, along with similar graduate seminars I took later at summer schools in Canada. The students were usually in their mid-twenties or older, highly motivated, and part of a postgraduate community in which they met together for coffee, supper or parties (and I was often invited). As we argued and discussed literary theory during the seminars, I thought to myself how much I would have been stimulated by such teaching arrangements if they had existed when I was at Cambridge.

Course assessment, though, brought me many problems. On my first visit to my room in the English department I was delighted when an American student, whose name I had better not reveal, dropped by to talk to me about my Forster course, for which he had already enrolled. We talked for half an hour, and his enthusiasm impressed me. When my class started he dominated the seminars, and soon I was tactfully asking him to hold back. To my amazement his first piece of written work proved of below average quality, poorly written with little feeling for sentence structure. I awarded him a 'C', a grade lower than that required by students who hoped to proceed to graduate school. Distraught, he attended my office hours regularly, but when he submitted his second piece of written work it was no better than the first. When I told him I had given him a 'C' again, his manner changed. He turned truculent and belligerent, and bullied me by insisting that no other tutor had allocated him such low grades, and that he could not understand what I wanted. He blamed me for failing to teach him my requirements. When this bullying did not work, and it became clear after a few more weeks that I could not be intimidated, the student withdrew from my course on medical grounds (trumped up, I believed) so he would not have to enter a low grade in his records. In the following semester he could enrol for a different course whose tutor might prove more lenient.

I grew to dislike intensely the American system of course assessment. There was no external examiner to check my grades, and I found the easy, informal relationships I took for granted in my tutorials in England very difficult to establish. I could never be sure whether the students were being honest with me, or whether they were just trying to impress. At Berkeley if a student was awarded a string of low grades he or she would be forced to withdraw, and transfer to a less prestigious institution; for ambitious students entry to graduate school in the best universities depended on regular achievement of 'A' grades. I had many problems. A quiet young man whose contributions to my seminars were naive submitted a typed essay on Ezra Pound of outstandingly high quality. As I marked it, whenever I wanted to record a note of dissent in the margin I noticed that usually someone else's pencilled comments had been rubbed out. I called the student in to see me, and suggested he had submitted an essay written by another student for another tutor. He denied my accusation, and told me he and his flat-mate always exchanged essays so they could criticize each other's work with pencilled comments. I did not believe him. I had arranged to end the course with a written examination, so I decided to wait to see how he performed when he was unaided. His exam paper was a borderline B/C, in no way reflecting the brilliance of the paper on Ezra Pound. I gave him a 'B' for the course. When I met him in the corridor of the English department he accused me of marking him down because I thought he had cheated. Maybe I was wrong, and he did write the Pound essay. I still worry about my decision. But these incidents taught me the difficulties of course assessment, and, when later G.C.S.E. was introduced in England, made me sceptical about the virtues of any system of examining which depends on 100 per cent coursework. A teacher can never be sure how much help a pupil has received from family or friends.

Berkeley professors discussed the problems continually, and issued warning notices about plagiarism. Professor Muscatine recounted how a girl who had failed to submit the necessary written work for his course arrived one day at his room scantily dressed. It was the custom at Berkeley to take office hours with the door open so students could see if you were engaged. 'I would do anything for you,' the girl said, 'if you would give me a "B" for your course.' He stood up, quietly closed the door, and bent over her. 'Work, for instance?' he enquired.

Teaching at Berkeley proved so much easier than at Hull because the students, maybe due to the course assessment system, were so determined to participate. Accustomed to the reticence of English students, I prepared my first freshman English composition class with care, choosing a large number of controversial passages in prose and verse so that as soon as the discussion flagged I could introduce another excerpt. As soon as I read the first passage, the American students took over, and fifty minutes later they were still arguing about the first issue. My task had been simply to act as chairman of this vigorous debate. Of course, American students often talk on subjects about which they know little, without due attention to evidence. In *The House of Intellect* Jacques Barzun said that in the American seminar the right answers were supposed to come out of pooled ignorance. Yet American willingness to participate makes teaching a delight.

When I returned to England I took my first tutorial at the University of Hull, still euphoric about my teaching in the United States. I immediately realized that most of the students did not expect to contribute to the discussion. I tried to arouse their interest by introducing controversial topics, such as the nuclear deterrent, but they said little. After thirty minutes I noticed one boy looking out of the window. I longed to be back at Berkeley.

Our two older children attended the local Berkeley state school, where they enjoyed class-rooms in which their own talk was encouraged far more than in England. The head was given extra facilities and staff so he could also teach in the University education department. To enlist working heads to participate in the instruction of apprentice-teachers seemed to me an admirable arrangement, worth copying in Britain.

The San Francisco Bay Area suffered from major race problems. Our house on McGee was situated in a twilight zone, with blacks and whites mixed together. Our neighbour, Danny, was half black, half Indian, a social worker closely involved with racial problems as the coloured community asserted its rights. We became close friends with his wife and family, and we used to go dancing together at the Claremont Hotel. From Danny I learnt for the first time the problems of neighbourhood schools, that a comprehensive system of education does not necessarily create equality of opportunity. Pupils in the poor areas near San Francisco Bay were almost entirely from the black community, while on the pleasant hills above the campus nearly everyone was white. The schools for black children offered far less chance of entry into higher education. My neighbour told me that bright boys in the black community would realize about the age of thirteen that they had little chance of a good education. In their frustration it was not unusual for them to turn to crime.

We experienced an alarming example of this during the second semester. During a rain storm a black youngster, about sixteen years of age, knocked at our front door. Jean was alone in the house with our youngest, Celia. He explained that he had fallen over while running for a bus, and wanted to phone for a taxi to get to work. Jean invited him in, with typical English politeness, and after he had phoned invited him to make himself comfortable in our front room. I arrived home a few minutes later, and noticing his muddy overalls and hands invited him to wash in the bathroom. He kept standing up nervously and glancing out the window until the yellow taxi-cab bore him away.

The next day a detective, urbane and courteous, arrived at our door. With several accomplices our quiet visitor had raided a store, threatened the cashier with a gun, and dashed off with hundreds of dollar notes in a getaway car. A few blocks away the car hit bollards, and broke down. Dropping dollar notes which blew away in the wind (none were ever returned, the police informed us), the men scrambled away, running across rain-soaked backyards. From our house the boy went straight home in his taxi, and so was easily traced. Jean and I had to attend an identity parade at the police station. We were seated in darkness, so we could not be seen by the four black men who stood before us, strong lights trained on their faces. We identified him easily. As he was taken away, attended by huge policemen, his slim figure looked forlorn.

In letters to friends in Hull we recounted this incident, and it was soon much exaggerated. Ray Brett wrote to us to ask if it was true that we had been held up at gun-point in the desert. This happening was adapted by David Lodge for his novel *Changing Places*. He arrived with his family in Berkeley just before we left, having spent the year on a scholarship which enabled him to travel to several campuses across the States. David had been free of teaching commitments, while I had worked hard, preparing new courses, marking assessed essays and teaching three days a week. Surprisingly we both agreed that I had probably enjoyed a more profitable year. He had been rather like a tourist, an outsider, at the universities he visited, while after ten months Jean and I had made many close friend – John Jordan, who eventually became chairman at Berkeley, and Louis Simpson, whose collection of poems, *At the End of the Open Road*, won the Pulitzer prize in 1963. David decided to return to teach at Berkeley, but he arrived back in the worst year for student disturbances, and found life in California nothing like so paradisal as we had suggested. His frenetic year provided him with the material for *Changing Places*, his first really successful novel.

For Jean and me, though, our year at Berkeley was the happiest of our lives. I cannot do justice to the beauty of San Francisco, so often described. On a typical day, after my first hour's teaching, I would sit with my students sipping coffee on a terrace overlooking the Bay, with the famous fog drifting through the Golden Gate to reveal the distant San Francisco skyline. I can never slough off the puritanism inherited from my Methodist upbringing, but California certainly made me more relaxed, more at peace with myself. Partly it was living so much out-of-doors, walking through Muir Woods, with its grand redwood sequoia trees, or paddling at Stinson Beach with the children, watching the sun go down over the Pacific.

The other professors of English invited us regularly to cocktail parties or supper. They were an extraordinarily distinguished group of people – Mark Schorer, Henry Nash Smith, Stanley Fish, John Jordan, Tom Parkinson, Jonas Barish, Maynard Mack, Frederick Crews, Louis Simpson, Gary Snyder and so many others. I learnt to respect their learning and sophistication. Most of them had taken the opportunity to spend extended periods of research in Europe, in London, Oxbridge, Paris or Rome, and knew Europe better than I did. I realized that with our lack of money for sabbaticals, few English academics would be able to rival their achievements. Their wide-ranging four-year undergraduate courses, plus often four or five years of research provided them with a rich background I could not hope to emulate. Once, at a dinner party of young professors, the conversation turned to Sartre and existentialism. After a few minutes I stayed silent. I realized that I was the only person present who had not had the advantage in recent years of taking a course on the subject taught by a specialist.

I learnt much from Gary Snyder, the Beat poet, who taught for one semester at Berkeley while I was there (or at least he was supposed to do. Once when I visited his room I found a notice on the door telling his students he would be away in New York for three weeks.) I had lunch with him once with John Montague, the Irish poet, out of doors at a small restaurant on Telegraph. I found in him a strange stillness of spirit, an acceptance of life, of the natural world, which I wished I could cultivate in my own life. When I returned to England I published Snyder's poems in *Critical Quarterly* pamphlets; during a speech at a live televised Oxford Union debate on education I recited his poem 'Mid-August at Sourdough Mountain Lookout', as an example of the pleasure of lyric verse I wanted all young people to enjoy:

> Down valley a smoke haze
> Three days heat, after five days rain
> Pitch glows on the fir-cones
> Across rocks and meadows
> Swarms of new flies.
>
> I cannot remember things I once read
> A few friends, but they are in cities.
> Drinking cold snow-water from a tin cup
> Looking down for miles
> Through high still air.

My idea was to seize my opportunity to present a little poetry to a huge television audience. Later in the debate, when Richard Crossman (then a Labour Party Shadow Minister) wittily savaged my speech he clearly had more grasp of audience requirements.

After teaching ended, Jean and I set out with our children in our little Rambler car on a two-month trip from La Jolla in southern California to Yosemite to the Grand Tetons and Yellowstone to New Haven and New York. At Yosemite we stayed at the Berkeley family camp, a line of wooden platforms for each family perched above a narrow stream in the forest. Jean and I slept on the platform outside, gazing up at the stars as we drifted off to sleep, while the children were snug and comfortable in a covered tent alongside. Again we were overwhelmed by Californian hospitality, with regular cocktail parties before dinner on the wooden platforms. The camp was organized with typical American efficiency. The cooks who served our food were students of catering from a San Francisco college, and their work at the holiday camp counted as part of the course. A few moments before any meal a tutor might arrive to assess the cooking, so our meals were always of the highest quality. After dinner the chief cook for the day would appear to take a bow as we clapped and cheered.

After this kind of experience I was to find it difficult to adapt back to the inefficiency and stagnation typical of British universities. There is an old joke about T.S. Eliot's *The Waste Land*. Was the man who wrote the poem American or English? The answer is English, because if he had been American he would have drained the waste land, and installed modern plumbing. In England if you suggest a new idea to a university committee you often find that everyone immediately puts forward reasons why it will not work. In America the professors always wanted to help you, to think out ways of ensuring your plan would succeed.

So back in Hull life for Jean and me seemed flat. We still wonder if we would have been well-advised to stay in the United States. I think not, though, for I feel completely at home only in England. I understand my own people, their instinctive assumptions, their social background, whereas in California I never lost my sense of being a visitor. Since 1965 my strategy has been to reside in England, but to make regular trips to the States. In subsequent years I accepted a series of invitations to teach at summer schools in Canada, partly so we could take our children on two- or three-week trips to the lake areas in New York State, or to the green hills of Vermont.

While we were away a new open-plan primary school had been built behind our house in Cottingham; children were allowed to choose their activities all day long, and there was no formal teaching. At first we were pleased for our children to enjoy such a progressive environment, but we soon learnt that the unstructured day meant that children, often bored, moved haphazardly from one activity to the next. I was applying for Chairs at other universities, and we were very pleased when my success at Manchester meant our children could return to more formal class-rooms. They attended both private and state schools, and eventually all three won university places. At my interview at Manchester I faced about twenty professors, most of whom knew little about my subject, so I enjoyed myself, in what was really a kind of impromptu seminar.

When I sat down the Vice-Chancellor's first question was to ask me what I thought of Berkeley as a university. He pronounced Berkeley in the English fashion (to rhyme with darkly), and for a desperate few seconds I wondered whether to imitate him or to draw attention to his mistake by using the American pronunciation. Fortunately I chose to do the latter.

Manchester, a large provincial university, was suffering in the mid-1960s because so many of its staff had moved away, several to posts at the new universities (Bernard Bergonzi, for example, had moved to Warwick). Like other large provincial universities the buildings were mostly ugly and ill-equipped, and, as the post-Robbins boom brought large sums of money for new developments, little thought had been given to the social needs of an academic community. In the English department many colleagues were still sharing rooms; the departmental library was locked up and rarely used. There was dust everywhere, and blank walls with no pictures. Registration of first-year students involved long queues and form-filling, with no other academic activity for the first two weeks. Remembering my own uncertainties during my first days at Pembroke, I introduced wine parties and lectures in the first week, which I gave myself. Through Manchester City Rutherston loan collection I covered the walls with pictures (or at least some of them). John Jump, my co-professor of literature, was a most conscientious, clear-minded teacher, a man of infinite generosity who accepted his chronic illness – Hodgkin's disease – with great courage, acting as Dean and Pro-Vice Chancellor before he died in 1976.

Jean and I bought a four-bedroom house with a large garden in Cheadle Hulme, and I settled down to the regular routines of teaching and administration. In 1969 I had little idea that my life would suddenly be transformed, and that soon I would be leading a right-wing national campaign to reverse the Labour Party's educational policies. But I was unusual in that I had been granted special insights into the great educational controversies of the late 1960s. At Berkeley I had witnessed the ill-will created among the general public by student sit-ins. At the new school behind our house in Cottingham I had witnessed the failure of permissive education, when working-class children (the majority at this school) are denied the carefully structured teaching they need if they are to develop skills in literacy and numeracy.

Also at Berkeley my neighbour Danny had explained to me the problems that face a universal comprehensive school system. His arguments would have been accepted by most members of the Labour Party in the 1950s, but in 1965, when I returned from California, Anthony Crosland's famous Circular 10/65 compelled local authorities to submit schemes for comprehensive schools. Both the Conservative and Labour Parties discovered that parents believed comprehensive schools would raise standards, and provide new opportunities for all children; the pro-comprehensive campaign was therefore a vote winner. Previously there had been useful discussions among Labour Party politicians about the problems of neighbourhood schools, like those I had witnessed at Berkeley. Richard Crossman preferred middle schools for nine- to thirteen-year-olds, followed by a variety of upper schools in which the grammar school tradition would be maintained. This has always been my own preferred option. Emmanuel Shinwell thought it ridiculous to allow the rich to send their children to public schools while taking away the grammar schools which, he said, are for many working class boys the stepping stone to the universities and a useful career. Harold Wilson declared that the grammar schools would be abolished over his dead body. In the 1960s, as the arguments about comprehensive schools and progressive education grew fiercer, I still regarded myself as a moderate, but the media insisted on dividing the camps into warring factions. As utopian dreams and political expediency joined together in the Labour Party's advocacy of revolutionary educational changes, the Party for which I had voted and campaigned seemed to have disappeared. After the Black Paper was published I gave a talk to a local group of parents brought together by John Izbicki, education correspondent for the *Daily Telegraph*. I explained that I could see little difference between my views and those of Hugh Gaitskell. Someone at the back of the hall shouted out: 'He's dead.'

# 7

# *The First Black Paper*

Obedience to the force of gravity. The greatest sin.
Simone Weil

At our-sixth form conferences in the 1960s I normally gave the last lecture, a deliberately provocative performance about politics and literature in the post-1945 period. In those days our student audiences clapped enthusiastically, and I often received an ovation which lasted at least a minute. I was proud and vain about my successes as a university teacher.

Within a few days in March 1969 this world collapsed, and among undergraduates I found myself the most hated professor in the country, nicknamed by left-wingers as the Enoch Powell of education. In student debates I was vilified as the leading opponent of the student revolution which was supposed to be bringing new light to outmoded university traditions. I received hate mail, often obscenities on postcards which I immediately consigned to the wastepaper bin. At the University of Sussex at Brighton a dart board in the Students' Union sported a photograph of me affixed over the bull's eye. Such japes may seem trivial, but I was deeply shocked, and all my subsequent career has been dominated by the nightmare of those extraordinary weeks.

University staff were almost always supportive, and most shared my disgust for student violence. Vincent Knowles, my Registrar at Manchester University, kept a copy of the Black Paper in a drawer in his desk; he took it out to soothe his nerves whenever he was particularly depressed by another student sit-in on a trivial issue. But my career was permanently altered. In the 1970s Professor

142

R.L. Brett found himself appointed to a committee set up at Hull University to elect a new Vice-Chancellor. He put my name forward, and travelled specially to Cheadle Hulme to discuss my possible candidature. Later he told me that as soon as the fatal words 'Black Paper' were uttered my name was removed from the list.

Why did Tony Dyson and I decide to publish the first Black Paper? In one sense the whole controversy was a kind of historical accident, and I have often wondered how educational ideology and teaching practice in schools would have fared without the Black Papers. In July 1968 Tony and I went for a walk on Hampstead Heath. Tony was sharing a house near Hampstead tube station, and I usually stayed with him on my visits to London. In 1968 we were discussing, as usual, our financial problems. The subscription to the Critical Quarterly Society had remained since 1963 at two guineas, and during our walk on Hampstead Heath we decided we must increase this in 1969. We agreed we would announce this in the spring issue of *Critical Survey*, and that therefore this must be of especially high quality so that our members would be persuaded to resubscribe. After much discussion, part serious, part fanciful and lighthearted, we determined to make the *Critical Survey* a special issue on education. We were both angry about the student sit-ins which were headline news at the time, and which we believed were causing harm to the status of universities and to freedom of speech. Our original intention was to deal exclusively with universities, and only as the weeks progressed did we decide to include articles on comprehensives and progressive education. As a joke Tony suggested we should call the pamphlet a Black Paper, in contrast to government White Papers. A crucial difference would be that ours would cost the electorate nothing.

After our walk on Hampstead Heath Tony and I started to assemble contributors in our usual fashion. We wrote to people whom we thought would join us in opposition to student rebellion, but we did not prescribe any programme of reform. We took for granted that, as usual in *C.Q.*, our writers would disagree. It was only as the contributions arrived that we realized there was considerable uniformity of view. After the Black Paper was published, an opponent on a television programme pointed out triumphantly to me that our contributors were inconsistent. It had never occurred to me that a group of intelligent people writing about education would concur in every detail. That there was so much common ground proves how strong was the 1968 reaction against egalitarianism and disruption in the universities.

At the end of July, Tony Dyson wrote to Robert Conquest, famous author of *The Great Terror*, who in addition to his spoof on *Lucky Jim* had also published a poem and an essay on science fiction in *C.Q.* We explained our idea, and asked him to suggest other contributors. In a letter of 2 August, he put forward the names of Philip Larkin, Kingsley Amis, Walter James (editor of *The Times Educational Supplement*), John Sparrow and the Pro-Vice-Chancellor of Bath University whom he had never met but who had just written a good letter in the *Daily Telegraph*. We started corresponding with all of these, except Philip Larkin, whom I knew from my Hull days would be unlikely to write a prose piece on education. On 29 August Tony and I gave lunch to Robert Conquest in London to discuss further names. Tony wrote to friends such as Professor C.L. Mowat at Bangor. Our editing proceeded in this fashion, by picking up suggestions from a variety of sources. John Sparrow, Warden of All Souls, agreed to contribute. He told us about G.F. Hudson, a Fellow of St Antony's, who had just read a paper on the Berkeley student uprisings to a small group of friends at Oxford. Hudson agreed to adapt his paper for our pamphlet. Robert Conquest suggested John Gross, recently editor of *The Times Literary Supplement*, and from him we were given the name of Professor William Walsh at Leeds. We invited Donald Mclachlan, a freelance journalist, after reading an article by him in the *Sunday Telegraph*, and he agreed we might reprint this. We also arranged to reprint an article by Bryan Wilson, of All Souls, Oxford, first published in *The British Universities Annual*. Only Tony and I knew the total plan, and later accusations that we were a well-organized political conspiracy were untrue. Many contributors never met each other, and they did not see each other's articles until publication day.

In September we decided on a major shift of policy. As we sent out our letters and followed these up with telephone calls we were constantly advised that disruption in the universities needed to be related to youth culture and to the fashion for progressive education in the schools. We felt we ought to include some teachers among our writers, and so we sent out a circular to invite a number of head teachers of independent and grammar schools to contribute. We composed a special manifesto for this circularization, and with the omission of the final short paragraph this became the first page of the Black Paper. We called our proposed pamphlet 'Fight for Education: A Black Paper'. It is worth quoting this document sent out to teachers in full:

### Fight for Education

Since the war revolutionary changes have taken place in English education – the introduction of free play methods in primary schools, comprehensive schemes, the expansion of higher education, the experimental courses at new universities. There are powerful arguments in favour of such changes, but particularly in the last year or two, many people have become increasingly unhappy about certain aspects of the general trend. Anarchy is becoming fashionable, and in papers such as the *Guardian* and *New Statesman* writers take it for granted that fundamental changes in the student/teacher relationship are inevitable. The teacher is no longer regarded as the exponent of the great achievements of past civilisation; his job is to 'decode' the 'radical critique of the young' (in the words of Roger Poole, a university lecturer, in the *Guardian*, 15 October 1968). Politicians and even Vice-Chancellors have been imitating the fashion, and there is great danger that the traditional high standards of English education are being overthrown. At primary school some teachers are taking to an extreme the belief that children must not be told anything, but must find out for themselves. At the post-eleven stage there is a strong impetus to abolish streaming, and the grammar school concepts of discipline and work are treated with contempt. In the universities, students are claiming the right to control syllabuses, to abolish examinations, and even to become involved in appointing their own teachers. At a recent demonstration in a new university, students objected to being taught History,

Literature or Science, and asked to be taught LIFE. There is a feeling that excellence in education is snobbish or undemocratic and that, for example, we should do away with class divisions in university honours degrees.

Much of this agitation could be dismissed as extremist nonsense, if it were not that major administrative decisions are resulting from these so-called 'liberal' views. The new fashionable anarchy flies in the face of human nature, for it holds that children and students will work from natural inclination rather than the desire for reward. It also, like other anarchisms, tends to be more authoritarian than the system it seeks to replace. Parents, children, students and teachers are to be forced to accept the new changes whether they like them or not.

Our purpose is not to resist the exciting challenge of new ideas but to make clear that certain theories now thought to be new and progressive are in fact old-fashioned, and products of a bankrupt romanticism. We believe that people in powerful administrative positions need to know more about the facts of education today, and that they should not be allowed to think that opponents of the revolutionary changes now being proposed are irrational or prejudiced.

When I re-read this today I am struck by a shift in the tone of argument. The first two sentences and the last paragraph are balanced and moderate. We admit that there are 'powerful arguments' in favour of the new reforms, and in subsequent radio and TV debates I often quoted these when accused of extremism. But with the words 'Anarchy is becoming fashionable' our argument turns increasingly hortatory, and we even assert that 'the grammar school concepts of discipline and work are treated with contempt'. The change of tone from moderation to denunciation brings into prominence a problem which runs through the Black Papers. Tony and I, as I have suggested, regarded ourselves as moderate progressives; we were reformers opposed to a rigid selection system at eleven-plus, and in the forefront of new teaching methods in sixth forms and universities. At the same time we were dismayed by the extremism of 1968, and believed great damage was being inflicted on education at all levels. In the ensuing campaign there was a constant tension between our sympathy for reform and our indignation at the extraordinary changes being proposed daily in the newspapers and in educational journals. We already felt that a great betrayal was taking place.

On 14 May 1969, after the Black Paper was published, Professor William Walsh wrote to me, refusing to contribute to the second Black Paper:

> I am, as you will realise, interested in the philosophical contradictions inherent in current progressive notions but not necessarily opposed to specific kinds of teaching methods. And again, as you point out, this is quite clear to anyone who reads the pieces in the pamphlet attentively, and I have had all sorts of curious attributions of ideas to me. I saw your nice comment in *Encounter* and also the point made in the *Sunday Times* review. I am sure that you are absolutely right to do what you have done and I have no regrets at all of appearing in it, especially as I think my own views are clearly put.

Professor Walsh's problem reflects my own ambiguities about the impact of the first Black Paper. In orchestrating the campaign, my difficulty was to balance the invective of intransigent traditionalists with a sympathetic and generous attitude to some progressive reforms. I was not always successful.

In the Black Paper we included a section called 'Signs of the Times' and another called 'Demolition: Work in Progress'. In these we collected snippets from the Press, including, for example, letters to *The Times* or *Guardian* alongside items from local newspapers. Reading these I am still shocked by what was going on in 1968, and I recall why I felt so strongly that a Black Paper was needed. 'Signs of the Times' begins with an item from the *Manchester Evening News* of 13 November 1968:

> Teachers who break the rules at a Cheshire primary school risk being found out and 'punished' – by the children. For a school council sits once a week to hear complaints about school meals and discipline . . .

Teachers who jumped the break-time queue recently at the tuck-shop were reported and got a severe 'ticking off'. Leading the school at the 250-pupil Ludworth County Primary School, Marple, are two ten-year-olds . . .

The idea stems from the belief by headmaster Dr John Pye that society is turning out too many robots instead of teaching young people to think more for themselves.

'We have a pretty free approach in school and this gives children the chance to speak up for themselves without the fear of being crushed by authority,' he said today.

Such news items were common. After the Black Paper campaign began it was often claimed that many schools, perhaps the majority, were still largely unaffected by the new progressive ideas. I believe we were right to insist that all the publicity in the media was devoted to praise of progressive reforms, and that as a consequence the ethos of many schools was changing rapidly. Teachers were being persuaded into reforms about whose efficacy they were often secretly in doubt. Schools varied considerably in their response to fashion, and generalizations about the educational scene can always be countered by contrary examples.

As recently as 1988 a head of a primary school claimed in a letter to *The Times Educational Supplement* that 'schools where children wander around aimlessly all day choosing to do whatever takes their fancy' never existed and that the Black Paperites attacked a kind of school which no one could identify (*T.E.S*, 1 January 1988, p. 10). My children attended such a school in Cottingham in 1965, and the trend continued at least until the William Tyndale scandal of 1976. The Black Paper campaign did much to slow down and reverse this fashion. In the mid-1970s many teachers told me that after 1969 the most extreme progressive doctrines were no longer urged so vociferously by advisers and inspectors.

When the Black Papers were being published my close friend Alan Young was teaching at Didsbury College of Education. On our journeys to watch Manchester United he regaled me with many anecdotes about progressive methods in schools in the Manchester area. At one open-plan school he found white crosses marked on the floor. 'What are these for?' he asked. The reply came: 'In the hurly-burly teachers often crowd together on one side of the room. They are required to return regularly to their assigned mark so the children can spread out again.' At another school he found an older teacher sitting in the cloak-room. She told him: 'I come here to recover from the noise. I need these five-minute doses of silence.'

That Dr Pye's school council led by ten-year-olds was not an eccentricity is shown by the second item in 'Signs of the Times'. On 29 December 1968 the *Sunday Telegraph* reported that popularly-elected school councils consisting equally of teachers and pupils, with the head teacher relegated to an advisory role, were among proposals to be considered at a national meeting of secondary school pupils in London. The campaign was said to claim considerable support among assistant teachers.

'Demolition: Work in Progress' began with an excerpt from the *Guardian*, 24 December 1968, which quoted a report entitled 'Discipline in secondary schools', prepared by a working party from the London branch of the Association of Assistant Masters. This described a slow but certain deterioration in general discipline, which took the form of chronic class-room misbehaviour. The decline in standards was ascribed to a situation where young people were becoming more rebellious than ever before, while society and its leaders were increasingly permissive.

The next item was taken from a parent's letter to his local newspaper about a conversation with the teacher of his seven-year-old son who was proving a slow learner. The teacher told him: 'We allow the child to please himself about sums. If he doesn't want to do sums, then he can choose something else. This way the child will only do sums when he himself is ready for them.' The parent took his child away, and sent him to a traditional school, where he thrived. After the Plowden Report of 1967 such permissive ideas became increasingly dominant. The progressive ethos was advocated at almost all teachers' conferences by those who thought themselves in the forefront of new ideas.

The quotations about university disruption remind me how deeply upsetting this period proved for most academics. On 4 December 1968, *The Times* reported that Mr Jenkins, Chancellor of the Exchequer, was constantly interrupted by students as he spoke on the democratic system in a live BBC television programme from the University of East Anglia. At one point Mr Jenkins and Mr Robin Day, the chairman, were showered with pamphlets. Towards the end of the seventy-five-minute programme, Mr Day told a student, who strode to the rostrum, loudly complaining: 'I would be grateful if you would not try your bullying fascist tactics on me.'

On 12 December, the *Daily Telegraph* reported that Professor Patrick Meredith of Leeds University Department of Psychology had said that he was going to burn all the files he used for helping to find jobs for students. Freedom from invasion of his office could no longer be assured. On 6 December *The Times* reported that 'one sit-in by university students – at Birmingham – ended yesterday. Another one began – at Bristol.'

In these sections of comments and quotations only one refers to the grammar versus comprehensive school issue, and for Tony and me this rated a low priority, compared with the sit-ins at universities. Our central concern was with the breakdown of traditional authority in both schools and higher education. 'Signs of the Times' included an excerpt from the *Guardian*, 17 October, in which Simon Hoggart, a young journalist and the son of our advisory editor, described how a left-wing don closely associated with student revolt protested that his students were leading him. 'This was a brilliant man who continually admitted his own ignorance and asked his pupils to lead him out of it.' An article in the *Guardian* two days before this provides a good example of what had become fashionable among students and younger members of staff. Roger Poole, later a lecturer at Nottingham University, explained that the universities had been entrusted with the job of decoding the turbulent criticism and self-criticism of the young:

A university cannot fail of its purpose if it decodes these messages aright, and directs all that flood of energy towards a sane and responsible 1969. It is beyond anyone's capabilities to 'read off' accurately the signs for longer than that, for in 1970 they will all be different again. But the university too is in a perpetual process of *becoming*.

In 'Demolition: Work in Progress' we introduced some antidotes to this fashionable rhetoric. In *The Times Educational Supplement*, 9 August 1968, Professor J.W.L. Adams wrote: 'Self-expression often is talked about, but few people have stopped to ask what "self" is and if there are good and bad ways of expressing it.'

These quotations from newspapers, together with eighteen articles in different tones and forms made the Black Paper a new kind of polemic. Bryan Wilson's article was about 6,000 words in length. In contrast to this carefully worked out academic-style paper, essays of 1,000 to 1,500 words by Kingsley Amis, Angus Maude or John Sparrow were journalistic, personal and trenchant. These mounted the attack from different levels, with the items from newspapers providing the background evidence. There were even some humorous items: ('Ask the young: they always know. Old Proverb'; 'At primary school children are taught nothing; at secondary school they discuss what they have been taught.') The impact of the Black Paper was partly because of this combination of popular polemic with careful academic reasoning. It turned out to be a type of pamphleteering which infuriated its opponents.

Our circular to schools produced articles from R.R. Pedley, head of St Dunstan's College, on the comprehensive issue, and J.M. Cobban, head of Abingdon School, on the importance of direct-grant schools. Pedley suggested that I should write to Miss G.F. Browne, head of Wyborne Primary School. I did so, but she provided only a few notes which I stuck at the bottom of a page in small print. Undoubtedly the article which caused most furore was that on freedom in junior schools by Miss C.M. Johnson, head of Prendergast Grammar School. When Tony and I received her article we wondered whether it was worth printing. Her arguments seemed just pleasant, obvious common sense, and we only decided to publish because the pamphlet was so obviously thin in its coverage of progressive education. Our reaction shows that though Tony and I were angry at the fashionable reports in newspapers, we had no idea how Miss Johnson's simple reflections would offend the progressive establishment. These are the criticisms which so angered Mr Short, the Secretary of State. The essay is worth extensive quotation:

No one would wish to return to the days when junior school children were rigidly confined to their rows of desks and learnt long lists of largely unrelated facts. But what is happening now? The restrictions of the old 11+ have almost disappeared, but the resulting freedom has been used in a multiplicity of ways. The children moving on to secondary schools present a bewildering problem even among the brightest groups.

Some at eleven can write fluently and imaginatively paying due attention to paragraphing, punctuation and spelling with none of their enthusiasm dampened. Others, of comparable intelligence, write illegibly, have no idea of arrangement of work and are thoroughly frustrated. Unfortunately the numbers in the latter category increase year by year ...

According to some present-day psychologists, all teaching of young children must be child centred: the teaching must grow from the child's interests and not be limited by any time-table divisions. Freedom of expression is all important and the method of conveying it is relatively unimportant. So far so good, but at what point should the child learn that correctness and accuracy have their place? All may be well at the junior school stage, but the freedom of the look and say method of reading, of the outpouring of ideas without arrangement or plan has disastrous results at a later stage. For instance, when learning a foreign language, one incorrect letter may well alter the whole meaning of a sentence.

Some of my friends in junior schools tell me that marking and correcting is a thing of the past as it may bring a sense of failure to a child. So one sees mistakes becoming firmly implanted in the child's mind. Many schools arrange projects for their children and some begin through this to learn the excitement of independent research and the joy of exploring in the library. Others undertake the work but do little more than copy passages from the encyclopaedia and stick cut out pictures in their books ...

To go back a stage further: at nursery level, the matron of a baby's home is told by the visiting inspector that her nursery is too tidy because she trains her under fives to put away their toys at the end of each day. In a nursery class another inspector says it is wrong to forbid children to take home toys which do not belong to them . . .

The world is a noisy, chaotic and restless place, yet in schools we see the same lack of quiet encouraged. It is putting a great strain on young children to leave them constantly to make decisions with rarely any time in the day when they are quiet and listening. This feeling was expressed in a delightfully naive manner by a little 11 year old, beginning life in an ordered secondary school, who said she liked her new school because discipline was allowed . . .

The child who has been free to wander in his junior school much as he pleases, fails to see at a later stage why he should not wander further afield. Many children who come before juvenile courts have committed their offences during school hours, although the truancy is rarely known at the school. The boy has been present for registration and then has disappeared . . .

Many of my colleagues who are working in secondary schools would agree that the children who are the most well balanced and who make the steadiest progress, are those who come from the junior schools where the children have had plenty of opportunity for independent, free study, but who have learnt the importance of listening and concentrating and who have found the satisfaction which comes from doing something, at whatever standard, really well.

It is generally accepted that the home is the strongest influence on a child's development so the child from the inadequate home, more than any other, needs security, an ordered school-life, sensible discipline and quiet.

On radio and television I often quoted the story about the little girl who liked her new school because discipline was allowed. As I read this essay today I suppose that behind its simple language one basic assumption provoked the abuse with which it was greeted. Miss Johnson presumes that the breakdown of authority in schools is directly responsible for the increase in truancy, selfishness and vandalism among adolescents. Well-intentioned reformers such as Lady Plowden or Sir Alec Clegg were being held responsible for a major deterioration in moral standards. No wonder the article provoked such rage. I hold just as strongly today as in 1969 that Miss Johnson was right, and that the abdication of authority by teachers has fundamentally damaged our society.

A 1987 survey carried out by the Professional Association of Teachers found thirty-two per cent of the 1,500 teachers who responded had been physically attacked by a pupil and five per cent by a parent. Eighty-six per cent said that class-room violence was increasing, and ninety-four per cent believed that indiscipline was becoming more commonplace. Eighty per cent had been subjected to 'offensive verbal abuse'. Attitudes to authority have changed in the family as well as in the school, of course, but I am convinced that the breakdown of good order in our society, particularly the steep rise in crime among children and young people, derives in part from the relaxation of discipline in schools. Later I was to find an essay by Hannah Arendt in *Between Past and Future* (1961) which provided philosophic underpinning for this point of view. Hannah Arendt's views on education were highlighted in *Black Paper 1977* (see p.217).

In November we wrote to Angus Maude after reading his views in the newspapers. This was a momentous decision, because it linked our work with a prominent Conservative MP. Angus Maude was the only politician who contributed to the first Black Paper, and some supporters of our campaign have suggested that we would have been better advised to confine ourselves to teachers and academics. Tony and I did not suspect, however, that our pamphlet would create such an extraordinary national controversy. We asked Angus Maude simply because he wrote well, and we agreed with what he said. When his article arrived in the *C.Q.* office we decided to place it first because it so splendidly summed up the case against egalitarianism. I do not regret the invitation to Angus Maude. In the early months of 1969 he gave us good advice on publicity, and without him our pamphlet might not have received so much attention. Already in 1968 Tony and I had realized that we could not avoid politics. After the Black Paper was published, a close friend of mine, a university professor at a provincial university, accused me of betraying the traditional values of academic neutrality. I was worried by his attack, but I remain sure that the present low esteem in which universities are held partly results from the failure of academics in the late 1960s to fight a political campaign. The 'neutrality' of which my friend boasted was in reality an illusion, for university education depends on ideas of selectivity which were being undermined by political reformers on the left of the Labour Party. Academics who pride themselves on taking a non-political stance are in fact opting out from their democratic responsibilities. Obviously whether one supports the Labour or Conservative Party depends on a host of factors, but one's attitude to egalitarianism in education must play some part in the decision.

The response to our letters to schools was so encouraging that Tony and I became increasingly ambitious. We sent advertisements, including the 'manifesto' to every professor in Britain and to every head teacher. In February we arranged a lunch and then a dinner, both in London, at which contributors met to discuss publicity. Not all attended, and at this stage Tony and I were mainly assisted by Kingsley Amis, Robert Conquest and Angus Maude. We decided to hold a Press conference at 5 p.m. on 12 March at Brown's Hotel (famous in American novels) because we thought the venue would intrigue the education correspondents. At this Press conference Amis, Conquest and Maude played leading roles, while Tony and I, inexperienced in these affairs, kept comparatively silent.

Not only did the Black Paper range from knockabout comedy to serious academic articles; it also tackled the three different major educational problems I described at the end of the last chapter: the introduction of free expression in schools, the Labour Party's plans for comprehensive education, and the student demands to participate in university government. In the first article Angus Maude brought these together by expounding with exemplary lucidity the ideological fundamentals of progressive education to which we were all opposed. His article begins:

> Taking a long view, one must conclude that the most serious danger facing Britain is the threat to the *quality* of education at all levels. The motive force behind this threat is the ideology of egalitarianism.

Maude contended that the reformers who cherished the highest ideals, who were emotionally committed to the concept of equality, were the most dangerous. Their sentimentalities were weakening the essential toughness on which quality in education depends:

> (the egalitarian) complains bitterly of the excessive 'competitive-ness' of the conventional system of education, and claims that his reforms would remove the 'stresses' from which children are alleged to suffer. Not only does he dislike class marks and competitive examinations, he has a horror of any test which some children might fail. This leads him on to decry the importance of academic standards and discipline – and indeed of learning itself. He will advocate a variety of 'new teaching methods', which in fact absolve anyone from teaching and anyone from having to learn.
>
> The egalitarian rationalizes his dislike of academic disciplines by talking of 'education for social living'. He prefers this to real learning, because it is impossible for any recognizable elite to emerge from anything so woolly and unmeasurable. The idea is to remove from the educational process anything which calls for effort and incites children to excel. Some children must be held back, in order to avoid 'discouraging' the rest.
>
> No system of education based on this philosophy of emotional prejudice can possibly provide a useful preparation for life as it actually has to be lived. When the adolescent who has been coddled along in this way finally has to face the realities of life, he is liable to disappointments, frustrations and resentments far more searing than those which the educational reformers claim to have spared him at school.

He attacked in particular the 1967 Reith lectures given by Dr Edmund Leach, Provost of King's College, Cambridge, in which it was argued that removing competitiveness from education would result in a less competitive society.

This is perhaps the central point at issue in all debates about the Black Papers. The socialist, following in the steps of Rousseau, believes that changes in the organization of schools will transform the nature of children. The conservative holds that human nature is instinctively competitive, that high standards can only be achieved when children are motivated by ambition for success, and that virtuous behaviour depends to a large extent on training and discipline. My own sympathy for the conservative position goes back to the crucial moment during my time at Cambridge when I read C.S. Lewis's *Screwtape Letters*.

Maude particularly criticized the belief that the worthy ideal of equality of opportunity can be achieved quickly, quoting Bagehot; the latter wrote of the menace of philanthropists who have 'inherited from their barbarous forefathers a wild passion for instant action'. If the egalitarian is allowed his way he will create a more inefficient society than we have already. Worse still, he will destroy our culture, with his pretence that intellect and cultivation do not matter. Maude insisted that teaching inevitably creates an élite, for children vary in their talents, and to try to hide such unpalatable facts does great harm to society:

> No society can abandon all toughness in its educational system without, in the end, becoming soft itself. If it becomes soft, it will not survive. There is no hope for a people, none of whom has been taught to do anything properly or to think any problem through, with rigour, to its essence.

Maude concluded by demanding that the egalitarians, whose ideas of 'social justice' are prescriptions for mediocrity and anarchy, must be prevented from having any control over the education of the young. Tony and I were impressed by this essay, which helped us to focus more precisely the reasons for our discontents. Maude's criticisms seem to me just as relevant today as when he wrote it twenty-four years ago.

Maude's article was followed by Kingsley Amis on 'Pernicious Participation'. His first sentence reads:

> A student, being (if anything) engaged in the acquiring of knowledge, is not in a position to decide which bits of knowledge it is best for him to acquire, or how his performance in the acquisition of knowledge can most properly be assessed, or who is qualified to help him in this activity.

He continues: 'Who can understand the importance of Roman law, or anatomy, or calculus, if he has not mastered them?' He finished his essay by repeating his famous remark that 'more has meant worse'; Amis wrote that the universities were full of students who do not understand what study is about, and who are painfully bewildered by the whole business and purpose of university life.

Amis put the issue more starkly than I might have wished. In 1969 and still today I know he is right to argue that the university has failed to adapt to the needs of a wider range of students. My own view is that the new universities missed a great opportunity by aping the old (their early reforming intentions rendered bland and relatively insignificant once traditional staff were appointed), and that creative writing and drama and visual arts and music ought to be at the centre of courses in the Arts. I return to this theme in my final chapters.

I also agree with Amis that student participation brought few benefits and many ill consequences. Students are useful members of hall of residence committees, for example, where discussions take place on their day-to-day living conditions, but their presence on Senate and Council is often of dubious value. Most students are too ignorant of the business to participate. Some never turn up. Those who do speak are nearly all left-wing ideologues preparing for a career in politics. The result for university administration is that much time is wasted, and that astute vice-chancellors have removed real power to private discussion and small committees. In his Black Paper article, G.F. Hudson draws a distinction between matters of accommodation, catering, health and welfare, on the one hand, and matters of curriculum, degrees, research and appointments and emoluments of staff on the other, in which students should not be involved. This sums up the Black Paper view. In some ways student participation has reduced the power of the non-professorial staff, as crucial financial and administrative decisions have been quietly taken away from committees with student members.

Robert Conquest's article, 'Undotheboys Hall' started with a major misprint, introduced by a printer's error after a page-proof correction. Conquest wanted to illustrate that an educated man must possess a certain minimum of general knowledge. In the Black Paper this reads:

Even if he knows very little about science and cannot add or subtract, he must have heard of Mendel and Kepler. Even if he is tone deaf he must know something about Debussy and Verdi; even if he is a pure sociologist he must be aware of Circe and the Minotaur of Kent and Montaigne, of Titus Oates and Tiberius Gracchus.

No one ever mentioned this mistake. Perhaps no one dared to expose their ignorance about the Minotaur of Kent. The sentence should read: 'of Circe and the Minotaur, of Kant and Montaigne'. In subsequent years Tony and I have found the Minotaur of Kent a friendly beast which often manifests itself in our letters to console us when proof errors crop up in our publications.

Robert Conquest attacked what he called the pseudo-discipline of sociology. To learn to talk polysyllabically, he says, is not to learn to talk rationally. In opposition to Simon Hoggart and Roger Poole in 'Signs of the Times', he emphasized the 'apprentice' role of the undergraduate:

When one is told that the task of education is to teach people to think critically about established values and institutions, one can say that there is a sense in which this is true. But it is impossible to think critically about attitudes, however much one wishes to prove them obsolete, if one has not learned what they are. Teaching, therefore, must here too involve providing a knowledge – and a real knowledge – of the culture of the present and past.

He extended his strictures to the teaching of literature, drawing on the experiences of his wife. She had discovered that, in the secondary school where she taught, the English staff, instead of teaching literature, presumed they were teaching 'life'. Thus fiction about barrow boys on the Old Kent Road was regarded as the right thing to teach the children of the area. The children had no desire to read low quality novels of this sort, even if any could be found, and preferred *Treasure Island*.

Conquest attacked the fashion for encouraging children to write free 'verse', regardless of rhythm or form, inaccurate in punctuation, but supposedly a genuine emotional response to their own experiences. Children forced to do these things for a teacher will be heard in the playground singing or reciting old 'street game' ballads, even making up their own versions, to a genuine rhythm and form. Black Paper contributors were often accused of opposing the development of a child's imagination and of advocating a return to parrot learning. This was not true. Like Conquest we believed that a child's adventures in the use of language depend upon craft, upon training which includes the use of traditional form. The requirements for the National Curriculum in English put forward by my Working Party in 1989 reflect not some change of heart in me, but what I already believed when the Black Papers were published.

Student sit-ins in Britain were treated by Conquest with contempt:

> And when these radical students choose to exercise their animus by preference against their own universities, on the extremely arguable ground that that is the place to start, one notes that it is a matter of taking on the most bumbling and pathetic lot of elderly gentlemen to be found. Paris students at least fight the Garde Mobile. Ours boldly confront those beetle-browed thugs Professor X. and Mr Y., the modern equivalents of Dr Spooner and Dr Dodgson.

This kind of exasperated wit naturally provoked some emotional reactions.

In 'The Berkeley Fashion', G.F. Hudson surveyed the influence of American student protest on British institutions. What is new, he says, is not the inclination of students to play a part in politics; in 1937 several hundred students marched down the High Street in Oxford shouting 'Arms for Spain'. But these students would have been as meek as could be if they had received a summons to appear before the Proctors or the College Dean. Dons were still regarded with a certain awe: they were accepted as *in loco parentis*.

In the 1960s parental authority had been eroded to such an extent that a fashionable slogan urged students to trust no one over thirty. For this reason militants could draw on emotional sympathy from moderate students. The great change in the 1960s was that it was found in practice that direct action against university authorities could be very effective. Small minorities could through sit-ins force administrators to introduce major changes. If a vice-chancellor tried to impose his authority through punishments he might provoke even larger demonstrations and disruptions. A small minority of militants could be formidable if the majority did nothing to stop it; if its actions were frequently crowned with success the indifference of the majority was gradually transformed into support.

The next two articles were by academics from the London School of Economics, which by 1968 had become notorious for its student riots. Imre Lakatos, a mathematician with a considerable international reputation, allowed us to print an open letter he had sent to the Director of L.S.E.

Lakatos came from an unusual background. As an undergraduate in Germany he had witnessed the erosion of academic autonomy by the demands of Nazi students for the suppression of 'Jewish-liberal-Marxist influence' expressed in the syllabuses. Later he was a graduate student at Moscow University when resolutions of the Central Committee of the Communist Party were imposed on syllabuses in genetics, and dissenters were condemned to death. In his letter he also recalled how Russian students demanded that Einstein's 'bourgeois relativism' (i.e. his relativity theory) should be suppressed, and that those who taught such courses should confess their crimes in public. He linked such memories with the humiliation of university professors by the students of Peking University during the 'cultural revolution'.

Lakatos thought that events in Britain would end in similar suppressions if the campaign for student participation was not halted. Like Hudson, he wanted students to participate in decisions about their welfare, and he acknowledged their right to criticize syllabuses and teaching. However, he knew from his background in Germany and Russia that the fragile plant of academic autonomy soon withers. Also like Hudson he foresaw that the real danger might come from the government rather than the students. Demands for student interference in academic policy-making could lead to demands for government interference:

This is perhaps the most important reason why we should resist student power while accepting student freedom to criticise: because we resist government power while accepting government freedom to criticise.

Outside Britain, academic autonomy was being assaulted with different degrees of vehemence and success, the most recent examples being the purge of Greek universities by the junta of colonels and the dismissal of seven liberal-Zionist professors of Warsaw University. Like the Jewish professors during my time at Berkeley, Lakatos foresaw sinister dangers in student riots. He did not claim that university traditions will *necessarily* be destroyed within a few years if we adopt a policy of appeasement. For him, though, it was a miracle that the university tradition was ever established, and we would have to fight against its gradual erosion all the time against demands from either students or government.

D.C. Watt had been a lecturer in history at L.S.E. His article consisted of a careful analysis of the damage done to L.S.E. after the Robbins Report of 1963 by unthinking plans for expansion. He forecast what Lord Annan and others have been saying in the 1980s: 'The scale of university expansion projected in those years was wildly beyond the national capacity to pay for it.' Already by 1969 the staff-student ratio at L.S.E. had risen sharply, with consequent breakdowns of communication, while money for promotions and equipment had run out.

Watt extended his critique to the creation of new universities on the Oxbridge model in the outskirts of Baedeker towns where lodgings could be expected to be in the shortest of supply, and the local catchment area of students extremely limited. The Oxbridge model was suited only to a tiny élite, and was quite inappropriate for a major expansion of the student population.

Like Hudson and Lakatos, Watt foresaw that the future threat to academic freedom would come from government as well as from student militants. As I have said before, one reason for the immense success of the Black Paper was that it forcibly expressed ideas held by large numbers of people previously muzzled by the progressive establishment. Hudson, Lakatos and Watt prepared their articles without consulting each other and without editorial guidance, yet in their different ways they deduced that student rebellion would end in government control of the universities.

The first Black Paper thus began with a series of brief, trenchant essays on egalitarianism and student revolt. These were followed by an article by me on examinations, acting as a bridge to the central section of the pamphlet, which was devoted to schools. Articles on direct-grant, public and comprehensive schools were followed by Miss Johnson on progressive education. After these essays the concluding section was devoted to general material on the idea of the university and the cultural and social trends underlying student revolt.

In 1968 there was a vigorous campaign by students and junior staff to get rid of university examinations, or at least to move away from traditional exams to course assessment. In my article I pointed out, as R.H. Tawney argued long ago, it is inherent in professional work – and a first degree from a university is the *sine qua non* for entering many professions – that the public is not in a position to judge the quality of performance which it must take on trust. Passing exams before entering a profession is a necessary protection for the public. Before a head appoints a teacher of French, he needs proof that a candidate has reached an acceptable standard. If a specialist is wanted for sixth-form work it is a great help to know that one applicant has an upper second class honours degree and another only a third. In professions such as medicine or architecture, qualifications must have authority, for a complex society depends on such safeguards and classifications.

My article accepted the need for moderate reforms, even some use of course assessment, but my Berkeley year had instructed me in the weaknesses of the American system. American undergraduates told me that course assessment restricted their freedom to think for themselves. If a teacher proved a martinet, a student iconoclast could inevitably expect low marks. Course assessment could also create more strain than conventional exams, for the student is placed under continual pressure. In the late 1980s many children taking the new G.C.S.E. found this to be true. And what does 'cheating' mean? If an essay is to be graded as part of a university honours requirement, then the student who submits his work without asking for advice is either a fool or a saint. If a student is married, and the wife or husband is a graduate, may they discuss essay topics together?

Course assessment in the schools works in favour of middle-class children, whose parents can provide their offspring with various kinds of help. My experiences at Wintringham demonstrated to me that only public exams can reveal to sixth-formers that their approach to their subject is inadequate, and that their teachers may be giving poor advice. When exams involve 100 per cent coursework, students may never learn the truth about their abilities until it is too late. A left-wing friend of mine who teaches at the University of California at La Jolla explained to me a great disadvantage of the American system of course assessment. At high schools many working-class children with a regular string of 'A' grades are shocked on arrival at university to find that their performance is weaker than that of middle-class students with an average of 'B' from the high school. On two occasions the consequent depression had ended in attempts at suicide.

R.R. Pedley (not Professor Robin Pedley to whom I refer later) made a frontal attack on the replacement of grammar schools by a system of eleven to eighteen comprehensives. His article was called 'Comprehensive Disaster', and he did not mince his words. Pedley insisted that able children in the company of their peers find an atmosphere, an ethos, specially relevant to them, and so receive a stimulus and an incentive which fully stretches their abilities. His stress on the importance of the peer group appealed to me because of my memories of Wintringham and Pembroke. My failures and successes had depended to a large extent on the degree of support I received from friends such as Tony Dyson. This argument is not often mentioned today. A boy or girl in the sixth form is unlikely to reach high standards without the daily stimulus of children of similar ability. Recently a parent told me how sad he was because his son, who had the ability to go to university, had chosen to leave his comprehensive school at the age of sixteen. He had yielded to pressure from his peer group, all of whom were leaving to take up employment.

Pedley addressed himself to the neighbourhood school problems of which I first became aware at Berkeley. In the 1980s and 1990s the social divisions created by neighbourhood comprehensives are well-known. In his public speeches Sir Rhodes Boyson has continually drawn attention to the influence of a good comprehensive on house prices, yet in the period from 1969 to 1975 I found it very difficult to persuade anyone to listen to this argument. On a three-part *Panorama* television programme on secondary education in 1970 I drew attention forcibly to the problem of the neighbourhood school; when the programme was transmitted, though, this section had been completely excised. In 1975 I was interviewed by a bright graduate journalist working for the *Guardian*. Typical of her generation, she had never heard of the neighbourhood school argument, and I felt I persuaded her to change her mind. During the Black Paper campaign we were faced by idealists who feared rational discussion, and who often amazed me by their willingness to close their minds to all objections to their programmes of reform. Pedley acknowledged that in some underpopulated parts of the country comprehensive schools were inevitable, and throughout the Black Paper campaign I insisted that in country areas a comprehensive school was probably the best form of education. The Black Paper authors liked to think of themselves as pragmatic rather than doctrinaire.

Pedley's article was followed by that of Miss Johnson; together they attracted more attention than all the previous articles on student revolt. The section ended with a piece by A.M. Hardie, Pro-Vice-Chancellor at the University of Bath. He advocated the kind of discipline of study I recalled at Nunsthorpe. Hardie pointed out that many teachers who paid lip service to modern methods, particularly when the inspector called, resorted to more systematic and well-tried means when behind their own class-room doors. Professor Hardie wanted a broader 'A' level exam, perhaps similar to the Scottish model, with students taking courses in both sciences and arts. This was one of the many moderate reforms put forward in the Black Paper which were never mentioned by the media.

The final section began with an anonymous article, signed 'B', which advocated the traditional liberal values of academic study. The author was a university professor who so feared student reprisals that he dared not reveal his name. When preparing this book I wrote to him, asking if I could name him, but he refused.

His first sentence reads: 'It is, I believe, no exaggeration to say that over the past five years or so the English universities have deteriorated considerably as cultural environments.' He found a seriously diminished confidence in the ideal of education itself among many university teachers. 'B' wrote that this decline was 'a manifest signal of the unhappy fortunes of that belief in culture, civilisation and disinterested criticism that the university has particularly stood for in English society'. In the post-expansion climate, emphasis had moved away from the university's prime function, which should be 'to civilize, to refine, self-consciously to "make" itself a culture, to provide that context of tolerance and openness to ideas that is primary and prior to the value of any given idea in itself'. Liberal ideas were threatened both by the intolerance of student militants and by problems created by expansion – financial setbacks, over-rationalist architects, and bad planning. This article is the one closest to the original intention of the Black Paper when Tony and I devised our plans on Hampstead Heath. The university is seen as a profoundly delicate and complex community, whose most important features cannot be costed. Neither the government nor the extremist student lobby had a marked interest in the survival of the university in its liberal guise. The strong feeling of moderates such as this professor comes out when he talks of how the traditional tolerance of the campus has been threatened in 1968 by 'new forms of extremist left-wing fanaticism and fascism'.

Bryan Wilson's essay on youth culture was largely ignored. He was at pains to acknowledge that the new students were not less intelligent than the previous small élite of the pre-expansion days. The problem of the late 1960s was that the culture of the university itself had been transformed, particularly by the split between generations created by youth culture. Wilson ascribed this mainly to the entertainment industry, where sensationalism thrived in opposition to university ideals of inculcated restraint, internalized discipline and steady acquisition of taste and knowledge:

The growth of dissident entertainment values and of the youth culture is part of the context of contemporary student troubles. Spock-ism in childrearing; 'free expression' in early education;

the permissive morality advocated by self-styled 'liberals', are other elements. Students today have been much more exposed to these influences than could have been the case in the past.

More has meant worse, Wilson suggests, not so much because people of less intellectual capacity had been admitted, but because the new students were less committed, less adequately socialized for the university experience and less prepared to take on university values. All this happened when because of expansion and financial cuts universities were less able to communicate their values.

Wilson's essay was followed by a short article by Tony Dyson which summed up the concluding section with a quotation from Goya: 'the sleep of reason brings forth monsters'. As Tony and I read more and more in the educational field we were shocked by the utopian simplicities of progressive ideology, particularly the thinking that derived from A.S. Neill's *Summerhill*, with its belief that children are 'innately wise and realistic'. This utopianism was completely at odds with the modern literature we were discussing with teachers at *Critical Quarterly* conferences – Kafka, *The Waste Land*, Sylvia Plath's *Ariel*, Beckett's *Waiting for Godot*. Tony ended the Black Paper with the prophecy that a bankrupt and dangerous romanticism (Blake's 'The road of excess leads to the palace of wisdom' had become a popular student slogan) would be more likely to create Belsen rather than Utopia. As well as the two Black Papers, 1969 was also the year of the sensational killings in California directed by Charles Manson.

# 8
# *Responses to the First Black Paper*

Raving politics, never at rest – as this poor earth's pale history
runs, –
What is it all but a trouble of ants in the gleam of a million million
of suns?

'Vastness', Tennyson

The covers for *Critical Quarterly* were designed by Ted Burrill, a
teacher at Hull Technical College. For the Black Paper he excelled,
with a design of a crowd of grey, Lowry-like children splashed over
by huge black blots. On several occasions during debates it was
suggested by our opponents that the violence of our rhetoric was
matched by the violence of the cover.

I suppose if I edited the Black Paper now I might tone down the
more extreme language. Some contributors – D.C. Watt or William
Walsh – would have preferred a pamphlet written in more judicious
and restrained tones. Not surprisingly, most education journalists
confined their attention to the extravagant elements and ignored
the solid arguments. But the exasperation of Robert Conquest, or
the fierce criticisms of Angus Maude, reflected the genuine anger
of thousands of teachers and parents who welcomed the Black
Paper. In 'University Unrest' in the Black Paper John Gross felt
it to be urgent for teachers and students who were committed to
traditional civilized standards to fight for better Press coverage.
The abuse heaped on the Black Paper created its own reaction,
and made it easier for more moderate voices to be heard. When
the media has become dominated by a set of fashionable ideas,
this hold can probably only be broken by some sensational event

like a Black Paper. We created a swing against the assumptions of the 1960s which might not have occurred if we had only published academic-style essays. When in our letter to MPs Tony and I asserted that 'disastrous mistakes' were being made in education I do not think we were exaggerating.

Today the breakdown of discipline in inner-city comprehensives is a direct result of the sicknesses which afflicted the schools in the 1960s. In November 1988 a report compiled by the Tavistock Institute of Human Relations showed that there were 535 reported attacks on staff in inner-London schools and colleges in one academic year. Today teachers at comprehensive schools tell me that hardly a day passes without rudeness from some pupil, and that they have few sanctions to cope with this problem. This would have been out of the question when I taught at Immingham Secondary Modern School.

Even before the Press conference at Brown's Hotel in London on 12 March the Black Paper had begun to attract attention. We had never heard of Press embargoes, and so sent the pamphlet for review in our usual way. Free copies were sent to every MP, directors of education, vice-chancellors, members of the U.G.C. and heads of Oxbridge colleges. Several weeks before the publication date we started sending out advertisements to schools, and by early March we had orders for several thousands. Immediately there were leading articles in *The Times* (5 March) and the *Daily Telegraph* (11 March).

The choice of Brown's Hotel for the Press conference was Angus Maude's idea. About thirty education journalists attended. Stuart Maclure, soon to become editor of *The Times Educational Supplement*, was there and so was Brian MacArthur, representing *The Times*. Many Black Paper contributors attended, including Miss Johnson, Imre Lakatos and D.C. Watt, none of whom I had met before. As I explained in my last chapter, Tony and I left most of the talking to Angus Maude, Kingsley Amis and Robert Conquest. The questions were fierce, particularly from Stuart Maclure, and at times a touch acrimonious.

After the Press conference, lengthy reviews appeared in journals and newspapers such as the *Spectator, New Society*, the *Sunday Times* and the *Observer*. Kingsley Amis contributed a feature as guest columnist for the *Daily Express* (19 March). The Black Paper, also called 'Fight for Education', was covered extensively in the educational press.

On 7 March Lord Snow gave the inaugural Clayesmore lecture at Clayesmore School in Dorset. This was reviewed in *The Times*, together with the Black Paper, by Brian MacArthur on 8 March. Like us, Lord Snow dealt with egalitarianism, warning his audience that we were in danger of not educating our most gifted children to the height of their talent. He conceded that élitism was an ugly word, and recalled that throughout the 1930s he had campaigned against the restriction of educational opportunities to too small a proportion of the population. In 1969, however, opposition to élitism had taken on destructive meanings such as lack of regard for academic excellence, or ignorance of the conditions which produced it. He described the Kolmogorov boarding school attached to Moscow University, which selected and trained the best young Russian mathematicians, a kind of selectivity essential for high standards: 'Egalitarianism, like élitism, has two faces, one ugly, one benign. It is good to believe that men are equal in the sight of God. It is ugly to try to achieve this by cutting down the tall poppies, as the Australians say.' Lord Snow thought that any parent whose child had a chance of becoming a pianist like Richter, but whose social conscience insisted that he was treated like anyone else instead of sending him to the Yehudi Menuhin school, was depriving both the world and his son.

In his *Times* review Brian MacArthur treated Lord Snow with sympathy, but the Black Paper with contempt, quoting a leading article in *Teachers' World* on the 'Goon-like illogicality' of claims that student unrest might partly originate in the new primary school approaches to education: 'Teachers', MacArthur wrote, 'would be puzzled at some omissions. There was, for instance no argument that long hair sapped energy for study, that mini-skirts distracted high-flyers, and that cold baths prevented thoughts about Raquel Welch.' This kind of send-up was typical of many educational journalists who often repeated that research had shown that the new progressive methods of teaching were raising standards. The great betrayal of education in the 1960s was very much fostered by this kind of media coverage.

On 23 March the *Observer* published a major article, 'Education: the backlash starts', by Stuart Maclure, at that time still editor of *Education*. The nature of the 'backlash' became a popular subject for debate. Maclure saw the Black Paper as an onslaught on liberal ideas in education by dons and schoolmasters 'who want to restate as vigorously as they can the old-fashioned virtues of intellectual rigour and academic scholarship'. After a detailed summary of Black Paper philosophy he accused us of nostalgia for the past: 'But the main weakness of the whole argument is that its claim to intellectual toughness is fundamentally bogus. It is not imbued with earthy realism but a romantic nostalgia for a time when advanced education was only available for the well-to-do or exceptionally bright.' For Maclure the expansion of education at secondary and higher level was inevitable: 'Coming to terms with mass education certainly doesn't mean retreating into the fortress of the academic curriculum. It doesn't mean fitting an academic straitjacket on the primary and secondary schools and insisting that every child should grow up within it.' This article provoked a series of letters.

On 6 April the *Observer* published the following letter from me:

I'm sure the contributors to the Black Paper, 'Fight for Education', would happily agree that there are many excellent primary schools; but the problem for parents is this. In one school a good head teacher combines the best of old and new methods. The children are allowed plenty of freedom, but their learning is carefully structured and guided by sensible teachers. In another school, perhaps in fine buildings with colourful displays on parents' day, the children are left too much to their own devices, and move haphazardly from one activity to the next. Their written work is seldom corrected.

The impression of many people in education is that the latter kind of school is increasing in number. The result, as recent letters in *The Times Educational Supplement* have testified, is that children are backward in maths and English when they reach the secondary school.

Now that the 11 plus is to be abolished, and the power of

inspectors has been reduced, how are parents to judge what is going on? Already educated parents are making up for the deficiencies of schools by teaching their children at home, but this is grossly unfair to most working-class children.

In my view, parents must insist on proper inspection and testing of primary school methods. Otherwise schools can be ruined by new fashions and gimmicks, and parents will find out too late.

I think very few people would disagree with that letter today; the balance between freedom and structure is to be found in the recommendations of the National Curriculum English Working Group, and its treatment of discovery methods is close to that of Professor Robin Alexander in his Leeds report of 1991.

In the same issue of the *Observer* which carried Maclure's article, Professor Julius Gould of Nottingham University reviewed the Black Paper in the literary section: 'Cox and Dyson have produced a timely polemic – but its zeal may be counter-productive. What they stress (and I am sure that they are right) is that educational "thought" has rested far too much upon tendentious, anti-intellectual rubbish and that bad "thought" has driven out good.' Later it was often claimed that before Mr Short's April speech the Black Paper attracted little interest. This is not true, as I hope I have demonstrated. After the Secretary of State's outburst, the nature of the comments changed.

Mr Short's speech to the National Union of Teachers conference at Douglas, Isle of Man, on 8 April produced headlines in all the national newspapers, from the *Daily Mirror* (Short hits out at 'education backlash'), to the *Daily Express* (Short slams the classroom critics), to the *Guardian* (Minister attacks 'backlash' against school freedom). Mr Short also attacked a recent speech Lord Snow had made in New York. *The Times Educational Supplement* gave this summary of Mr Short's speech:

The backlash should be seen in its wider context as a massive lurch in society towards reaction, 'the reaction of racism, of demands for capital and corporal punishment, of the ending of the welfare state and now of reaction in education'.

It was much more than an attack on the comprehensive secondary school – it was an attack on liberal ideas in education generally.

'To those of us who have been brought up in the free progressive atmosphere of English education much of the Black Paper appears to be archaic rubbish, but we should be extremely foolish if we ignored it or underestimated the impact it may make, because it is so ridiculously and outrageously behind the times.'

In his criticism of Lord Snow, Mr Short said that the suggestion that racial and ethnic factors affected ability and achievement was 'reminiscent of Dr Goebbels'.

Why did Mr Short flare up in this extraordinary manner? Cynical observers at the time suggested that he was offering abuse of the Black Paper as an alternative to a pay rise. Representatives of teachers at the Douglas conference were concerned about 193 part-time teachers at Coventry who were likely to be sacked, and speakers from Bristol, London, Oldham and Kingston demanded that Mr Short should reverse his financial cuts. His speech turned their wrath onto the Black Paper, and he was given a standing ovation.

Several MPs told me that Mr Short was quite genuine in his horror at the contents of the Black Paper. He thought that 'we could have egalitarianism without sacrificing the gifts of the more able', and saw the Black Paper as a major threat to such ideals.

After Mr Short's speech the wildest untruths were printed about the Black Paper. The *Guardian* (7 May) said Enoch Powell was a contributor. He was not. The *Guardian* Miscellany (10 May) referred to the authors as 'the tightly-knit group of "Black Paper" Rightists', and mentioned specifically Warden Sparrow, Kingsley Amis and myself. The *Guardian* later published a letter from me pointing out that I had never met Warden Sparrow, and that I had met Kingsley Amis only twice. *Private Eye* said that Peregrine Worsthorne was a contributor, and that the Black Paper was a plot hatched by Worsthorne, Bernard Levin, Amis and Conquest against Sir Edward Boyle. This was all fantasy. I had never met either Peregrine Worsthorne or Bernard

Levin, and they had nothing to do with the preparation of the Black Paper.

The change of tone after Mr Short's speech is amusingly illustrated by *The Sunday Times*. On 16 March John Raymond reviewed the Black Paper in the usual way in the literary pages. He was full of praise: '"How far", ask the editors, "are we witnessing a progressive collapse of education?" An impressive team of dons, schoolteachers, writers and journalists set out to answer this largely rhetorical question. Their candour is refreshing, their jeremiads incisive and stimulating, and their reactions by no means as predictable as the distinguished list of names suggests.' On the Sunday (13 April) following Mr Short's speech, a leading article said the exact opposite: 'Much of the Black Paper was tendentious cliché supported by superficiality piled on superficiality.'

These untruths and wild comments very much harmed the Black Paper campaign, as was intended. In June 1971, in a live television debate on education at the Oxford Union (the one where I read the Gary Snyder poem) with Richard Crossman, Shirley Williams and Norman St John Stevas, Crossman admitted that he had not read the Black Papers, and that his information came entirely from the newspapers. He was typical of many people who did not read the pamphlet, but took their opinions from inaccurate newspaper reports. This, of course, is a common problem.

I was outraged and dismayed by Mr Short's speech, particularly by accusations which linked Tony and me with racism and authoritarianism, and which told thousands of teachers and parents who read the newspaper reports that we were anti-liberal. When one considers Tony's courage in starting his campaign for homosexual reform it was an extraordinary falsification. Until 1989 I could not slough off this authoritarian image, and I have every right to blame Mr Short for exaggerations which damaged my public reputation for twenty years. It was not until 1984, when I began a series of twenty-two monthly back-page articles for *The Times Educational Supplement*, that I was able to speak to teachers direct, and to persuade many of them that I am proud to call myself a liberal.

After Mr Short's speech the arguments continued for several weeks on radio and television and in the newspapers, and there were even interchanges in the House of Commons (6 May, *Hansard*, 259–62):

> *Mr Evelyn King*: When the Secretary of State describes the expression of quite moderate opinion by eminent thinkers such as Kingsley Amis and the Warden of All Souls as the 'blackest day in education for 100 years', does not this sound a little unbalanced? Does the Prime Minister think that intellectual argument is assisted by Ministerial hysterics of that kind?
>
> *The Prime Minister*: What the hon. Gentleman regards as a moderate statement and what the rest of us regard as moderate are not exactly the same. The paper which was castigated by my right hon. Friend is a document calling into question all the advances in education policy – (Interruption).
>
> *Mr Speaker*: Order. This is on an educational topic.
>
> *The Prime Minister*: – carried through by my right hon. Friend with the support of the Front Bench opposite, and if the hon. Member for Dorset South (Mr King) does not agree with those advances the fault obviously lies in him . . . I totally reject, as my right hon. Friend in the speech which is the subject of this Question, the attitudes and arguments used in this so-called 'black paper' about the whole liberal progress in education carried forward for over twenty years now.

In the *Spectator* (17 April) Denis Brogan expostulated against the way Mr Short had treated the Black Paper as if it were a new edition of *Mein Kampf*. He defended the humane qualities of Lord Snow, who in New York, while addressing a totally Jewish audience, had referred to the possible intrinsic superiority of Jewish genes as part of their intellectual equipment. For Mr Short to compare these words to those of Dr Goebbels was the height of absurdity. In the same issue of the *Spectator* Auberon Waugh said Mr Short had invented a dragon out of the Black Paper just as Don Quixote worked off his urge for social justice against a windmill. As defence and attack continued, I found that all the support for the Black Paper could not efface the images of racism and authoritarianism which had sunk deep into the imagination of progressive teachers.

At the eye of the storm, Tony and I found ourselves in an almost impossible position. Hundreds of letters and orders for the Black Paper arrived at our Radcliffe Avenue office. We were answering letters in the newspapers, and giving interviews to journalists. On Radio 4 (8 April) I said that Mr Short 'doesn't know what liberal means'. When asked whether I agreed with Mr Short that the issue was 'authoritarianism versus democracy', I replied that although I was against élitism in social terms, 'in education you must accept that some children have special abilities in mathematics or in music or athletics and they need special training'. I was to say these things again and again in public, but often felt that once I was tarnished with a fascist image nice distinctions about liberalism and élitism were usually ignored.

Within a couple of weeks of Mr Short's speech Tony and I had decided to publish a second Black Paper. Our first pamphlet had been repeatedly accused of ignoring the facts. The second, scheduled for October, was intended to rebut this charge. The first Black Paper had been thin on progressive education and comprehensive schools, and we would put this right.

We were told repeatedly that statistics proved that progressive education worked better than traditional methods, and that comprehensive schools would raise the standards of all children. When we investigated these claims we were astonished by the naiveté of major documents such as the Plowden Report (1967) or Professor Robin Pedley's Penguin book *The Comprehensive School* (1964). The Plowden Report pointed out that reading standards of eleven- and fifteen-year-olds had improved since 1948, and this was used as a triumphant vindication of progressive teaching methods (paragraph 585). Leading educationalists such as Sir Alec Clegg, or Mr Short himself, quoted these figures against the Black Paper (*The Times*, 18 July 1969), and they had very much influenced sweeping changes in school organization. But because of evacuation and call-up of teachers during the war, standards in 1948 were particularly low. Statistics based on this year were bound to give a false impression. In *Crisis in the Classroom* (1968), Keith Gardner, a leading British expert on reading, explained how the Plowden figures had obscured what was in reality a disturbing situation, and commented: 'Our costly present system apparently achieves little more, in terms of reading ability, than the years of economic depression . . .' (p.21). I soon realized that in educational disputes there are few reliable authorities, and that political change is often swayed by fashion. Gardner's work was ignored by Sir Alec Clegg and Mr Short. To publicize the truth was justification for the subsequent Black Papers, which included careful analysis of Professor Pedley's statistics.

We gathered together contributors for the second Black Paper in our usual way, asking previous contributors for suggestions, and sending invitations to teachers who had written letters of support. In the third week of April we received the following letter from a London head who was unknown to us. His name was Dr Rhodes Boyson, and it proved to be a significant moment in Black Paper history:

Dear Sirs,
When I called on Dr W.H. Chaloner last week at Manchester University I mentioned that I should like to see Professor Cox but he was unfortunately out at the time. I read *Fight for Education* which you edited and also noted from the press that you intend to bring out a further issue which will chiefly be concerned with comprehensive schools.

As a head of a comprehensive school (and ex-head of a secondary modern and a grammar school) and as a person who writes regularly and with considerable concern opposing fashionable tendencies in education, I obviously view your next project with both interest and concern. I am worried about standards in comprehensive schools as I made clear in my chapter, Defence of Tradition, in *Crisis in the Classroom* published last autumn but I do hope that there is a scrupulously fair analysis in your next publication.

I thought the article by R.R. Pedley was unfair to Wandsworth – the intake there among the academic band is nothing like Chislehurst and Sidcup, and to compare the achievements of the two schools without realising this suggests the same lack of critical faculties which other writers in your publication so rightly deplore. Direct Grant school heads writing on junior schools are not going to impress the teaching profession, and

this plays into the hands of someone like the Rt. Hon. Edward
Short who can then condemn all the articles as reactionary.
Then the real problems and failures of many comprehensive
schools can be conveniently forgotten by their advocates!

An issue on comprehensives is undoubtedly required but it
will certainly need care. I fear a blanket condemnation of all such
schools by many writers which instead of helping to pin-point the
failures will simply rally support for them in this age which seems
to see all issues as progressive or reactionary as the present press
reaction to your publication and yourselves has already shown.

I should welcome a discussion with one of you on this problem
of an issue on comprehensive schools. I often visit Manchester
since I shall fight for the Parliamentary seat of Eccles at the
next general election and I have to visit Norwich on May 24.
Alternatively I should gladly meet one of you in London.

> With kindest regards,
> Yours sincerely,
> Dr Rhodes Boyson

Soon afterwards I met Dr Boyson in Manchester (where he had
taken his doctorate) and he agreed to contribute to Black Paper
Two. It has been suggested that Dr Boyson hijacked the campaign,
and that his influence led to a hardening of attitudes, a change of
emphasis from the liberal to the authoritarian. I believe this is
an exaggeration. Dr Boyson's ideas about education have always
been more complex than the usual caricatures allow. He proved
a tough debater, with ebullient energy. He knew intimately the
conditions of schools in London, and was never frightened by
the insults which commonly greeted Black Paper authors when
they appeared in public. Dr Boyson's influence became dominant
after 1970, and without him the campaign would have probably
lost impetus in the early 1970s. His great success was in changing
attitudes in the Conservative party; during the 1970s he spoke at
grass-roots meetings all round the country. The new realism in
education of the 1980s was to some extent his achievement, and
even his opponents were forced to shift their ground.

Over the years Rhodes has been turned into an ogre by left-wing writers. I found him honest and passionate in his defence of high standards of education for working-class children. His high spirits were irrepressible; his first meeting with Florette, his second wife, is typical. Florette had applied for a teaching position at the school where he was head. After she entered the school she asked a male teacher in the corridor for directions to the head's room. When she faced Rhodes for her interview, she found that he had been the man in the corridor. He had dashed round a back way so he could surprise her. During Black Paper campaigns I often stayed the night at their house in Pinner, and they were always hospitable and generous. When we worked together Rhodes was tough in support of his opinions, but willing to make compromises when I disagreed. In 1992 he came out strongly in favour of the Workers' Education Association. As usual, the media turned a human being into a caricature.

While all the preparations for the new pamphlet were continuing I was teaching at Manchester University, organizing our sixth-form and teacher conferences, and editing *Critical Quarterly*. Attempts to persuade a commercial publisher to take over a new Black Paper (we tried Penguin, Faber, and Oxford University Press) failed because the publishers feared adverse reaction from teachers. We had to handle all the administration ourselves. That summer Tony took up an invitation to teach a summer school at Sir George Williams University, Montreal, and he was away for six weeks in July and August. I managed to deliver all the material to Hull Printers by the end of July, and then departed with my wife and family for a much-needed camping holiday in France.

The second Black Paper was published in October, with a press conference at the Waldorf Hotel. On this occasion there were about 100 journalists present, with radio and television interviews taking place immediately afterwards. The *Daily Telegraph* printed some material in the days before publication, and this provided the *Critical Quarterly* with a useful fee. The new pamphlet was 160 pages, twice the length of the first; we kept the price as low as possible for maximum sales, and charged only ten shillings. *Critical Quarterly* made little profit on the Black Papers because we were not prepared for their success, and as a small private organization we could not exploit their potential. We reckon we sold 50,000 copies of *Black Paper Two*, but in the turmoil after publication our records were not kept precisely. I have a letter of 14 October which records an order for 2,000 copies from Dillon's of London.

On 15 April, Richard Hoggart, then a professor at Birmingham, wrote to me to resign as a *Critical Quarterly* adviser. He is the most generous of men, and his letter stressed his continuing friendship. He felt, though, that as a Labour supporter he would be placed in a false position if his name remained on our masthead: 'It's just as well not to let one's *public* alignments get too confused'. A postscript said: 'I dictated this *before* the Sec. of State blew his top so excessively'. All the publicity after Short's speech placed great pressure on Tony and me. I used to wake up at six in the morning with a lurch in my stomach as I wondered what further abuse would be heaped upon us in the morning's newspapers. I found the break-up of my relationship with Richard Hoggart as an editor particularly distressing.

# 9
# *Black Paper Two*

You keep both Rule and Energy in view,
Much power in each, most in the balanced two.
'To Yvor Winters, 1955', Thom Gunn

The second Black Paper provoked as much publicity as the first. We chose to repeat the form we had devised for the first pamphlet, with short polemical articles balanced by longer essays in a more academic style. Once again we included quotations from newspapers ('Signs of the times'), and added a collection of letters from teachers and parents. The pamphlet ended with a survey of responses to *Black Paper One* written by Kingsley Amis and Robert Conquest, and called: 'The Anti-Sex, Croquet-Playing, Statistic-Snubbing, Boyle-Baiting, Black Fascist Paper'.

The same cover design was repeated, only this time the Lowry-like figures were in red, splashed over by black dots as before. At the last minute we rejected a different design, feeling it was too provocative. This consisted of a collage in red of words which students in higher education had mis-spelt on examination papers marked by Black Paper authors during the previous couple of years. These words included: speach, buisness, bycical, happend, suseptable, compatition, cearial, villen, priviledge, delaid, weakning, utterley, waisting, dispises, souly etc.

Since April I had read Jacques Barzun's *The House of Intellect* (1959), and discovered that central Black Paper ideas were reflected in Barzun's witty and humane advocacy of traditional education. We started our pamphlet with a long quotation from *The House of Intellect*:

181

In our century, the worshippers of innocence have similarly laid on the future the task of repairing all their mistakes. But forgetting that innocence petted and prolonged can only make dupes and cynics, they have produced conditions in which strength other than physical cannot grow. The notion that 'free growth' and 'integrity' in the young require the absence of formal manners – no thanks and no subordination, no regard for time or fitness, no patience with difficulty or distaste, no feelings or reverence or pride, and in many 'excellent' households, no respect for objects and no constraint of cleanliness – that anarchical notion seems curious only till we see it as a first step in liberation from power and its attendant responsibility. Those who are reared in this permissive atmosphere seem embarrassed by, almost afraid of, human respect.

Other quotations from *The House of Intellect* were interwoven with the text:

(speaking of a 'free discussion') . . . no preparation is made – no readings, no definitions or summaries given out in class, nothing but a 'free' discussion by the group to ascertain what a scientist is. The right answer is supposed to come out of pooled ignorance.

Our current discussion of education in America is thus of peculiar interest, because we, dissatisfied with our handiwork, are seeking to change just at the time when England, France and Germany are courageously starting to repeat our mistakes.

As one student remarked when rebuked for an illegible scribble, 'well, it's my handwriting, isn't it?'

We obtained permission to reprint these extracts from Barzun's publisher, Secker and Warburg, but I did not write to Barzun direct. Passing through London immediately after the Black Paper was published, he was startled to find that he seemed to be leading an educational revolution. Later we became friends, and he contributed articles to subsequent Black Papers. In 1972 he invited me to read a paper on examinations at the Chicago Conference of the Open Court Publication Company's Advisory

Board. In 1981 he arranged for me to participate in a seminar in Aspen, Colorado, to consider proposals for a new curriculum for American schools (the Padaea project), organized by Mortimer Adler, editor of the *Encylopaedia Britannica*. There were many such pressure groups in the United States and Australia, and I was often to visit and to receive visits and support from their members. The reaction against the permissive teaching methods of the 1960s was an international phenomenon.

Many books about education are written in bureaucratic prose, colourless and rhythmically inert. We were determined that the new Black Paper should not fall into this category. In addition to the pieces from Barzun's *The House of Intellect*, other inflammatory quotations were placed at the end of articles. From W.H. Auden's *City Without Walls* (1969), we took these lines:

> In semi-literate countries
> demagogues pay
> court to teenagers.

A friend at Hull University reported to me that Philip Larkin had written a barbed couplet about student revolt at the London School of Economics and at Essex, where Dr Sloman was Vice-Chancellor:

> When the Russian tanks roll westward, what defence for you
> and me?
> Colonel Sloman's Essex Rifles? The Light Horse of L.S.E.?

I wrote to Philip, and persuaded him to let me print this.

The excerpts from newspapers demonstrate the extraordinary atmosphere of 1969, as progressive ideas were taken to further extremes. The influence of A.S. Neill's *Summerhill* was worldwide. In April 1969 the *Evening Standard* printed the following account of a progressive kindergarten in West Germany:

> The 'anti-authoritarian' kindergarten was set up last year. There are now eleven. They are being financed by the West Berlin parliament as an 'interesting experiment'.

A main idea of the kindergarten is to develop in infants a healthy contempt for authority. Teachers refrain from commands like 'Wipe your nose', 'Leave the room' or 'Be quiet'. Such commands, say the advocates, 'destroy the child's spontaneity and make him into a cowardly and submissive subject of the state'.

Another feature is the 'loving room', where infants of both sexes can, if they wish, explore the first stages of sex. If he wants, little Fritz can escort little Heidi to her home and sleep with her overnight.

Today this wild story reads almost like a spoof, but there is no doubt that *Summerhill* ideas were being put into practice in this incredible manner. More restrained descriptions of what was happening are typified in the following letter we published from a parent:

We have had personal experience of the introduction of vertical streaming into the local infant school. For four terms, our son had been taught along with children of his own age. He was very happy at school and seemed to be making excellent progress. Then, vertical streaming was introduced, and all formal group teaching came to an end. Every day, his class of about forty-five children, ages ranging from four plus to seven plus, was encouraged to use the mass of equipment available. Theoretically, each child circulated from one activity to another and learnt from his own experience. In practice, our own child seemed to be learning nothing at all, was baffled by the whole thing and began to get completely bored with school. He spent hours doing French knitting. I suspect that his teacher would have been appalled to know exactly how much of his time had been spent in this way, but with forty-four other children to contend with, how could she be expected to know?

Even the daily story became a rare event, because the story which would suit the younger children merely bored the older ones. Written maths was completely abolished and the children were very rarely heard to read.

We went twice to see the headmistress. She assured us that there was not in fact as much difference in ability between the five-year-old and the seven-year-old as we imagined. We find this quite impossible to believe.

After two and a half terms of this, we could stand it no longer and decided to send our son, now aged seven, to a different school. Here, he is in the top class of infants, and, once again, is full of enthusiasm for all the new and exciting things he is learning about.

This letter from a parent was typical of large numbers which were sent to me at Manchester and to Tony at our Radcliffe Avenue office. What was happening, I would now agree, is that progressive ideas were being applied indiscriminately and in ignorance by teachers ill-equipped to understand the problems of vertical streaming. That the difficulties often stemmed from bad training in colleges of education was illustrated by numerous letters we received from teachers:

1. I trained from 1950–52, and even at that time the wind of change was beginning to blow through our colleges. The 'in phrase' at that time was 'free expression' and any attempt at formal teaching was strictly taboo. I well remember how appalled my infant Tutor was when I asked her how one set about teaching reading. Briefly, her reply was that one must never 'teach' reading. If one's classroom was sufficiently interesting, reading would 'emerge'.
2. I did a two-year teacher training course at the age of thirty-eight. Since leaving college I've spent five years in juniors. . . . The first question I was asked at an interview for a junior post on leaving college was 'What do you know about teaching reading to children?' In my innocence, I answered 'nothing'. We had had exactly three quarters of an hour on reading methods in the two years I spent at college.

Newspapers in the late 1960s were full of letters and features about low standards; no doubt there was exaggeration, but the evidence from the letters is that teachers were inadequately trained. Other letters and news items drew attention to the problems of comprehensives on split sites, and to the continuation of student rebellion: 'Obscene chantings were also spreading. At the L.S.E. students have stood face to face with lecturers chanting obscenities.' (*The Times*, May 1969).

As with our first Black Paper we started with a letter to MPs. This was a much better researched document than the first one, with various kinds of evidence of low standards in reading and arithmetic. I have always disliked arguments about whether standards are going up or down, for the facts are so difficult to evaluate. The main thing to say is that standards are always too low, and that those of us who work in education must endeavour to improve them. We were forced to engage in this argument because our opponents insisted research had shown that progressive teaching and a system of comprehensive schools inevitably raised standards. We quoted Professor Peters in *Perspectives on Plowden* (1969), who declared that many strong claims had been made for learning by discovery, but almost none of these had been empirically substantiated or even clearly tested in an experiment (p.12). We referred to a number of writers – Cyril Burt, S.H. Froome, Joyce Morris, Betty Root, Nancy W. Green, Maya Pines, William Van Der Eyken – who in various ways cast doubt on the success of discovery methods. My aim in assembling this material was to show that newspaper assumptions were untrue. I have since been accused of giving only one side of the argument. At that time I felt that I must bring together material which would blow away fashionable assumptions. This was polemic, not a PhD.

Teaching, we said, should combine the best of formal and informal methods. We praised Jerome S. Bruner, who in 'The Growth of the Mind' (*American Psychologist*, December 1965) explained the difference between the learning processes among juvenile baboons, primitive tribes and a civilized society. In the complex society 'there is knowledge and skill in the culture far in excess of what any one individual knows. And so, increasingly, there develops an economical technique of instructing the young based heavily on *telling* out of context rather than *showing* in context.'

We used this article to rebut the simplicities of the Plowden Report, which argued that 'finding out' had proved to be better for children than 'being told'. We did not reject discovery methods, but said that the Plowden doctrines were ossifying into dogma, often applied unthinkingly in schools. *Telling,* we said, may take various forms. It may consist of letting children find out for themselves in a carefully structured environment. It may involve straightforward explanation, of a mathematical process for example, by a teacher standing in front of a class. Good teaching demands a flexible use of all methods of *telling,* of teacher intervention. I repeated this idea of balance in many letters and articles and radio interviews. It was not, however, until the publication of my Report for the National Curriculum in English for primary schools in 1988 that I succeeded in persuading the profession that these were indeed my views.

In this introductory letter we once again drew attention to the problems faced by neighbourhood schools, the problem of establishing sufficiently large sixth forms in comprehensive schools, and the difficulties caused by split sites. We acknowledged that the eleven-plus needed reform, suggesting that thirteen would be a more appropriate age for selection. Selection should be linked to machinery to ensure that late developers would have every chance of transfer. Over the years it has been very annoying for me to read so often that the Black Papers supported the eleven-plus. We also described research which showed that pupils of high quality leave comprehensive schools at an earlier age than those of similar ability in other maintained schools; these findings have been confirmed by surveys in the 1980s.

We endorsed private education as a necessary feature of our liberties, essential in a society where there are so many dangers of coercion and control by central government. As realistically as we could, we explained what would happen if private schools were declared illegal. Would it be forbidden for parents to send their children to a private school in Ireland or Switzerland, for instance, or for them to pay a tutor to give private lessons in their home? One of our correspondents envisaged an England where teachers would be smuggled into the houses of the rich by underground tunnels, and concealed from informers and state spies in teacher-holes.

We ended by quoting an article in *New Society* which said that the Black Paper had broken the consensus on education. In reply to Mr Short's egalitarianism, we reaffirmed the central doctrine of our first pamphlet: you can have equality or equality of opportunity; you can't have both.

*Black Paper Two* began with long articles by Cyril Burt, Richard Lynn and H.J. Eysenck dealing with fundamental education issues, especially the case for selection. We continued with a section called 'Comprehensive Disaster', with articles from Tibor Szamuely, Rhodes Boyson and Ralph Harris, General Director of the Institute of Economic Affairs. The next section, 'Primary School: Moving Progressively Backwards', featured a major article, probably the most influential in this Black Paper, by G.H. Bantock on 'Discovery Methods'. This was accompanied by articles from several teachers. The final section, 'Universities: The House of Intellect', brought together essays by D.C. Watt, John Sparrow, Max Beloff, Michael Swann and Angus Maude. It is significant that so many famous people were willing to support the Black Paper campaign.

Professor Cyril Burt (Emeritus Professor of Psychology, London) contributed an essay called 'The Mental Differences between Children'. This was written with that lucidity and force of rhetoric which characterized all his letters to me. In my next chapter I deal with the attempts to destroy his reputation (see pp. 203–205). He summarized the history of the belief that all children are born with the same intelligence, and declared that such beliefs were reactionary: 'They are advocated – as they always have been – not on the basis of experimental trial or factual evidence, but as deductions from certain ideological theories.' He dealt briefly with the history of thought from Helvetius to Rousseau, from Pestalozzi to Froebel and Piaget: 'All these earlier pioneers would have heartily endorsed the aphorisms of the present-day "progressives" – "The teacher should never say 'No'". "Each child should choose his own subject and his own mode of approach", – and the popular slogans of "free discipline", "learning by discovery", and "mixing together all social classes in a common school".'

To combat this ideology Burt described the scientific evidence for intellectual differences between individuals, beginning with the attempts of Francis Galton in the Victorian period to measure mental abilities. In the disputes about the influence of heredity versus environment, nature versus nurture, the evidence from both neurological findings as well as from the studies of identical twins in orphanages is that there is a strong co-relation – certainly over fifty per cent – between the abilities of a child and its genetic stock. The inheritance of mental abilities depends on Mendelian principles (we inherit characteristics from our family stock, not just our mother and father), and this explains why sometimes bright parents may have less intelligent children and ordinary innkeepers or blacksmiths or cobblers have produced a Kepler, Faraday or Marlowe. All research continually shows that like begets like.

In an article in 1988 in *The Times* (29 October), 'Obscuring the braingap', Peter Brimelow, senior editor of *Forbes Magazine*, described how most experts today believe that intelligence is a useful concept, that it can be tested in a reasonably scientific way, and that to some degree it is hereditary. Because of the claims that Burt was a fake, many ordinary educated people think that the idea of the heritability of IQ has been discredited. 'But Burt's results, if they were fakes, have been independently replicated.' (Brimelow was reviewing *The I.Q. Controversy, the Media and Public Policy*, by Mark Snydeman and Stanley Rothman.) The attacks on Burt have made scientists afraid to publicize their research, but Burt's views on heritability are generally accepted.

For Burt the development of IQ tests was a means of achieving social justice, as he made clear in his Black Paper article. Hundreds of children from poverty-stricken or illiterate homes were rescued from this background because IQ tests discovered their innate ability, enabling them to be selected for grammar schools. Burt acknowledged that the eleven-plus examination was about ten per cent inaccurate, and urged that testing of innate intelligence should take place at regular intervals during the primary school stages.

The violent reaction to the Black Papers was partly because they mentioned the unmentionable, and deeply offended central tenets of progressive ideology. This was certainly true of the second article in *Black Paper Two*, Richard Lynn's 'Comprehensives and Equality'.

Lynn (Research Professor of Psychology, Dublin) wrote in a belligerent style which expressed the anger felt by many of our supporters at what they saw as an unnecessary and foolish undermining of academic standards. Lynn described the weaknesses of the American comprehensive system, where graduates of high quality were less likely than in Britain to choose teaching as a profession: 'In 1966 only four per cent of Harvard graduates entered school teaching (in the private schools?) as against fourteen per cent from Cambridge in England.' According to Lynn, the grammar and independent schools provided an attractive career to high-quality graduates which would not exist to the same extent in comprehensives.

Like Burt, Lynn stressed that children are born with different innate abilities, and that the organization of schools must reflect this: 'false premises lead to false remedies and ultimately to disappointment'. He forecast a new barbarism if quality was not preserved in education.

Lynn also broke taboos. He stated boldly that the culture of the intelligent, which involves the pleasure of reading Milton and George Eliot, of listening to Bach or Mozart, will never be the culture of the majority. This culture should be available to all who can enjoy its gifts, but a system of mixed ability teaching and slack discipline would reduce the numbers who enjoyed the traditional culture.

Lynn described the voucher system, which would promote, he believed, parental choice. Ralph Harris, whose influence on Mrs Thatcher brought him a peerage in 1979, also referred to the voucher plans in his article in *Black Paper Two*. Thus began a debate about parental rights, which continued until the Education Reform Act of 1988 introduced the possibility that schools could opt out from local authority control.

In the third article, 'The Rise of the Mediocracy', H.J. Eysenck (Professor of Psychology, London) put forward a general principle: every adult citizen has the right to have been educated to the limit of his or her natural abilities. Unfortunately this desideratum conflicts with the social need to train a proper supply of teachers, doctors, engineers, lawyers etc, and with the lack of sufficient funds to allow all people to undertake expensive university courses. The result is inevitably selection, the attempt, as justly as possible, to provide opportunities for those most suited to profit.

Eysenck repeated Burt's claim that IQ tests helped able working-class children to be given special teaching, and that this was a recipe for social justice. Like Burt, Eysenck repeated the claims of researchers such as Jensen and others that the heredity factors in IQ tend to be about seventy-five per cent. When in Northumberland IQ tests were first introduced there was an immediate and spectacular rise in the number of children from rural backgrounds, where schools were often inadequate, who passed the entrance examination for grammar school. Eysenck thought that the Labour Party ought to welcome IQ tests and selection as the best means of promoting academic success for working-class children, but left-wing people had a deep emotional fear of élitism. They found repugnant the truth that some children are innately cleverer than others, framing their policies not on this truth but on their ideological commitments. Both Burt and Eysenck made scrupulous reference to the fallibility of testing, but argued that it was the best means of achieving social justice. Eysenck ended by arguing for more money to improve the quality of tests. Without tests, he said, we shall witness the rise of mediocrity.

Tibor Szamuely (lecturer in politics, Reading University) began the section on comprehensive schools with an essay based on his own personal experiences. He attended school and university in Moscow; for nearly ten years he was a lecturer and then professor at Budapest University (including one year as Vice-Rector). His wife worked as a teacher in a Moscow secondary school and as a lecturer at Budapest University. Their children attended Hungarian schools for eight years. 'So,' he wrote, 'I know what I am talking about when I say that comprehensive education in this country will *inevitably lead to far greater social inequality than exists at present.*'

Szamuely quoted numerous articles published in Russia and Hungary which showed that able working-class children in these communist countries stood much less chance of entry into higher education than the middle and professional classes. The reason was that comprehensives become neighbourhood schools. Szamuely also drew attention to the way Stalin threw out the child-centred experiments of the 1920s when these were shown to have failed. He returned Russia to a uniform and rigid system of conventional schooling.

Rhodes Boyson's article followed. It is one of his best, and offers a balanced assessment which little accords with his present-day public image. He outlines the essential conditions for the success of a comprehensive school. The article which followed showed how at places such as Cheltenham and Enfield reorganization had been rushed through which did not meet these essential conditions. Boyson described how he had worked as head of a secondary modern school, a streamed comprehensive and a grammar school before he took over the headship of Highbury Grove, a purpose-built comprehensive boys' school in Inner London. He imposed a disciplined and regulated framework where the Arts and sporting activities flourished, but where boys, staff and parents knew that standards of achievement and percentage pass rates mattered. Learning needs discipline, he said, not the atmosphere of a Butlin's Holiday Camp, a remark he was to repeat on numerous future occasions. His school included children in all ability bands; he placed great emphasis on academic success, but also on the civilized values of tolerant concern for individuals, helping boys to feel that they mattered, even if they were in the lower bands, and that they belonged to the school. He listed five essential conditions if a comprehensive was to succeed:

1.  The new school must be based on a well-respected existing school.
2.  Special buildings must be erected on one site.
3.  There must be a balanced ability intake.
4.  There must be at least 1,400 pupils.
5.  There must be good staffing both in qualifications and with senior teachers of sufficient stature both to take decisions and to delegate responsibility.

Even after *Black Paper Two* the Press continued to say that we were opposed to all forms of comprehensive school. Boyson's article proves this was not true. If his prescriptions had been obeyed the comprehensive school ideal would not have fallen so quickly into disrepute. He wrote: 'Pressure for the creation of a comprehensive system to satisfy political beliefs is producing a hotch-potch and completely confused secondary educational system in this country.' A boys' comprehensive such as Highbury Grove must possess a sixth form large enough 'to carry some forty-five to fifty boys in each of the lower and upper sixth on two and three "A" level courses'. This, as a recent I.L.E.A. Report had shown, was the minimum number of boys required if ten to twelve 'A' level subjects were to be offered and taught in economic teaching groups. This could only be achieved in schools with an entry of 360 boys each year if one accepted the present current figure that an eighth of an age group can take two or more 'A' levels; this meant a school of 2,000. Boyson insisted that only a large comprehensive school could support a truly viable sixth form. Later, in the 1970s, as heads found so many difficulties in the organization of large comprehensives, Rhodes Boyson came to think that there was a design fault in the system. He then believed that a comprehensive was likely to fail either because it was too large and impersonal or because its sixth-form provision was too small. In January 1967 the average size of a comprehensive was 800 pupils, with an average total sixth form number of only fifty-eight students. I quote all these details to show how Black Paper articles tried to tackle realistically the problems of school reorganization, while our opponents largely ignored serious discussions of these issues.

The next group of articles described how comprehensives had been formed too quickly on split sites, and often with vast wastage of existing resources such as laboratories. A comprehensive school teacher described the pressure on staff on a split site as they rushed from class-room to class-room, often moving from a remedial reading group to an 'A' level class. In large schools, where the children often could not recognize the head, they became bewildered by the crowds, with none of the community spirit of the smaller schools. Fatigue among the staff was giving way to depression and anger. This forecast what was to happen all over the country during the next decades. After a brief period of time, some local authorities realized their mistakes, and reorganized again, with further upheavals for the staff. Manchester, for example, was soon forced to abandon most of its eleven to eighteen comprehensives, and replace them with eleven to sixteen schools, topped up with sixth-form colleges.

Also in this section on secondary education we printed an essay by Professor Arthur Pollard (Hull University) who had long experience as Chief Examiner in English for the Joint

Matriculation Board in Manchester. He showed that there was no statistical evidence that a fully comprehensive system would raise the standards already achieved by the secondary modern/grammar school arrangements. He pointed out that examining boards passed the same percentage of candidates each year, regardless of the numbers who entered (Grade A – ten per cent, B – fifteen per cent, C – ten per cent, D – fifteen per cent, E – twenty per cent). This meant that the argument that the increased number of passes showed that standards were rising was untrue. It simply meant that the number of candidates being entered was rising. As more girls stayed on at school, the pass rate, including the high grades, must inevitably rise. This had nothing to do with school organization. Misuse of statistics continued through the 1970s. Another common form of deception is for a school to announce that 100 per cent have passed in some 'A' level subject. This may mean that only two or three were entered, in contrast to a school with a similar socio-economic background where thirty were entered but only twenty passed. Today, whenever I read in a newspaper that standards have improved or declined, I tend to presume the statistics are meaningless.

After the secondary school material came Professor Geoffrey Bantock's crucially important article on progressive education and discovery methods. It has been reprinted and quoted on many occasions, and undoubtedly had a great influence on professional opinion in the schools. By the late 1970s I was often told that the excesses of unstructured learning had disappeared, and the importance of Bantock's article was cited as of major importance in persuading teachers to change their minds.

Bantock began by describing a BBC television programme designed to show off modern methods. A class of children were seen at work by the side of the Thames, under the direction of a teacher. Some were discovering evidence of tidal behaviour, while others were examining examples of the local flora and fauna. One child, for example, had captured a number of leeches in a large test tube. Others, after digging in the mud beside the river, had found a piece of an old pipe and part of the jawbone of a horse. A small group was measuring the height of a bridge with a piece of weighted string. The film then moved to the class-room, where the findings were being discussed with the teacher. The piece of old pipe was of historical interest, for example, while the horse's jawbone would help the children to learn about anatomy.

Welcoming the children's enjoyment of such trips, the arousal of their interest and the importance of concrete experience as a basis for learning, Bantock had serious reservations. He thought some parts of the lesson were inappropriate. The leeches form part and parcel of the natural life of the riverside, and though the river as a phenomenon together with its attendant plant and biological life does not constitute a conventional school 'subject' in itself – it involves geographical, botanical and biological studies, among others – 'it is sufficient of an entity as an identifiable element in the environment to make it, in all its heterogeneity, a reasonable object of study, especially for young children'. But the jawbone and the old pipe are not part of the natural environment of the river. They are there by accident, and could easily have been found on a piece of waste ground. They have no *structural* relationship to the river; 'now the danger of this sort of treatment is that it fosters what might be termed a magpie curriculum'. Anything constitutes an experience, and the children pursue any hare that attracts their temporary interest. There is no order to their work, and much of it will soon be forgotten.

This emphasis on structure is at the heart of Bantock's evaluation of discovery methods. He declared that the so-called new methods do not constitute anything very new in the history of teaching. Socrates employs a recognizable form of such methods in the *Meno*, and much recent pedagogy looks back to Rousseau's *Emile*.

In societies in which technical and scientific understanding is little advanced, most teaching involves only the passing of traditional wisdom, of sacred texts or useful skills, mainly by rote learning: 'The aim, in brief, is the transmission and the perpetuation of the culture.' With the coming of technical and scientific development, the basis of the new learning is sense experience and induction from it. The certainty of the old knowledge is destroyed. Rousseau himself was profoundly affected by the growing prestige of science, and so applied the methods of scientific observation of nature to his ideas of child development. Like the scientist who studies nature at first hand, the child must not be given received wisdom but allowed spontaneously to develop his or her own forms of thinking from his or her own concrete experiences. This thinking lies behind the doctrine that children should not read until they are ready and want to read. Both Rousseau and the progressive teacher of the 1960s were confused in their presentation of these ideas; sometimes they say the child should be left undisturbed, and sometimes they stress the need for the teacher to prepare the child's surroundings so that he or she discovers the right things in the right sequence. So a doctrine of liberty for the child moves rapidly to a doctrine that the teacher should interfere in an authoritarian manner.

Like many progressives, Rousseau seems unsympathetic towards verbal instruction. Rousseau says: 'Give your scholar no verbal lessons; he should be taught by experience alone.' Bantock explains that Rousseau was reacting against meaningless rote learning, and against Renaissance humanist learning which was so exclusively verbal it was often beyond the capacity of a child to grasp.

Bantock strongly criticizes this fear of verbal instruction. Rousseau 'seems to think that words always have something to which they refer, and that unless the thing to which the word refers has been "experienced", they simply constitute meaningless noises to the children'. Bantock explains why this is not true. Children can derive considerable joy out of uses of words, which, in Rousseau's sense, they cannot be said to understand. An extreme example is 'nonsense' words; poetic statements also often do not invite complete 'understanding'. A child can appreciate a great deal of Shakespeare without understanding many central meanings.

Above all, the mind needs to bring to the experience a set of relevant concepts in terms of which the experience can be given some meaning: 'Consciousness that an experience is being undergone only arises if the child has at his disposal a set of mental tools which enables him to order the bewildering mess of impressions in the external world in some meaningful way.' Children from primitive tribes who have never seen a moving film are unable to see anything significant on the screen because they have not learnt to distinguish two-dimensional moving figures and objects into discrete meaningful shapes having some relevance to the real world.

This brings Bantock to the heart of the problem, the way children develop the mental structure of relevant concepts they apply to the environment. The problem is to determine how and when structure should be introduced into children's learning situations. Informality must at some stage be replaced by formality, and structured learning must replace the haphazard magpie curriculum. Such structures must be imposed by the teacher if the child is to develop as a learner: 'Really to enjoy some aspect of the environment necessitates learning to recognise certain features – the architecture of cities and towns, insect life in field and hedgerow, to take two random examples – and really to pursue some such study in depth, so that experiences within the chosen field become genuinely meaningful.' Bad academic teaching can be dull and useless, but, in fact:

> academic subjects, so called, have evolved as they have simply because they have proved to be the most economical and lucid ways of handling the undifferentiated mass of phenomena we experience in the natural and social worlds around us or in the internal life of our feelings and emotions.

Rousseau's injunction: 'Let him not be taught science; let him discover it' is absurd. It throws away our cultural heritage, what indeed makes us human: our ability to build on the findings of others, to package information in assimilable form and to determine rationally efficient means for accepted ends.

Children indeed learn a great deal from the concrete, from direct sensory experience, but Bantock insists, and in the Black Paper we put his words in italics: '*It must indeed be said quite categorically that the superiority of discovery methods cannot at present be justified on grounds of empirical research.*' Discovery methods need to be collated with carefully presented and meaningful but quite formal instruction. '*There is, in fact, no one way.*' A good teacher must use both formal and informal methods of instruction.

This balanced approach was reflected in the accompanying essays by primary school head teachers. Mrs D.M. Pinn, head of Henrietta Barnett Junior School, had previously worked as a college of education lecturer in primary education. She explained that in the late 1960s teachers were chosen for headships or positions of responsibility when they advocated the 'freeing' of the school. Naturally, when promotion depended on being progressive, teachers moved in that direction, even against their own previous successful class-room practice. Much of the problem derived from college of education lecturers who had no primary school teaching experience, and who often had not taught in any class-room for a considerable number of years. Mrs Pinn proposed that all college lecturers should remain in post for no more than five years, and then return to the class-room for at least a year.

In his article on modern maths S.H. Froome (Head, St Jude's School, Englefield Green) drew attention to the danger of introducing new ideas which could not be put into practice by the average teacher. The new modern maths could only be taught by experienced, competent and dedicated teachers 'who not only have the genius to supervise forty little individuals each working at a different speed but also have the mathematical expertise as well to guide the children fully to comprehend the graded concepts which are continually encountered'. Most old-fashioned teachers found the daily task of setting and marking sums easy to perform, and even the less charismatic could instil some skills in their pupils.

The section on universities attracted almost no attention. This was sad because it included some splendid defences of academic freedom. These were not in tune with the illiberal caricature of the Black Papers spread abroad by Mr Short and his followers, so those who preferred to see issues in simple confrontational terms ignored these essays. Max Beloff (at that time Gladstone Professor of Government and Public Administration, Oxford, later first Principal of the Independent University College at Buckingham) wrote about the declining freedom of Oxford to manage its own affairs, and the danger of government interference. The inevitable reliance on government subsidies for research in the natural sciences had led to new pressure away from the humanities, away, for example, from compulsory language requirements. Lord Beloff repeated his pleas for intellectual independence in 1988, when he played a major role in persuading the Government to modify its Education Reform Bill and to add clauses preserving academic freedom. In 1992 in the House of Lords he once again successfully opposed government attempts to assume power over the content of university courses.

The article I quoted most in my subsequent speeches was that by Michael Swann (then Principal and Vice-Chancellor at Edinburgh University). He drew careful distinctions between student representation on the non-academic side and student consultation on the academic side. Like Amis in the first Black Paper, he pointed out – a blinding flash of the obvious – that only those who are expert in a subject can determine the syllabus. We should allow students power in their daily and social affairs, and we should consult them on academic matters such as teaching standards, but there are 'no reasons for including students on Senate that do not apply with equal force to Government'. He wanted a university senate totally free from direct outside pressures, a senate which would operate as 'the protector of academic autonomy and freedom of thought'.

Michael Swann finished with a peroration with which I often ended my own public speeches. It makes an appropriate conclusion to this chapter. He had been talking about the great problems of the world – the misuse of science, the growth of impersonal management of our lives by government:

> The young are right to be deeply concerned; but they are wrong to imagine that there is some short cut to a golden future. We have, in the Universities, a compelling responsibility to bring home to our students the most painful lesson mankind has learnt throughout civilization, that there is no short cut.
>
> It is only scientists, doctors, vets and agriculturalists who have been trained with the full force of their very demanding disciplines, who can relieve suffering and help to end starvation. It is only men and women who have had the toughest education in the disciplines that impinge on man and society, in the Arts, the Social Sciences, in Law, and in Divinity – who can gain the knowledge and acquire the insight to make a fresh contribution to the appalling problems that beset us all over the world.
>
> The best *we* can do therefore is to give our students the fullest, most rigorous education that lies in our power. The best *they* can do for the generations to come, is to learn all they possibly can

from us. As educators we must help them to stand at the level of our own eyes, in the hope that they will then see further than we can, and do better than we have done. But we help no one if we allow them to imagine for one moment that there is some quick way of doing better than all the great minds of the past. There is not.

# 10
# *Pressure Group Activities*

Living at the full stretch of their perfectionist fancy,
modern men of ideas loathe the world they know.

*The House of Intellect*, Jacques Barzun

The responses to *Black Paper Two* were particularly nasty, though
at the crowded Press conference at the Waldorf Hotel on Tuesday
7 October, I thought all was going very well. Most contributors
attended, including G.H. Bantock, Rhodes Boyson, Ralph Harris,
Angus Maude, Arthur Pollard and Tibor Szamuely. Afterwards
Bob Conquest, Kingsley Amis, Tony and I adjourned for a
celebratory lunch. I dominated this Press conference, chairing
the meeting, answering questions and expressing forcibly our
central arguments about progressive education, comprehensive
schools and student revolt. Before our lunch, I gave radio and
television interviews during which I felt I had been allowed to
represent our case fairly.

The next day's newspapers were a great shock to me, from which
I have never fully recovered. I had not realized that the Press were
not especially interested in a clear summary of our arguments, but
only wanted a story. In our introductory letter to MPs, Tony and
I had said that as experienced external examiners at colleges of
education we found that the best students were excellent, but that
a disturbing percentage at the bottom were semi-literate: 'It is rare
for a student to fail because of semi-literacy.' During the Press
conference a middle-aged man in a dark suit (I never discovered
his identity) asked me if this meant that as an external examiner
I had passed students who should have failed. Undoubtedly he

201

asked this question with the deliberate intention of providing the journalists with the story they needed. Robert Conquest and others assured me afterwards that my answer was clear and unequivocal, and that no other Black Paper contributor realized the danger implicit in the question. I replied that it is the duty of the external examiner to impose national standards, for it is grossly unfair if he or she suddenly fails an extra twenty per cent or so of students, while other nearby colleges are maintaining the conventional pass-rate. I was only responsible for English. On several occasions I had failed a student in English only to discover later that high marks in Education had balanced out my mark to produce an overall pass. I had fought at discussions of borderline cases for an increase in the failure rate, and in my examiner's reports had urged that national standards should be raised.

The next day most newspapers made this headline news. I was accused, particularly in the *Guardian*, of 'hypocrisy' for passing students who should have failed. The *Daily Telegraph* headline for 8 October read: 'Professor Passed Students Who Had Failed'. This accusation was repeated for weeks afterwards, and used deliberately to turn attention away from our substantial arguments on educational issues. I became even more determined to win this great educational battle, but felt exhausted by the emotional problems created for me by this personal abuse. Whereas after *Black Paper One* I read every newspaper, and sent letters in all directions to correct errors and to answer false arguments, I now concentrated on major inaccuracies in the quality Press, and stopped looking at the tabloids.

I wish I were more thick-skinned (as Rhodes Boyson proved to be), but anyone who has been pilloried by the Press for weeks and months will know that the strain can become almost unbearable. Repeated telephone calls from journalists, apparently friendly and comforting, demand careful answers if one is not to be misinterpreted once again. These calls often come at inopportune moments, when one is offguard; once Simon Hoggart rang me after midnight when I was fast asleep after he had read a story about me in the late night edition of the *Daily Telegraph*. I had to devise a way of life to keep myself sane, and to prevent myself from giving way to violent reactions over the phone which could only be counter-productive. One of Rhodes Boyson's favourite sayings is that if you can't stand the heat you should get out of the kitchen. I was convinced I must fight on, but it was not easy. A year later, in 1970, Professor Harry Rée of York University made similar points about exam standards at colleges of education, and was subjected to similar abuse for passing students who should have failed. This incident helped to heal my wound, for I felt not quite so isolated in my stand on this issue.

While this was happening to me, Professor Cyril Burt was also suffering from a spate of abuse in the newspapers. In the *Sunday Times* (12 October) a full page feature attacked the Black Paper, particularly our statistics. The article referred to Professor Burt's claim in *Black Paper Two* that 'the average attainments in reading, spelling, mechanical and problem arithmetic are now appreciably lower than they were fifty-five years ago'. The *Sunday Times* stated that Professor Burt had written that statistics supporting his claim would be published in a scholarly article in the *Irish Journal of Education*, but 'the editor of that journal says he has neither published nor received any article from Professor Burt which would substantiate his remarkable claim'. The implication that he had made it all up was frequently repeated and accepted by many teachers, as Black Paper contributors discovered when they addressed public meetings. The story was repeated in letters in *The Times Educational Supplement* and the *Observer*.

The report in the *Sunday Times* was untrue, a complete fabrication. Dr Thomas Kellaghan, editor of the *Irish Journal of Education*, immediately (15 October) wrote a letter to the *Sunday Times* saying that Professor Burt's article did exist, and was about to be published. This letter was not printed. Eventually in December the *Sunday Times* published a letter from me giving the truth; the Personal Assistant to the Editor wrote to me: 'Our information about non-publication of Professor Burt's article came from two very reliable sources in the educational world and our correspondent did not think it necessary to check with him directly. He agrees now he should have done so.' When after Christmas the article was published with the statistics, it was well reported in the *T.E.S.* and *The Times*. But the damage had been done. The story had been told everywhere, and the idea that Black

Paper statistics had been made up was repeated for months afterwards.

Other attacks were made on Sir Cyril Burt, and he replied in letters in the *Observer* and in the *T.E.S.* In all my dealings with him I found him co-operative, generous and clear-minded. Although he was eighty-six years old, he wrote his letters to me in a firm long hand, dealing with each point succinctly. The tone of his letters suggested to me a man of good sense, not in the least the con-man and psychopath portrayed in the BBC documentary *The Intelligence Man* in January 1984. His subsequent letters, which I still possess, were similarly considerate, offering suggestions but willing to give way to me if I opted for an alternative course of action. During the crucial first weeks after *Black Paper Two* was published it obviously helped our opponents considerably that the debate centred on whether I was a hypocrite and whether Sir Cyril Burt was senile.

I was not altogether surprised when in 1976, five years after Sir Cyril died, he was once again accused in the newspapers of fraud. His evidence for the influence of heredity enraged those teachers and academics who believed that the environment in which a child is brought up is what primarily determines its intelligence; that if children could be reared in more similar social circumstances the difference in their intelligence levels would be largely ironed out. Such people wanted to believe that Sir Cyril was a fraud, and were willing to accept the flimsiest evidence.

When Professor L.S. Hearnshaw, who at first seemed neutral, came down firmly in his biography of 1979 on the side of Burt's detractors, many of Burt's earlier supporters, including Professor Eysenck, changed their minds. But in 1987 in articles in *Social Policy and Administration* (Spring 1987) and in the *Sunday Telegraph* (2 August) Ronald Fletcher, Emeritus Professor of Sociology at Reading University, showed that much of the evidence directed against Burt was false: 'A great injustice has been done,' he wrote. In 1989 Robert B. Joynson published *The Burt Affair*, in which he exonerated Burt from the charges made against him. Fletcher's own book, *The Cyril Burt Scandal*, was published in 1991. The reviewers almost unanimously agreed that Burt was innocent.

There is no point in my repeating here the detailed arguments of Fletcher and Joynson. I feel they are likely to be right for a number of reasons. When Hearnshaw was preparing his biography I sent him all my Burt correspondence and my evidence about the untruths of 1969, with copies of my letters and the replies from the *Sunday Times*. To my amazement he made no mention of any of this material in his biography. My own belief is that Sir Cyril Burt was a great and honest man, and that as more people study the facts they will agree with Fletcher and Joynson.

During the aftermath of the publication of *Black Paper Two* it was repeatedly asserted that research had proved that comprehensive schools would raise academic standards. The main source for this claim was Professor Robin Pedley's Penguin book, *The Comprehensive School* (revised edition, 1969). I found a young statistician, John Todd, from Balliol College, Oxford, to examine the evidence, and we published his findings in the third Black Paper in November 1970.

Once again I was amazed by the naiveté of the research whose results were being used to validate major political changes in the British educational system. Not only Labour Party politicians such as Mr Short but also Conservatives such as Lord Butler quoted Pedley's statistics during the Black Paper controversies. Professor Pedley's sample for his research covered only sixty-seven of the national total of 745 comprehensive schools in 1968. He based his statistics on a questionnaire sent to those schools, but only seventy-three per cent replied. For so emotionally and politically charged a question as the examination performance of comprehensive schools by a researcher nationally famous as their champion, it would not be surprising if the schools which replied had more favourable results than those which did not. The schools in the sample are unevenly distributed over the country, and excluded all comprehensives in the Inner London Education Authority; forty-one of the schools were in country towns (twenty-two of them in Wales) against only twenty-six in cities, suburbs and industrial conurbations. Having made this selection of comprehensives, Professor Pedley compared their examination results with those of *all* other State grant-maintained schools (i.e. schools other than direct grant and independent schools). In addition, Professor Pedley counted a grade one pass at C.S.E. as being an 'O' level pass from the schools in his sample of comprehensives; this was not done for the maintained school results. It is not surprising that the exam results of his carefully chosen group of comprehensives were slightly higher than those from the whole of the state-maintained sector.

In spite of the obvious inadequacy of this research, it was quoted constantly as conclusive evidence that Black Paper criticisms of a comprehensive system could be brushed aside. In the 1960s the education journalists had formed themselves into what they called the Education Correspondents Group. In April 1969, Tudor David of *Education* was Chairman, and Roy Nash of the *Daily Mail* Deputy Chairman. The Honorary Secretary was Peter Newell of *The Times Educational Supplement*, and the committee members were Nicholas Bagnall (*Sunday Telegraph*), Anne Corbett (*New Society*), Bruce Kemble (*Daily Express*), Brian MacArthur (*The Times*) and Shirley Toulson (the *Teacher*). There were about thirty full members and twenty-eight associate members (the list which I possess contains crossings-out of two or three names so I do not know the exact numbers). Full members included Stuart Maclure and Peter Wilby (he is now with the *Independent on Sunday*).

From my meetings with education correspondents at that time I realized that many were strong advocates for comprehensive schools; that almost all of them took for granted that Pedley's book was authoritative. Their meetings enabled the more able, such as MacArthur, Wilby and Maclure, to impose their convictions on the others. I began to realize that I could only win the education battle if I found some way of ensuring better coverage in the Press, for parents, teachers and politicians took their opinions from what they read in newspapers such as *The Times*, the *Daily Telegraph*, the *Guardian*, the *Sunday Telegraph*, the *Observer* and the *Sunday Times*. The consensus in almost all these papers against Black Paper arguments would be very difficult to break. There existed no authoritative body whose pronouncements on educational research were respected, and this gave the education correspondents their special power.

I determined on various kinds of campaigning. First, I would try to persuade large numbers of people to sign manifestoes which I would publish in the Press, so that everyone would realize that my supporters were not cranks but must be taken seriously. We would also publish further Black Papers, and eventually sponsor a variety of additional pamphlets and books. I had discovered that if education correspondents are sent a short, pithy handout they usually publish it; if I wanted to change the minds of newspaper readers I must organize regular publications so that our opponents did not hog all the space. Next, the hundreds of supporters who were writing letters to us must be organized into some kind of national body, whose regular conferences and activities would be reported in the Press. Finally, together with other supporters, I would appear as often as possible on radio and television, and write regular articles for the newspapers. Rhodes Boyson took a major role in all these activities, and in the mid-1970s became the most popular Conservative Party speaker after Mrs Thatcher, in constant demand from constituencies all over the country.

For the next eighteen years I pursued these policies, year by year, through a series of failures and successes until, in 1988, the Education Reform Act provided an appropriate culmination for my work. It is now often said that the Black Papers plus this continued pressure group activity changed the agenda for the education debate, and converted the Conservative Party to Black Paper philosophy.

At first the campaign created more problems than rewards. With other Black Paper contributors, particularly John Sparrow, Warden of All Souls, Oxford, I prepared a manifesto on 'Freedom in the Academic Community'. I persuaded 154 academic staff from different universities to sign the document (the manifesto is printed in Appendix A at the end of this book). Our intention was to publish this in *The Times*, and we had obtained the editor's agreement. In early November 1970 Sparrow began to doubt the wisdom of this venture, and so publication was delayed. As student militancy had cooled down in the autumn term, would we be accused of rekindling the fires? While we were in this awkward position (I was arguing for immediate publication), members of staff at York University leaked the document to their students and to the education journalists. On Sunday 22 November, this 'secret' document made headline news, even the main front page story in the *Sunday Telegraph*. With Sparrow's agreement, I immediately authorized publication of the manifesto in *The Times* the next day. In the late morning Jean and I had taken the children for a day in the Derbyshire countryside, and so I was not at the end of a telephone when radio and television tried to cover the event for the evening programmes. This was fortunate, for I would have found it difficult to discuss a document which *The Times* had yet to publish. The manifesto was received with fury by the National Union of Students; on the Monday it was published they passed an emergency resolution at their conference at Margate claiming that our call for the discipline of students who took part in sit-ins was 'a threat to campus freedom'.

My plan was to collect more signatures, and to print the document again, possibly with 1,000 signatures from university academic staff, in advertisements in the newspapers. I persuaded well-wishers in other universities to circulate the document to people who might wish to sign. Unfortunately this work was interrupted by the postal strike in January 1971, which prevented me from collecting further signatures. By early January I had gathered just over 700 signatures. In April, when the strike was over, several supporters were dubious about the value of a further confrontation, and so I let the campaign lapse. By this time I was slightly punch drunk after all the personal abuse I had received for organizing the manifesto.

I regret this decision now. It is still true in the 1990s that universities have lost the freedom to invite guests to speak on any controversial topic. In the later 1980s well-known politicians, such as Leon Brittan, were prevented by militant students from addressing meetings. I continue to deplore such interference with freedom of speech. Violent intimidation of speakers by students has permanently damaged the reputation of universities, and this provides one explanation for public doubts about the value of investing large sums of money in higher education.

*Black Paper Three* was published on Friday 27 November 1970. It was a sign of the change in the consensus of opinion that it was treated far more rationally than the previous two, and even achieved enthusiastic reviews in *New Society* and the *Economist*. The education journalists were beginning to take our views seriously, and to recognize that we were winning over thousands of followers.

Since *Black Paper Two* the Conservatives had won an election, and Mrs Thatcher had taken over as Secretary of State for Education. This third pamphlet was subtitled 'Goodbye Mr Short' (intended to recall *Goodbye Mr Chips*, but the joke fell flat). The Black Papers figured quite largely in the debates in the House of Commons which followed the General Election, particularly after Mrs Thatcher's withdrawal of Circular 10/65, which had enforced comprehensive education on local authorities. We lost money on this third pamphlet. We had printed a large number, but the postal strike in January stopped orders for two months, and, of course, when normal postal services were resumed there was no longer any publicity in the newspapers. Also the moderate tone of many reviews, instead of invective and contempt, attracted less interest among prospective buyers.

We repeated the successful mix of articles we had used before, and many contributors – Sir Cyril Burt, Richard Lynn, Arthur Pollard, Rhodes Boyson, G.H. Bantock – appeared again. We had already put forward our main arguments in the first two Black Papers, and by and large this new one repeated what we had said before. I was pleased to publish an article on reading by Jacques Barzun; the loyal support of such a distinguished American scholar for many subsequent years strengthened my resolve. Tony and I had dinner with him at the Hilton in London, and I arranged for him to visit my home in Cheadle Hulme. I knew that my Vice-Chancellor, Sir Mansfield Cooper, was a great admirer of Barzun's writings, so I arranged a dinner at the Midland Hotel in Manchester. This was my idea, but I had not realized the bill would be so enormous. I was very relieved when Sir Mansfield took for granted that he was paying.

Kingsley Amis and Robert Conquest contributed 'A Short Educational Dictionary', a condensed version of which had appeared in the *Daily Telegraph* on the previous day. This included definitions such as the following:

*Academic*: (Pejorative) Used of knowledge difficult to master, irrelevant to contemporary reality and deriving from dead or elderly 'authorities'.
*Continuous assessment*: The method whereby teachers can ensure

that their favourites are accepted for further education without arbitrary or irrelevant tests.

*Democracy*: 1) The system prevailing in North Vietnam, China, Cuba etc. 2) The running of a university on the basis of suitably revolutionary students having a decisive voice in all matters. Participatory democracy implies conducting a state, a university, or any other organisation not by the mass vote of the apathetic and bourgeois majority, but by the conscientious, concerned minority.

*Marcuse*: Expression, mainly Irish, Brooklyn etc., meaning 'attend to what I am about to say'.

*Punctuation*: Arbitrary system of dividing written words (obsolescent).

*Teach*: Impose irrelevant facts and bourgeois indoctrination upon.

The final article, 'Why do the Critics so Furiously Rage Together . . . and Imagine a Vain Thing?', was by Marjorie Bremner, a writer on psychology and politics; this brilliantly analysed the elements of evangelical religious fanaticism among our opponents:

> Those who would use the schools to build a Utopia find other people (who are concerned with providing intellectual education and who disagree with the utopists about school organisation, teaching methods etc.) are not merely misguided. They are, to the former, morally wicked men and women who are trying to block the establishment of a Utopia: sinners, denying to 'the little children' access to Heaven. The dispute becomes moral, religious, separatist, polarised. All 'the Light' is on one side; all the powers of Darkness on the other. And so it is that the passionate denunciations of the Black Papers are couched in a fervent, violent, chiliastic vein. Against such zealotry, rational argument is unavailing. It can only convince the already convinced, the rationally amenable, those open to argument. Many critics of the Black Papers are clearly closed to it.

Bremner provided numerous examples of how for some of our critics 'what was actually *written* in the Black Paper was not only uninteresting, it was dull by comparison with what they could invent'. This split between the actual Black Paper doctrine and the caricature invented by our opponents remained a problem for me for the next eighteen years. To my surprise my work for the National Curriculum finally alerted people to my true beliefs.

Ralph Harris, Director of the Institute of Economic Affairs, had supported the Black Papers strongly. In 1971 Tony Dyson and I discussed with him, Rhodes Boyson, and Norris and Ross McWhirter (famous for their *Guinness Book of Records*) a plan to publish Black Papers on everything: the National Health Service, nationalization, the Trade Unions, the Armed Forces and so on. We enjoyed frenetic conversations, in which we created, like magic, one new idea per minute. At first I was willing to co-operate, but one sudden twist in our discussions persuaded me to resign from the project. When we were considering possible members of a committee, it was suggested that Angus Maude was not sufficiently right-wing. I gasped, and realized I was being inveigled into a project which might well run down public services for the poor and the disadvantaged.

After I withdrew, the Constitutional Book Club and the Churchill Press were started, with most impetus provided by Rhodes Boyson. A number of books were published, the most famous being *Rape of Reason* (1975), a vivid account of the damage done to education by militant students and staff at the Polytechnic of North London, written by Keith Jacka, Caroline Cox and John Marks. During the resulting controversy I drafted but did not send a one-sentence letter to *The Times*: 'Caroline Cox is not my wife'. Many people took it for granted that we must be related. Other books brought out by the Constitutional Book Club dealt with nationalization and the welfare state, and these helped to swing public opinion towards the radical reforms introduced by Mrs Thatcher in 1979.

I am glad I resigned, but it meant that I moved myself away from the centre of power at a crucial moment in the campaign. Like many academics, I prefer to work alone, and to publish my own ideas in my own essays and books. Working with other people involves compromise; it is so easy to soothe one's conscience by withdrawal or resignation. I resigned on one further occasion when I felt I was becoming associated with ultra-right-wing philosophy.

This was in 1980, after I had spent a year studying and teaching in California and Tennessee. On my return in the autumn of 1980, I attended a meeting of the Centre for Policy Studies Education Group, chaired by Caroline Cox (now Lady Cox), and very much dominated by Sir Alfred Sherman. I found his ideas about market forces deeply antipathetic, for such analogies cannot be properly applied to schools, and so I never attended again. Once again I worried about whether withdrawal simply meant leaving real decision-making in the hands of others.

Tony and I thought seriously about involvement in politics, and in 1970 I joined the Conservative Party, convinced that Labour Party policies were gravely damaging British education. Tony arranged a lunch at the Reform Club for Mrs Thatcher to meet several Black Paper contributors, and we sent her our various publications. On 3 August 1970 she wrote to me: 'I also regard myself as a "moderate" but anyone who believes as we do in excellence in education is liable to be called a right-wing extremist.'

In 1976 Leon Brittan acted as liaison officer between the Conservative Party and the academic community. I arranged for him to speak at Manchester University, and he stayed the night at my house. Jean and I were impressed by his intelligence and eloquence, and we stayed up until well after midnight, talking of education issues. In May that year he invited me with a small group of academics to lunch with Mrs Thatcher in the House of Commons, where she was now Leader of the Opposition. When he conducted us to her room, the academics hung back, and no one would enter first. This was so ridiculous I strode forward, and took her hand. But as I began to speak, she tugged me past her while I was in mid-flow, and I found myself standing alone beside the salmon mousse and hock. During the conversation over lunch we were far too self-conscious to engage in real debate, and Mrs Thatcher looked distant and cold. We discovered why when she interrupted us to watch the television news. She was taking part in an important debate in the House that afternoon, and her mind was taken up with her speech. I have later heard other Conservatives confirm that it was a habit of Mrs Thatcher to tug her guests past her at receptions.

Our major project in the 1970s was the founding of the

National Council for Educational Standards. In January 1972 Tony co-operated with Max Beloff, Rhodes Boyson and Tom Howarth (previously head of St Paul's School in London) to organize a conference at Pembroke College, Cambridge. I did not attend, because the dates, just before the school term, clashed with our *Critical Quarterly* sixth-form conference. Throughout these years I was taking my full load of teaching and administration at Manchester University, and often found difficulty in fitting in trips to conferences. The speakers at Pembroke included Jacques Barzun, G.H. Bantock, T.E.B. Howarth, Rhodes Boyson, L. Bruce Lockhart (head of Gresham's) and Stuart Froome. Max Beloff organized a seminar on university education, together with Dr Steven Watson (St Andrew's, Scotland).

The Press was invited, and the speeches were given good coverage. The first leader in the *Daily Mail* on 4 January was headed: 'It's Where You Live That Counts'. It began: 'One of the first questions that you ask an estate agent these days is: "What are the schools like round here?" Dr Rhodes Boyson, headmaster of one of London's best comprehensive schools, claims that comprehensives have led to a more vicious selection system than the eleven-plus.' The leader went on to summarize the neighbourhood school argument, and to support 'that brusque but over-maligned woman, Mrs Margaret Thatcher', who was said in the leader to agree with Boyson. This favourable Press coverage could not have happened in 1969; within those years we had accomplished a remarkable shift of opinion.

The Pembroke College proceedings were published as a booklet called *The Basic Unity of Education*, and Sir Desmond Lee, of Hughes Hall, Cambridge, became the Secretary of the newly-formed National Council for Educational Standards. The annual subscription was fifty pence, and very soon the Council had gathered over 1,500 associate members. I took over as Secretary and Treasurer in the mid-1970s. Throughout the 1970s, and until 1988, we organized regular conferences, usually at the Mostyn Hotel in London; these were always followed by extensive Press coverage. A second conference on primary education on 6 May 1972, at St Paul's School, London, attracted a large number; usually about eighty to 100 people attended our meetings.

In 1972 the National Council arranged a further conference in July at Gresham's School on Middle Schools. Evidence was also submitted to the Government's Inquiry into Reading Standards and the Use of English set up under the chairmanship of Sir Alan Bullock. Essays in newspapers and journals began to appear regularly, and as I look back I am amazed at the variety of our activities, largely a result of Tony's organizing zeal.

Over the years I often complained to Rhodes Boyson about the lack of volunteers willing to undertake administrative tasks; I was surprised that our small group could achieve such influence. He replied that in pressure group work this is a fact of life, and that a very few determined people can easily change public opinion – particularly when they are right! Our conferences were usually on Sundays, so the Press could report them on Monday, notoriously an off-day for news. We were repeating the process which had enabled a few progressives, such as Professor Brian Simon and Michael Armstrong, to win the battle for public support in the 1960s. In the 1980s I became convinced that we were becoming too successful, as I shall explain later.

After the collapse of Mr Heath's Government in 1974, Rhodes and I decided to publish two further Black Papers, the first in 1975 and the second in 1977. Tony Dyson had become seriously ill, and took no further part in our pressure group activities. We managed to persuade commercial publishers, first J.M. Dent and then Temple Smith, to publish the pamphlets for us, relieving me of the burden of administration. *Black Paper 1975* began with ten points – Black Paper Basics – which I reprint in Appendix B. In this pamphlet I could not resist a few humorous items, such as this piece of doggerel from W.H. Auden's *Epistle to a Grandson* (1972):

> Dare any call Permissiveness
> An educational success?
> Saner those class-rooms that I sat in,
> Compelled to study Greek and Latin.

There was also a not very successful comic piece from Amis and Conquest called 'I.L.E.A. Confidential'; but the new Black Papers were far more restrained in tone and more constructive than the previous three. I had learned the danger of giving the journalists easy copy.

Many previous Black Paper writers – Jacques Barzun, H.J. Eysenck, and Stuart Froome – contributed solid essays, but for me the most impressive contributions to *Black Paper 1975* were by Iris Murdoch, the novelist, Bernice Martin, a lecturer in Sociology at Bedford College, Geoffrey Bantock and Max Beloff.

Iris Murdoch, a Labour Party supporter, offered us a passionate but very lucid essay about the problems of the able working-class child in a comprehensive system which does not provide the stimulus of an academic environment and peer group:

> Why should socialist policy, of all things, be so grossly unjust to the underprivileged clever child, avid to learn, able to learn, and under non-selective education likely to pass in relaxed idle boredom those precious years when strenuous learning is a joy and when the whole intellectual and moral future of the human being is at stake?

I placed Iris Murdoch's article first, and arranged for it to be pre-published in the *Sunday Telegraph*.

Bernice Martin's 'The Mining of the Ivory Tower' examined the sociological and intellectual background of educational permissiveness, and described the dangerous irrationality of modern fashions. These ideas were further developed in her influential book, *A Sociology of Contemporary Cultural Change* (1981). In a little pamphlet, 'Education; The Next Decade', published by the Conservative Political Centre in 1981, I argued that progressive educationalists had appropriated Antonio Gramsci's idea of hegemony; this is the belief that revolutionary changes are achieved not only by the transfer of political and economic power, but by the creation of an alternative hegemony through new forms of experience and consciousness. Control of society can be achieved by gradual transformation of living styles, by radical changes in the organization of schools, for example. I quoted Bernice Martin's book at length, for I believe it sums up the underlying assumptions behind the attempt of progressive educationalists to transform our education system:

In the schools, too, this progressive movement involved a sharp attack on boundaries, categories, roles, rules and ritual and was characterized by a fundamental mistrust of institutions as such. Ivan Illich, the international prophet of deschooling, put the case most flamboyantly, though many teachers who had never read Illich and who would have been astonished to be thought of as part of a counter-culture, shared that generalized mistrust of the routinized and institutionalized in education. The merging of categories and elimination of boundaries was also something which few school-teachers held as an overt principle (unlike the student rebel leaders), but which simply happened to be taken on board with what they accepted as a liberal cargo. All-in comprehensive schools were favoured rather than specialist or selective schools, and co-education inexorably squeezed out the single-sex school.

Architectural boundaries were swept away (or rendered movable) in open-plan buildings and subject boundaries were eroded by new subject grouping. Pedagogically, the stress shifted from the pupil as recipient, 'vessel', or apprentice, to an insistence on his self-determination. Learning through exploration, feeling, self-discovery was ideologically preferred to the older, more classical models which assumed a hierarchy of skills, a structure of rules, sequences and rituals, and which endowed the teacher with the role of expert and authority on the basis of his superior knowledge and training. At the same time those rituals which traditionally embodied and expressed collective identity (communitas), group symbols such as uniform, speech day, school assembly, school sports and the house system, all fell out of favour as constricting individual liberty. Hierarchy, authority, and honourable achieved leadership roles (prefect, house captain, and so on), were also frowned on as anti-egalitarian. So instead of formal rituals of overall communitas, many schools came to be dominated by the symbolic vocabulary of anti-structure and new, informal rituals of peer-group conformity.

In part, these de-structuring moves have been an explicit ideological assertion of the superiority of openness, informality and fluidity over closure, formality and structure. In part, they have simply been a reaction against anything, however contingent, which appeared to have been linked with élite educational forms and practice.

Bernice Martin argued forcibly in the Black Paper that this lack of structure in progressive education particularly harmed working-class children. Similarly, in his article in the Black Paper, G.H. Bantock showed that fallacies in progressive thinking undermined its protagonists' efforts to achieve reforms. Progressives, he wrote, are committed to two contradictory sets of values. They believe in the importance of the individual, and this should persuade them to allow able children to advance as fast as possible. They also believe in equality, and this leads to collectivism, uniformity, instinctive faith in non-streaming. This confusion – a lack of clear educational goals – is a major cause of the failure of comprehensive education.

These arguments were central to Black Papers 1975 and 1977. I quoted passages such as these repeatedly in talks in all parts of England, and this work, I believe, helped to win the intellectual battle; by the time the Conservative Party took power in 1979 our thinking was well-known and influential with many Members of Parliament. I also often quoted Hannah Arendt's comments on child-centred education in her book, *Between Past and Future* (1961). Arendt explains that in the United States (long before the progressive revolution in Britain) the fashion for child-centred education led to all the rules of sound human reason being thrust aside. The abdication of authority by parents and teachers is unnatural. The authority that tells the individual child what to do and what not to do comes to rest with the child group itself; this creates a situation in which the adult stands helpless before the individual child, and out of contact with him. He can only tell him to do what he likes and then prevent the worst from happening. The real and normal relations between children and adults are thus broken off:

By being emancipated from the authority of adults the child has not been freed but has been subjected to a much more terrifying and truly tyrannical authority, the tyranny of the majority. In any case the result is that the children have been so to speak banished from the world of grown-ups. They are either thrown back upon themselves or handed over to the tyranny of their own group, against which, because of its numerical superiority, they cannot rebel, with which, because they are children, they cannot reason, and out of which they cannot flee to any other world because the world of adults is barred to them. The reaction of the children to this pressure tends to be either conformism or juvenile delinquency and is frequently a mixture of both.

Black Papers 1975 and 1977 try to offer specific proposals to implement our ideas. Max Beloff explained the policies and aims of the new University College of Buckingham, of which he had been elected Principal. Rhodes and I strongly advocated the establishment of national standards, with tests at ages seven, eleven and fourteen; these were introduced in the Education Reform Act of 1988.

In the mid-1970s two events in particular changed the climate of opinion in our favour: first, the publication of the Bennett Report, and second, the scandal at William Tyndale School. Dr Neville Bennett's Report on methods of teaching in primary schools was published in 1976. He showed that, within the space of a single school year, formally taught pupils moved ahead in reading and mathematical skills much more quickly than those in less formally-taught class-rooms. Afterwards, and not surprisingly, his statistics were questioned, but his study was only one among many which cast doubt on the validity of informal teaching methods.

In *Black Paper 1977* we insisted that we did not want to put the clock back to the 1930s, but argued that Bennett's research 'does support our demand for the best of both formal and informal methods, for more structure and teacher direction in schools'. Bennett's Report was extensively reported in the Press; the myth, so fashionable after the Plowden Report, that research had conclusively proved that children learnt best by discovery methods in an unstructured setting was therefore finally laid to rest.

In a review of the Bennett Report in *New Society* (April 1976), Professor Jerome Bruner, famous for his advocacy of discovery methods, acknowledged the great shift that was taking place in the climate of feeling, a change of mood which the Black Paper had helped to stimulate:

We are just at the end of an era in the human sciences in which concepts of self-direction, self-realization and self-reward lived unchallenged in a world where self-determination was the ideal. And indeed, this ideal is central to the democratic concept. But ends and means become confused: what of self-demand feeding schedules for babies? What of the 'innateness hypotheses', in whose name it was insisted that language is discovered and need not be taught? And what of the ever more dominating contemporary cultures of youth? The adult as model or teacher or friend is in eclipse. Common sense and technical inquiry are finally catching up with the romantic excess. It turns out the mother and her reactions are crucial for language acquisition and that self-demand in feeding and infant care leaves the child without a stable source of reciprocation. New studies are now pointing to the critical role of the adult tutor, in social and intellectual development. Early connection with a supporting world begins to emerge as a *leitmotif* for the development of later self-determination. And, indeed, one of the central issues is to assure the dispossessed that this connection is not destroyed by isolating alienation.

After the Bennett Report common sense began to prevail, and the best teachers acknowledged the need for structure and organization outlined by G.H. Bantock in his article in *Black Paper Two*.

The William Tyndale affair was even more influential. Angry parents at this progressive school in Islington forced the head, Mr Ellis, to hold a meeting to discuss his educational policies. For this event Mrs Dolly Walker, a teacher at the school, who advocated traditional methods, prepared a discussion document, a 'black paper' as it was later called in the newspapers. The resulting controversy led to a public Inquiry under the direction of a lawyer, Mr Robin Auld. The newspaper coverage exposed the worst features of progressive education, and created a reaction among parents to which politicians were quick to respond.

I persuaded Mrs Walker to contribute an essay to *Black Paper 1977*. When I met her I found her balanced and sensible, and her article turned out to be restrained in tone. It describes precisely what had been happening at William Tyndale. Her article reveals the hotch-potch of fashionable ideas which in the early 1970s were being purveyed by many colleges of education, and put into practice in the schools by young teachers. William Tyndale may have been an extreme example of progressive education, but it is absurd to suggest, as some teachers have done recently, that the events at this school were not being replicated elsewhere. Mrs Walker describes how at William Tyndale the basic skills of literacy and numeracy were not to be taught unless a child actually *wanted* to acquire those skills. When a worried mother came to the school to find out why her nine-year-old son was never given any work to do at school she was told that her son ought to know that it was up to him to *ask* his teacher for work; otherwise he could not be given any. One young teacher who was designated to take a reading group within the school's vertically streamed reading scheme wrote on the blackboard: 'I hate reading groups', and sent the children to play on the adventure playground instead. The head justified his rejection of formal teaching in arithmetic by saying that in any betting shop you could see men able to work out their winnings at high speed because they *wanted* to know the results. Those who wanted to learn mathematics would learn it for themselves. The example of the betting shop was commonplace in schools in the early 1970s; the truth that children learn best when their interest is engaged had been converted into a fanatical doctrine.

The parents were particularly distressed that their children were not reproved for swearing in school, even when they used the notorious four-letter words. This shocked the working-class women who helped with school meals. As at Berkeley, criticism of obscene language was viewed by the progressive teachers as 'unfair discrimination' against children from poor homes who were supposed to be aping their parents. This is a typical example of the ignorance of progressive, middle-class teachers when they apply their beliefs to the needs of working-class children. In the homes of the members of my family who are working-class I have never heard four-letter words; the men may use obscene language on a building site, but certainly not in front of their wives.

One inspector said that if William Tyndale had been left unchanged for another year it would have deteriorated into a *Lord of the Flies*. After the Auld Report the removal of the head reflected concern among parents that standards of numeracy and literacy were being neglected. In October 1976 Mr Callaghan, the Prime Minister, reacted to this mood in his famous Ruskin speech, in which he tried to initiate a great debate on education. He was responding to deep parental dissatisfaction with those Labour Party policies espoused at the end of the 1960s by Mr Short when he was Secretary of State for Education.

During all these years I appeared regularly on radio and television programmes such as *Word in Edgeways*, chaired by Brian Redhead, *Panorama* and *Man Alive*. My least successful encounter was the televised debate at the Oxford Union when I was savaged by Richard Crossman. My most successful was on 6 September 1973, on BBC 2 in a series called *Controversy*; it was chaired by Sir George Porter at the Royal Institution. As the principal speaker I was allowed to present a twelve-minute prepared speech on the topic, 'The Notion of Equality is a Threat to Education'. Three opponents – Dr A.H. Halsey, Nuffield College, Oxford, Dr Harry Judge, previously head of Banbury comprehensive and Brian Jackson, a well-known writer on progressive education – were allowed four minutes each to reply. An invited audience of about 150 then fired in questions and comments for about an hour.

The programme was pre-recorded on the Tuesday. At the start double doors were thrown open, and I entered the debating chamber to step up to the rostrum for my speech. I took deep breaths, strode in purposefully and made a splendid start to my speech. After thirty seconds the producer, Dominic Flessati, stopped the programme because the microphone hidden in my pocket was crackling. I found myself once more outside the double doors, now much more nervous.

Before the programme Dominic Flessati pointed out to me that because I stood on the rostrum whenever I spoke the cameras would return to me. The audience, at least those who asked questions, were mainly left-wing, but in this dominating position above their heads I managed to keep my temper and to answer their objections cogently and forcibly. The following Sunday in the *Observer* Clive James awarded the programme the highest accolade: 'You get a good debate only when the truth is shared out between both sides. So it was here, and the show crackled along throwing off illuminating sparks'. He described my opening speech as 'menacingly able', but thought I tired before the end, which is not surprising. During the next few days I received over fifty letters of support, including several from people of working-class origin. One wrote: 'As products of that strange thing, "the working class", we pray for protection from the Halseys who claim to speak for us.'

By the time of Mr Callaghan's speech, these public appearances, particularly those by Rhodes Boyson, had done much to swing public opinion to our side. After the Ruskin speech, I changed my mind about how the campaigns of the National Council for Educational Standards should be conducted. I felt that this change of heart from a Labour Prime Minister signalled that we might be in danger of pushing our opponents into an entrenched position, making it more difficult for them to move towards conciliation. I wanted the Labour Party to support a national curriculum, to re-assert the values of structure in schooling, and to fight for high standards of literacy and numeracy. Already, in September 1976, Mrs Shirley Williams, the new Secretary of State for Education, had admitted that large comprehensives were a mistake; she said that we needed to consider what kind of comprehensive worked best. My new concern to create a consensus brought about a major split in the National Council for Educational Standards, which in the 1980s began to separate into smaller groups.

In 1978 we registered N.C.E.S. as a charity, and this itself necessitated a change of policy, though not all our members were willing to co-operate with this. As a charity we were required by law to serve the cause of educational standards objectively, and not publish political polemics. Our sponsors included Professor Bantock, Lord Beloff, Baroness Cox, Professor Eysenck, Lord

Harris, Patrick Moore, the astronomer, and Philip Larkin (who when accepting my invitation expressed nervousness about allying himself to we 'jackbooted' characters). The trustees were myself, Baroness Cox, Tony Harris (headmaster, Clare Park School, Maidstone) and Laurie Norcross, who had taken over from Rhodes Boyson as head of Highbury Grove comprehensive school in London. Our secretary was Mrs Margaret Smith, who for the next ten years worked with amazing thoroughness to keep the venture afloat.

We started a new journal, the *Bulletin*, edited with panache by Stephen Woodley, a teacher at King's School, Canterbury. We also began a series of what we called the Kay-Shuttleworth Papers on Education, the first by Vernon Bognador (a supporter of the Liberal Party) and the second by Caroline Cox and John Marks. A major research project on examination results was undertaken under the direction of John Marks, Caroline Cox and Maciej Pomian-Srzednicki. This resulted in a number of controversial pamphlets on the relative achievements of comprehensives compared with areas which had kept the old grammar/secondary modern school divisions. Their research threw an unfavourable light on comprehensive education, and was greeted with the same kind of abuse to which I had grown accustomed during the Black Paper campaigns. They were supported by further N.C.E.S. pamphlets, such as R.W. Baldwin on *Secondary Schools, 1965–1979.*

After the Conservatives under Mrs Thatcher won the General Election in 1979, Rhodes Boyson became a Junior Minister at the Department of Education, and so played little further part in our organization. In the 1980s we continued to attract famous speakers to our Sunday conferences – Sir Keith Joseph and Mrs Angela Rumbold, for example – but I insisted that we must draw on a wider political spectrum. In January 1985 we organized a large residential conference at Sidney Sussex College, Cambridge, with our own speakers, Arthur Pollard and Patrick Hutton (head of Wolverhampton Grammar School). These two were balanced by Giles Radice, the Labour spokesman on education, and Anne Sofer, who performed the same duty for the Social Democratic Party. We printed the conference papers in a pamphlet, 'The

Search for Common Ground', and this 'common ground' became my aim in the late 1980s.

Unfortunately this policy divided my supporters. I have already mentioned my dislike for the work of the Centre for Policy Studies, and particularly for the opinions of Sir Alfred Sherman. After 1980 Baroness Cox and John Marks associated themselves increasingly with several right-wing groups. Margaret Smith and I tried to keep N.C.E.S. more moderate, and to ensure we obeyed the legal requirements of a charity. There were disagreements, and eventually a parting of the ways. Whereas in the 1960s almost all education pressure groups were progressive, in the 1980s our success had spawned a large number of pressure groups whose publications and conferences were reported in the newspapers. Members of the Friends of the Voucher campaign or the Queen's English Society attended our Sunday conferences; I feared that we would become associated with their views. After 1980 I had become convinced that schemes for parents to use a voucher to pay for the cost of their children's education at the school of their choice would not work in practice. They would create a new bureaucracy, and the children of poor parents in the inner cities would be left to stagnate in run-down comprehensives. According to the proponents of the voucher, such schools would either reform or wither away, but I worried about what would happen to the unfortunate children while this was happening. The process might take a long time.

In other crucial ways I felt that the new right-wing groups were in the wrong. As I have said before, I disliked talk about schools as if they operated like markets, the increasing emphasis on the utilitarian and the vocational. Moral crusades, such as those associated with Mrs Whitehouse, were intellectually superficial. After Mrs Whitehouse attacked the television reading by Tony Harrison of his poem 'V' (in which skin-heads use four-letter words in a poem which is highly moral), I was glad that *The Times* published a letter from me in support of Harrison. As the years passed it was very annoying to be continually addressing strangers at meetings who took for granted that my views were right-wing.

As the 1987 Election approached I was increasingly absorbed in Manchester University business (I was Dean of the Faculty of Arts from 1984 to 1986, and became a Pro-Vice-Chancellor in

1987). The disagreements with Baroness Cox and John Marks had led to their withdrawal from N.C.E.S. I was very pleased to be invited to join the Kingman Committee of Inquiry into the Teaching of English Language, and subsequently to chair the National Curriculum English Working Group. Mr Baker's Education Reform Act of 1988 had brought into law some central Black Paper doctrines. I felt that the National Council for Educational Standards had outlived its usefulness, and so I resigned as President. No one proved willing to undertake all the considerable administrative burdens, and the organization became defunct.

# 11
# *Return to Literature*

## Anniversary

FOR JEAN

We drop down to Le Lavandou,
  a dazzling beach,
    a hundred topless girls.
What a present!
  for my silver wedding,
    this rich variety of breasts.
I swim out to the raft
  wondering
    and then
a sudden apparition!
  Standing on the crispy waves
    a blonde windsurfer:
her lithesome body
  holds in balance
    a tugging purple sail.

A silver wedding diminishes
  us
    marks a small future
and what price our fidelity
  beside this bright company,
    pride of sense and easy love?
Yet when the Dutch boy
  puts mouth to breast,

touches a crotch,
his girl crouched blank-eyed on the sand,
    I'm distressed;
        I feel a loss
as if words fell out of language:
    intimacy,
        private grace.

Afternoon somnolence is broken
    by a yellow bus –
        a bevy of schoolgirls,
little breasts under regulation
    blue swimsuits;
        alert as birds
they sit cross-legged in line
    while their teachers
        mark out shallow water
with ropes and toggles and floats.
    A shifting of straw mats
        and collapse of sunshades –
the topless girls,
    ill at ease,
        drift away across the sand.

So our silver wedding ends
    beside a school at work,
        but we don't mind:
we've spent so many years
    with ropes and toggles and floats
        making a world safe for children.
We swim far out beyond the raft;
    from the shore you might think us
        a two-headed monster,
four eyes bobbing above the waves,
    yet at this vantage point
        we command perfect landscape.
Distant from the curving beach,
    blue hills of Le Lavandou,
        we are treading the deep waters.

Over the years my brother Derek had prospered. I often worried that while I was relishing the enchantments of Cambridge he was fenced in by office routines. After the war, grants were available for him to restart his career and go to university. We discussed this several times, but he would not take the plunge.

His hard work paid dividends, however, when in 1951 he was placed first in the Final Examination of the Institute of Chartered Accountants. This astonishing achievement for a Grimsby boy without university training and working almost entirely on his own enabled him to move to the prestigious Deloitte's in London.

Derek eventually became a partner and headed the tax department at Stoy Hayward, another well-known firm of London accountants. He took lodgings at Dulwich, arriving on his first day at Deloitte's on his sit-up-and-beg bicycle, but finding there was no obvious storage space. After a few years he rented a very comfortable flat on the seventh floor in Park Crescent, adjacent to Regent's Park; from there he could walk to work down Wigmore Street. For many years he enjoyed a wide circle of friends, ski-ing holidays and regular theatre and restaurant engagements. Jean and I often stayed in his spare bedroom on visits to London.

But all was not well. My own belief is that he never recovered from the death of our mother when he was thirteen. He feared intimacy with the opposite sex, and though he regularly escorted a series of women to parties or the theatre, he never went beyond friendship; I think he idealized our mother so much that no other woman could compete. Derek wanted a life of order and stability, and feared the messy compromises of close relationships. He kept a scrupulous record in a ledger of every relative and friend, and marked carefully in the appropriate column when he sent a Christmas or birthday card. The ledger, which I have in front of me as I write, includes records of about 200 people, with full details of gifts and cards from 1968 to 1975. In his flat everything was exceptionally well-organized; in the kitchen about thirty tins of soup were stacked in alphabetical order. As a young man I rebelled against his meticulous codes of conduct, his insistence, for example, that as a teetotaller he would not touch his food in a restaurant until he had a glass of water in front of him. As we grew older, however, we became very close, and even on day visits to London for university committees I would join him for tea in his flat before he drove me to Euston to catch a late train back to Manchester. He was very supportive during the Black Paper campaigns, sending me cuttings from newspapers which were on my side.

Just before Christmas 1974, when he was fifty years old, he went into hospital for a minor operation for varicose veins. On returning home, he declared he was feeling too weak to go to work, and we all presumed he was having a minor nervous breakdown. He would go into the office for a few days, and then break off again. Towards the end of March he complained of severe pains in the lower abdomen, but the three Harley Street doctors he consulted could find nothing wrong with him.

In the week before *Black Paper 1975* was published I stayed two nights at his flat while taking part in radio and television programmes. On Thursday evening, 17 April, I participated in a television debate on mixed ability teaching chaired by Ludovic Kennedy. I always enjoyed radio discussions, but disliked television confrontations; during them you must act a part, and smile and look as if you are winning. This is especially difficult if, like me, you have a long, lugubrious countenance. On this evening I had at last developed sufficient familiarity with television to overcome my nerves, and to converse in a relaxed manner, as if I was conducting a university tutorial. The programme went out live late in the evening. I arrived back at Derek's flat after 11 p.m. He had already gone to bed, but left me a scribbled note: 'You were excellent. Congratulations.'

At breakfast he was not well, and I was sad to leave him to catch the 10 a.m. train to Manchester, where I had teaching engagements in the afternoon. I wish I had stayed. The next day, in the afternoon, Derek climbed out of the seventh-floor flat window, and jumped.

The police rang, and Jean and I immediately decided that we would drive to Grimsby to break the news to my father. He was seventy-seven, and I worried that the shock might kill him. Our children were old enough to fend for themselves for one night.

In Ian McEwan's novel, *The Child in Time*, the main character, Stephen, sees a lorry disintegrate ahead of him on the road, and for a few seconds experiences a slowing of time, a sense of a fresh beginning, as he hurtles towards the crashed vehicle, knowing he may soon be dead. For a few seconds he enters a period in which all terms and conditions have changed, 'as though he was walking alone into a great city on a newly discovered planet'. When I read this account it recalled for me my own feelings after the telephone call from the police. I was bewildered, as if all existing categories of thought had dissolved and left me in some fashion unclothed, born into something new and alien. The sense of being born again into a different dimension stayed with me for over a year, until gradually work and conventional living restored me to accustomed, more comfortable habits of thought.

As we travelled towards Lincolnshire this bewilderment almost caused an accident. In 1975 the M62 was incomplete, and after the turn-offs for Leeds reverted to a two-lane highway. As lights approached from the opposite direction, I realized I had continued in the outer lane, and for a mile had been driving in the dark on the wrong side of the road. When we arrived at Laceby Road and broke the news to my father, I did not tell him it was suicide, but he guessed. He wept uncontrollably for a long time; perhaps this was fortunate. Telling my father that his eldest son was dead was the most distressing duty I have ever performed. Towards midnight Jean and I left him with my stepmother, and spent the night at Jean's mother's house in Henry Street. On Sunday we returned to Cheadle Hulme, taking my mother-in-law with us to cope with the children's meals while we travelled to London. On Monday the Black Paper was due to be published. I rang Rhodes Boyson, and arranged for him to take over all commitments to speak to the media, which he was well-qualified to do, and for my secretary to pass callers on to him. I was most anxious that my brother's suicide should not attract publicity, for that would have further wounded my father.

In London my first task was to identify the body at University College Hospital. I imagined that, as in the films, I would be taken to a morgue where a body covered with a sheet would lie on a table. Instead, after I left Jean in the waiting-room, I was conducted to a large ill-lit room where one side appeared like a gigantic filing-cabinet. The official who accompanied me pulled out a trolley-like structure where my brother was lying, and I felt slightly surprised that he was not breathing. I could only see the white face, unharmed except for a streak of blood across the nose. Beyond him I glimpsed another corpse, a woman who I thought must be the wife of the man in the waiting-room whose details had been recorded after mine. The official had turned away. After a quick glance I too turned away. I felt some symbolic action was called for, but could think of nothing.

After visits to the police and my brother's solicitor, we returned to Manchester. The next day I travelled back alone for the preliminary inquest. Manchester professors often joke that they only meet each other on the London train on their way to committees. After we passed through Rugby I visited the toilet, and discovered Bryan Carsberg (then Professor of Accounting and now Sir Bryan, Director General of Telecommunications) sitting at a table on his own. As he drew me into conversation, I could hardly tell him that the previous day I had identified my brother's body in a morgue and was now travelling to the inquest. Bryan was charming and sprightly, and we chatted for ten minutes or so. As we conversed it seemed heavily ironic that I should be exchanging pleasantries with a highly successful chartered accountant, the man my brother should have been, while he lay dead in that filing-cabinet contraption in the hospital.

After the inquest it was drizzling. I wandered out into the run-down area behind King's Cross Station. I came across a small, blackened church where I thought I might sit down to recover; but the wooden door was chained and padlocked.

Because he was an atheist Derek had left me strict instructions that there should be no religious service at his funeral. I disobeyed him, and did not find this a difficult decision. Now he was no more I knew my responsibility was to my father, who would have been even further distressed without the funeral service at his local Methodist church in Nunsthorpe. After the inquest the coroner released to me seventy pages of foolscap covered with my brother's notes to me after he had decided to commit suicide; his loneliness was implicit on every page. Weeks later I received a letter from Derek's doctor telling me that the autopsy had revealed a large cancer of his kidney, notoriously difficult, the doctor explained, to diagnose. In spite of our doubts, Derek had indeed been in great pain.

For almost a year afterwards I suffered from repeated dreams in which Bryan Carsberg was going about his business, assured and charming, while Derek was labouring in a back office on a meagre salary. I was my brother's executor and inherited his pension, so in my dream I worry about my brother's muted existence, and whether in law we should explain that I have inherited money from a man who is still alive. After the anniversary of my brother's death, in April 1976, these dreams troubled me less frequently, but they still occur occasionally.

Derek's suicide has affected me permanently, however. A few weeks afterwards I was billed to address 1,000 parents in Bradford who were opposed to the Labour Party's decision to remove financial support from direct grant schools. I would not claim I have never been nervous before such events; the adrenalin runs. But since my early experiences in the Royal Army Education Corps I have enjoyed addressing large audiences, and I know the temptations of the demagogue. On this occasion I was unsettled to discover that I was truly nervous, and I had difficulty in pulling myself together before I delivered my speech. I do not think I have ever completely recovered my self-confidence; since 1975 I have subjected myself less frequently to the ordeal of television confrontations. After this time, whenever I felt angry, even over matters which have nothing to do with me, such as a bad foul at a Manchester United football match, my hair would bristle and my cheeks flush.

I did accept an invitation to take part in three 35-minute television programmes under the chairmanship of Robin Day, a sequence called *The Sunday Debate*, on 15, 22 and 29 June, produced by John Eidinow. On 15 June we transmitted Part One live at 6.15 p.m., and after a short break recorded Part Two. On 29 June we transmitted Part Three live. The question for debate was 'Education: are we sacrificing quality for equality?' On my side was Bernice Martin (after several years of these confrontations I had learnt the advantage of having a woman to support me). Our opponents were Dr A.H. Halsey, once more, and Harry Rée, formerly Professor of Education at York University and then teaching at Woodberry Down School, a London comprehensive. In the first programme Bernice and I were allowed four minutes each to put our case, and then for fifteen minutes Halsey and Rée debated the issues with us. Programme Two followed the same pattern, with Halsey and Rée putting their case. In the final programme the debate was put into political context, with the Labour Party Secretary of State for Education, Fred Mulley, and the Conservative Shadow Spokesman on Education, Norman St John Stevas, joining us. I was impressed with Robin Day's professionalism, his thorough grasp of the subject. He told me he kept careful records of controversial matters, so before chairing a debate he could quickly check over the major facts and arguments.

I possess the transcript of these debates, and think Bernice and I did well, although at the time it all seemed strangely illusory. Before the recordings I stayed the Saturday night in Derek's flat (it took me four months to find someone to take over the lease). As I waited to set off for the television studio I sat in Derek's arm-chair by the window from which he jumped, feeling that my newborn identity existed quite separately from the rough-and-tumble of television debate. The arguments during the programme were not so very different from those of my *Controversy* television programme. After six years of campaigning the rhetoric of both sides was becoming too familiar.

There were moments of light relief. After the last programme with Fred Mulley and Norman St John Stevas we adjourned for drinks in the usual BBC courtesy suite. After chatting to St John Stevas, I was ushered by a sophisticated young female research assistant to my chauffeur-driven car, which transported me to Heathrow to catch the evening plane to Manchester. It was all like some glamorous film sequence. Jean, who had spent the weekend visiting her mother in Grimsby, met me at Manchester airport. I had been too nervous to eat anything before the programme, and was desperately hungry. Jean, presuming I would be handsomely wined and dined, had nothing suitable in the house for a quick meal. We stopped on Etchells Road at a takeaway shop, and so my glamorous Sunday ended queueing for fish-and-chips.

As the year progressed my highly-charged state of mind forced me to rethink my priorities. Presumably this influenced my decision after Mr Callaghan's Ruskin speech to play a less prominent role in educational politics. Like Razumov in Geneva in Conrad's *Under Western Eyes*, I turned to writing to explore my identity, and, I suppose, to impose some order and sense on to what had happened. I read plays such as *King Lear*, which I was teaching, with the kind of urgent, passionate response I had not experienced since adolescence.

I also started writing verse again. In the early 1960s, influenced by my work as poetry editor of *Critical Quarterly*, I had written a number of poems. I published just a few in journals such as *The Times Literary Supplement* and the *Kenyon Review*, but this creative energy soon withered. After Derek's death I spent hours working over drafts, and published a series in various British and American journals, particularly the *London Magazine*. Eventually I published two books of verse, *Every Common Sight* (1981) and *Two-Headed Monster* (1985). This activity seemed to me far more important than the literary criticism I had published in a book on Joseph Conrad in 1974. Both my books of poetry were well received, and in the *Spectator* Roy Fuller chose *Every Common Sight* as his Book of the Year. Encouraging letters from Philip Larkin, Ted Hughes, Charles Tomlinson and Louis Simpson meant a great deal to me, and helped me to continue.

When I start to write a poem I begin either with a memory of an actual event or with somebody else's personal experience by which I am particularly intrigued (for example, Mahler at dawn, as he began to compose, could not bear to see another human being: 'He longs to own two yokes of land, To sit alone in the middle.'). After I have selected an experience, a curious problem arises, which reveals my psychological conflicts. For some poems I choose a formal pattern, often with a rhyme scheme. This is the English side of my character, and I feel emotionally satisfied if I can complete such traditional exercises. On other occasions I imitate the style of William Carlos Williams, his experiments with triads, as in the poem about my silver wedding printed at the beginning of this chapter. I think my best poems are written in this freer form, more open to shifts of tone, more informal and colloquial. This is my Californian self, less puritanical, less in need of stability.

After Derek's suicide, I became absorbed by my experiments in verse. Whereas my Nunsthorpe and Wintringham training disciplined me always to be prompt and reliable, when I lose myself in a new poem I forget my other engagements. Since 1984, during my time as Dean of the Faculty of Arts and Pro-Vice-Chancellor, I have written less poetry; during the course of one day my mind cannot jump from the university's financial problems to the structure of my latest poem. But since 1975 I have found my various activities in promoting the Arts particularly satisfying, less contentious and personally upsetting than the educational debates.

In 1970 I had started a Poetry Centre at Manchester University, with a grant from the Arts Council. It was a bad time for such an ambitious project, for soon there was no extra money for the new buildings I had planned. W.H. Auden read his poetry at the opening of the Centre. When I met him at Piccadilly Station he was wearing carpet slippers, and looked wan. The reading took place on stage at the University Theatre, with a backdrop of a cavernous 1914–18 dugout on the Western Front for R.C. Sherriff's *Journey's End*. As his creased face pronounced the famous poems of the 1930s, it seemed an appropriately symbolic setting. I took an instant dislike to Auden, who was querulous and pernickety. Before the reading, a photographer who was obviously northern and working-class took a picture for *The Times*; Auden was sitting on a chair with his back to a white wall. Later, after the reading, as Auden was chatting to students in the tea lounge, the photographer returned to ask if he could take another picture, as *The Times* wanted something more appropriate to the occasion. Auden peremptorily dismissed him. I was disgusted, for this unsophisticated man was only trying to earn his living. Auden's witterings made me nervous.

I had invited Philip Larkin over from Hull for the day, and we all had lunch with the Vice-Chancellor in one of the University's small dining-rooms. On the way back to the railway stations with Auden and Larkin I absent-mindedly gave the taxi-driver the name of Larkin's station – Victoria – instead of Piccadilly, where Auden's train was soon due to leave. I realized only just in time that we were taking wrong turns, and I was glad to see Auden disappear down the platform.

In subsequent years I organized a series of readings, attended each time by several hundred students. Ted Hughes came a couple of times, and there were readings from Stephen Spender, Charles Tomlinson, Peter Porter, John Wain and Michael Schmidt. John Betjeman won my prize for the most gracious of readers. He walked with some difficulty, so after his reading in our Roscoe Theatre I took him out the back way to avoid the crowds. We walked up thirty stairs before I realized I had led him into the bowels of the building, and not towards the back exit. As I helped him down the stairs again, and into the crowds, he remained charming, trying not to cause me embarrassment. For an evening reading by Yevtuchenko I managed to draw an audience of about 300 in a lecture theatre whose full capacity was 470. He was very cross when he saw the empty seats, and informed me curtly that this never happened in Russia. R.S. Thomas gave a wonderfully lugubrious reading. His first poem began: 'Parents, I forgive you my life'. He stayed the night in my home; after his arrival, carrying a battered brown suitcase tied up with string, he descended the stairs with a present for my wife of six farm eggs in a little wicker basket. When I first met him at Hull, I found him sensitive, shy and very, very silent. But as he grew to know me well he relaxed, and talked animatedly about Welsh nationalism. I am proud that *Critical Quarterly* did so much to promote his work, for he has been seriously underrated.

The most important decision I took after I started the Poetry Centre at Manchester University was to invite Michael Schmidt and his collaborator, Peter Jones, to bring Carcanet Press from Oxford to Manchester. At that time Carcanet was a very small enterprise in grave financial difficulties. In 1972 we persuaded the Calouste Gulbenkian Foundation to award us a grant to bring Michael to Manchester, and subsequently he has been paid by the University to teach half-time as our Special Lecturer in Poetry. During the last twenty years this support has helped to keep Carcanet afloat as financial crisis has followed crisis. Some people might say, and I sympathize, that my support for Carcanet is my most significant contribution to English letters. As commercial publishers have withdrawn from certain areas of literature, Carcanet has published books of the highest quality, which, although they sell to a small readership, keep alive a concern for poetic form and literary tradition. Many poets have relied on Carcanet to publish their books after commercial publishers have deserted them. The publication of C.H. Sisson's *Under the Trojan Ditch* in 1974, for example, brought Sisson fame and a readership which he would never have achieved without Carcanet.

Michael is of American parentage, but was brought up in Mexico. He is a good poet, but, in my opinion, his best work is to be found in his two novels, *The Colonist* and *The Dresden Gate*. In both of these his imagination quickens to the rich colourful landscapes of Mexico. Although we are close friends, we disagree fundamentally in our judgment of poets. To put it in an over-simplified way, I am more concerned with the meanings of poems, while Michael is enraptured by language and prosody. I consider Philip Larkin, Ted Hughes, Thom Gunn, R.S. Thomas and Tony Harrison to be the most important post-1945 poets. Michael is less enthusiastic about Hughes, and would add C.H. Sisson, Donald Davie, W.S. Graham, Seamus Heaney, Geoffrey Hill, Jeffrey Wainwright and Derek Walcott to the list.

In his *Reading Modern Poetry*, Michael calls his approach 'aesthetic-historical', taking this term from Allen Tate. In this book he stresses the need for young readers to develop an ear for language; for him reading modern poetry 'entails an understanding "on the pulse" of the poetry of the past, and therefore a willing self-effacement before challenging new work'. My writings on modern literature tend to concentrate on matters such as the post-imperial depression in Larkin's verse, or the class struggles reflected in the language of Tony Harrison.

In 1973 Michael and I inaugurated a new, hardback, bi-annual journal, *Poetry Nation*, whose first editorial claimed that there was a need to respond to the renewed popularity and practice at that time 'of clear formal writing, a common bridling at vacuous public and private rhetoric'. Michael was the active editor, and I was glad to act as a sleeping partner, giving him moral support. After three years we were joined by C.H. Sisson and Donald Davie, and the magazine, now quarterly and in a paperback format, changed its name to *PN Review*. The new journal was intended to focus the poetic intelligence on a wider range of topics, including history, religion and politics. After a few issues I agreed amicably with Michael that I should withdraw. With my university and other commitments, I did not have sufficient time to read all the articles in advance, and attacks on my friends, Ted Hughes and Philip Larkin, had been printed without my prior knowledge. After this resignation I received from Donald Davie a letter accusing me of deserting the cause of poetic tradition. I threw it in the waste-paper basket.

Carcanet and *PN Review* still flourish. On black days I console myself by thinking of the large number of books which would never have been published if I had not invited Michael to Manchester.

After the publication of my book of poems, *Every Common Sight*, Ted Hughes wrote to me about how our contemporaries who read English at Pembroke wanted to write. With almost no exceptions, though, after three years of literary criticism they had been reduced to silence. I determined to try to change the teaching of English so that at all levels it would include the craft of writing. With Anne Cluysenaar of Sheffield Polytechnic, and Alan Young (an old friend with whom I attended Manchester United football matches, and previously a lecturer at Didsbury College of Education) I devised a Verbal Arts Manifesto. We persuaded the *Times Higher Education Supplement* to publish it. I collected forty-three signatures, including poets such as Ted Hughes, Douglas Dunn, Anne Stevenson and John Mole, novelists such as David Lodge and Malcolm Bradbury, and critics such as Raymond Williams, Richard Hoggart, Peter Abbs and David Craig (see Appendix C for the full Manifesto and signatories). I organized a special *Critical Quarterly* conference on the teaching of Verbal Arts, and lectured regularly on this theme. I always included a reading of one or two of my poems, for I argued that teachers of English should put their reputation on the line by offering their own writings for scrutiny by their students. The Verbal Arts Manifesto was followed by vigorous campaigning by Anne Cluysenaar, with numerous pamphlets and conferences. In 1986 I persuaded the novelist Maureen Duffy to edit a fiction section in *Critical Quarterly*, a reflection of my own shift of interest away from literary criticism. In 1987 I was appointed a member of the Kingman Committee, set up by the Conservative Government to advise on the teaching of English language, and in 1988 I chaired the National Curriculum Working Group for English. These commitments gave me the opportunity to introduce this emphasis on the craft of writing into the schools. In 1989 I explained my ideas at length in the

Collins English Dictionary Annual Lecture at the University of Strathclyde.

In this lecture, as on many other occasions, I quoted this crucial paragraph from the Verbal Arts Manifesto:

> Many teachers in Britain regard verbal arts, under the guise of 'creative writing', with suspicion because often there has been too much emphasis on free expression. True creativity in any art can best be developed within the framework of a thorough understanding of the nature and history of that art. The notion that verbal creation is somehow more self-indulgent, undisciplined or easy than other forms of creation is false. Responsible teaching is that which develops purposeful artistry in the handling of the medium. Verbal skill must be taught and practised in the curriculum, not left to chance, for it is one of the most important requirements for membership of a modern community.

In most schools and universities, as at Wintringham and Pembroke, the essay dominates the syllabus. I am not denying its great importance, as a means of evaluating evidence, developing critical arguments, organizing ideas in rational form. However, in my Collins lecture I said that the essay was usually a closed form, not allowing students to admit to confusion and uncertainty in their thinking, not allowing them to explore their ideas in imaginative and open-ended ways. The essay form had been dominated by scientific models of objectivity, and students often relied heavily on repetition of the views of their teachers or the critics; these views were often not in accord with their own personal response to the texts being studied. Images, ambiguity, dramatic tensions, all central features of twentieth-century modern literature, are not usually allowed, as the student is marked for coherence, order and objectivity.

I wanted all children in schools and students in higher education to be given the opportunity to write in a wide range of forms: diaries, formal letters, chronological accounts, reports, pamphlets, reviews (of books, television programmes, films or plays), essays, newspaper articles, biography, autobiography, poems, stories, playscripts. They should increasingly make their own decisions about their writing: what it is about, what form it should take, and to whom it is addressed. Instead of decontextualized exercises written only for perusal and marking by a teacher or lecturer, young people should write for a much wider range of purposes and audiences.

In the Collins lecture – and this was reflected in the National Curriculum Report – I also emphasized the importance of drafting, the *process* of writing as well as the final product. I wanted all pupils and students to revise and redraft their writing in response to their own or other people's reading of their texts. This collaboration should involve both their teachers and their peers. The normal university essay is handed in complete in final draft, and marked with a grade and a few sentences of comment from the tutor. This is not the way professional writers engage in their task, for almost invariably drafts are discussed and heavily revised after consultation. Language comes alive when our creative writings are intended for real readers, genuinely interested in what we have to say, responding in speech or writing to our failures and successes. I see no reason why these practices should not be introduced into higher education, even at postgraduate level. Large numbers of postgraduates in English suffer the same frustrations as I did at Pembroke. As they work in isolation from a real audience, their style often becomes clumsy and lifeless. I see no reason why, as in science, PhD students in English should not collaborate together and with their teachers on large-scale projects; drafts could be seen and evaluated by all members of the team, and individuals encouraged to contribute in a variety of forms, exploring meaning in language not prescribed and limited by the demands of the conventional essay. The loneliness of thesis writing as it is now practised leaves many students demoralized.

In the Ludwig Mond lecture at Manchester University, also in 1989, George Steiner talked about how scientists in their normal activities usually work in groups, undertaking research as a team. He spoke of how they can hope optimistically that they will solve problems, that by next week they may have moved forward in their understanding of their subject. In contrast, literary scholars often appear to be walking backwards, looking across history to the great works of Shakespeare or Racine or Goethe. As a result, teachers of the Arts often succumb to nostalgia for a lost golden age; this can develop into a passive frame of mind, a profound mistrust of any form of change in the literary canon or in their teaching practices.

We can overcome this passivity (and boredom in many students) only if we change our teaching practices, transforming our students from passive consumer to active maker. They should become members of a working community. They would look forward to next week, when they might publish a magazine, take part in a play, or complete a piece of writing which they would have discussed with friends and teachers. What at first might seem simple proposals to improve teaching methods involve important changes in cultural attitudes, new forms of collaboration and co-operation, new extensions of sympathy and imagination.

My period as Dean gave me extensive experience of chairing difficult committees. In 1988 I was to be given the opportunity to use these skills to determine how every child in State schools in England and Wales would be taught English. In this work I discovered a new confidence and finally exorcized my brother's ghost.

# 12
# *Kingman to Cox*

True ease in writing comes from art, not chance,
As those move easiest who have learned to dance.

*An Essay in Criticism*, Alexander Pope

The Kingman Committee was set up by Mr Kenneth Baker, Secretary of State for Education, to recommend a model of the English language, whether spoken or written, which would serve as the basis of how teachers are trained to understand how the English language works, and to recommend how the model should be made explicit to pupils. Often in 1987 I thought we would not reach any conclusions. We were such a strange assortment of people. Sir John Kingman had been trained as a mathematician. He proved an able chairman, but he knew little about the conflicts and passions that have riven the teaching of English language for decades; he had to feel his way forward slowly as these tensions surfaced among the Committee.

There were fourteen of us, in addition to Sir John. Professor Gillian Brown from Essex represented linguistics; she possessed a detailed and subtle understanding of the problems facing teachers of English language in schools. She was strongly supported by our Secretary, H.M.I. Peter Gannon, who had written books on language in schools. Antonia Byatt impressed by her considerable knowledge of English literature. She and I represented traditional views about the importance of literature; we were worried that the Committee would downgrade literature in the curriculum. We phoned each other regularly, wrote and criticized drafts, and met once at her home in Putney for detailed discussions.

242

There were some excellent teachers on the Committee: Leonard Ellis from North Riding College, Jeanne Strickland from Camden, Richard Knott from Berkshire, Pramila Le Hunte from North London. Then there were the writers: Patrick Kavanagh, Peter Levi, Robert Robinson and Keith Waterhouse. Waterhouse informed us that his main aim on the Committee was to ensure that inaccuracies such as 'ladie's' and 'potatoe's' were removed from signs in English streets. Robert Robinson, a man of considerable charm, was particularly useful at the drafting stage when he proved adept at spotting jargon and at reducing over-lengthy sentences.

At our early meetings (at Elizabeth House, near Waterloo) our discussions wandered all over the place, with anecdotes, meandering arguments and emotional polemics wasting precious time; we had to get to know each other. Gradually we began to formulate agreed ideas on language, particularly as we learnt to respect Gillian Brown's sharp mind and considerable knowledge of the subject. But Professor Henry Widdowson (from London University Institute of Education) proved a stumbling block. He feared we were being made to move too quickly; he continually requested that each point should be discussed at more length, that we should examine the assumptions that underpinned our assumptions. If in the closing stages he had not fallen ill with a back problem I do not think our Report would have been submitted. He declined to sign it, and composed a Note of Reservation. When the rest of us saw a draft of this Note we were distressed. It included some intemperate language about the inadequacies of the Report, which would surely have made headlines in the newspapers. It was arranged that representations should be made to him by letter and a visit. Fortunately Widdowson agreed to revise his draft, and it attracted little attention.

Immediately after the Report was published, Kenneth Baker summoned me to his room high up on the twelfth floor of Elizabeth House, overlooking Waterloo Station and the Thames. Behind a huge desk, flanked by several civil servants and Mrs Angela Rumbold, the Minister of State, he invited me to chair the National Curriculum English Working Group; when I accepted he looked extremely relieved. Afterwards I departed in the lift with Jane Benham, the young civil servant assigned to assist me in my task. My first words to her when we were alone were: 'We must be idiots to take this on.'

Our remit was to advise Mr Baker on attainment targets, programmes of study and associated assessment arrangements for English in the National Curriculum for the period of compulsory schooling, i.e. for *all* five- to sixteen-year-olds in State schools. English was defined as including both language and literature, and we were to take into account relevant aspects of drama, media studies, information technology and information handling. The framework for the National Curriculum had been set out in the Education Reform Act of 1988.

In my talks to teachers after our Report was published, I started by telling them that my first sentence would be inordinately long. I then read out the following:

> The English Working Group was asked to make pronouncements about all the major controversies in the teaching of English: how to teach reading (phonic methods or look and say?), how to teach spelling, handwriting and punctuation, how to promote enjoyment of reading, how to teach grammar and Standard English (spoken and written), how to cope with bilingual pupils, how to introduce drama, media studies and information technology into the curriculum, how to encourage speaking and listening, how to promote both imaginative writing and the ability to communicate in clear, vigorous English, how to devise a core curriculum for literature, how to assess all these things, how to advise on arrangements for children with special needs, and, last but not least, how to teach English in Wales.

Our first Report on the Primary stages, five- to eleven-year-olds, was due at the end of September, after only five months. Our final Report, dealing with all children from five to sixteen, was to be completed the following May. Neither I nor my Working Group was paid. I mention this as I have discovered that some teachers assume we all received fat fees. During the first weeks, as I woke at dawn in Cheadle Hulme and listened to the harsh screeching of our colony of magpies, I repeated to myself again and again that I must be an idiot to take this on.

But, in truth, I was wrong, and I enjoyed chairing this committee more than any other academic activity in which I have been engaged. I had been allocated an efficient back-up team from the civil service: Jane Benham (near the end of our work she was promoted and replaced by Martin Howarth), Michael Phipps and Jenny Bacon. They all impressed me with their loyalty to me and with their clarity of mind. After the stories that circulate about civil service chicanery, I can attest to the professionalism of my team. They were joined by Graham Frater, the Chief H.M. Inspector for English, more progressive in inclination than I am, but invaluable for his intimate understanding of the teaching profession. It was essential that our recommendations should arouse enthusiasm among the best teachers; if they disliked our plans, the National Curriculum would never be properly implemented in the class-room.

As chairman I like to move very quickly. At Manchester University I am gratified if when someone arrives a few minutes late I am already dealing with item five on the agenda. I am also very active in working for the results I want. In consultation with the civil servants, and with allies on the Committee, I would discuss in advance the problems of the next Committee session. We would establish clearly what we wished to achieve. There were therefore many long evening telephone calls. One common problem on such committees is that people who support you in private fall silent when the debate gets fierce. I had to persuade members that they must speak, and I had to rehearse them – tactfully – on the phone the night before. I controlled the final drafts, and this gives a chairman great power.

The Working Group itself was very small, only nine, including myself; we immediately struck up a rapport which carried us through without major upset until our work was completed. Professor Mike Stubbs, University of London Institute of Education, provided heavyweight intellectual backing; he prepared first drafts of chapters on knowledge about language, information technology and media studies. Linda Cookson, Senior Tutor, Central School of Speech and Drama, London, drafted our recommendations on drama. Professor David Skilton, of the new University of Wales College of Cardiff, coped with the Welsh dimension. Di Billups, Head of Broughton Junior School, South Humberside, Roger

Samways, Adviser for English and Drama, Dorset, and Brian Slough, Deputy Head, Kettering Boys' School, Northamptonshire, all contributed to our discussions and drafting sessions their considerable experience of the realities of the class-room. I paid a visit to Di Billups's school in Humberside, and found the discipline and structured programmes of learning not so very different from what I remembered at Nunsthorpe. But the encouragement of informal talk and imaginative writing, the colourful displays of children's work and the variety of books in the library reflected the good influences of progressive education – advantages I missed at my own primary school.

Another member of my original Working Group was Dr Charles Suckling, formerly General Manager (Research and Technology) with I.C.I. I had come to know and admire Charles when he was a member of the Kingman Committee. He was chosen to represent the business community, but his tolerance and considerable intelligence made him completely at home with teachers and academics. At the same time, his sharp, clear mind put all our assumptions to the test, particularly at the drafting stages.

Like the Kingman Committee, we met in Elizabeth House, the Department of Education and Science building, designed so incompetently by the discredited John Poulson that on hot days, with the windows open, sudden clatterings from the railway yards drowned our talk. We proceeded most expeditiously when we met for weekends at a conference centre at Lane End, near High Wycombe, starting after dinner on Friday and finishing with lunch on Sunday. We broke up into small groups to consider different curriculum problems, and to draft attainment targets, a very difficult task. On one occasion I visited each group; discovering that I was getting in their way I took myself off for a swim in Lane End's luxurious, heated indoor swimming pool. As I floated on my back, alone in the warm water, I congratulated myself that I had learnt the art of delegation.

Apparently Mr Baker had met Roald Dahl, the popular children's story writer, at a party; impressed by his opinions, Mr Baker invited him to join my Working Group. Roald Dahl attended the first meeting, which lasted over three hours. He wrote to me afterwards to explain that he had never served on a committee before, and that after a life of privacy spent mainly alone in his own room at work on his books he could not adapt. He would read the committee papers, and send comments, but he could not face any more meetings.

Very soon I realized that Roald Dahl was not in tune with my English Working Group's proposals (for example, he seemed to be advocating *no* advice from the teacher in a child's selection of books). I knew that if he expressed his adverse opinions to journalists when we reported in September he would dominate the headlines, and the Report might be irretrievably damaged. I wrote to Mr Baker to propose that he should tactfully suggest to Mr Dahl that, as he was not attending the Working Group's meetings, he should resign. I explained the danger of a September confrontation. A few days later Mr Baker was hosting a dinner to thank the Kingman Committee for their work. After coffee he drew me aside, quietly admitted I was right, and agreed that Roald Dahl must withdraw. 'Would you handle it?' he asked. Amused by Mr Baker's diplomatic skills, I composed a letter, and luckily by the end of July Mr Dahl had sent us a sensible letter of resignation.

After this letter was received I managed, with some difficulty, to persuade Mrs Rumbold and Mr Baker to invite Dr Katharine Perera, Senior Lecturer in Linguistics at Manchester University, to act as a replacement. They were worried that a new member might delay our work, and cause divisions. I had known Katharine for many years; she had chaired our House Committee when I was Dean of the Faculty of Arts. In common with all members of the Kingman Committee, I had been impressed by her presentation when she appeared before us to answer questions. She combined considerable teaching experience with class-room research on the teaching of English. She provided exactly the kind of expertise we needed, particularly as I had no training in linguistics. Angela Rumbold and Kenneth Baker, of course, knew very little about the teaching of English, and had little conception of the difficulties involved in preparing a National Curriculum. During my time as chairman of the Working Group I met the Secretary of State on only a few brief occasions, and was given no opportunity to discuss the curriculum in detail with either him or Mrs Rumbold.

Between committee meetings Katharine Perera and I often met

in the Stopford Room at the University to discuss problems over lunch. When the final draft was due for immediate return I joined her one hot Sunday in her garden at High Legh, near Knutsford. We worked at a fantastic rate, making last-minute alterations as we discovered, to our dismay, more and more mistakes. Her husband, Suria, served regular pots of tea and scones as time rushed by. Just before midnight I was standing outside her house waiting anxiously for the courier service (at a cost of fifty-eight pounds) which would ensure that our corrections arrived at Elizabeth House before breakfast the next day; they could then be included in the final version to be shown immediately to Mr Baker.

I found all this activity remarkably fulfilling. After my Black Paper battles, I now had the opportunity to determine how English would be taught in every State school in England and Wales, to ensure that a true balance was achieved between traditional and progressive modes of teaching.

I wanted our first Report, published in November 1988, to be written in a lively style, to avoid bureaucratic jargon, and to impart enthusiasm for literature. To attract interest I included names of specific authors. We printed a list of writers who might figure in the library of a good primary school, but made it clear that this list was not intended to be comprehensive: 'We stress again that we are not recommending as set texts the books of the authors listed.' Their books, we said, met our criteria for a primary school library, but 'we have no doubt that so too do those of many other authors who are favourites with children and teachers'. We left freedom for teachers to choose.

In our list of authors we did not include Enid Blyton or Captain W. E. Johns, author of the Biggles stories. Many teachers consider these two authors racist, and some find Enid Blyton's use of language narrow and undemanding. The media commentary on this first Report concentrated on this exclusion, and I was pilloried in the *Sunday Times* for blacklisting Enid Blyton's Noddy. In the tabloid press I became the villain who put his knife into Noddy and his boot into Biggles. Mr Baker told me he thought the decision to exclude Enid Blyton had proved a brilliant ploy to attract attention away from our more serious and controversial proposals.

In our final Report we decided to excise this list of authors because, as we explained, it attracted so much unfortunate attention. We recommended that Shakespeare should figure in all syllabuses for a National Curriculum, but that teachers must be free to choose which play or plays are studied. In the crucial programmes of study for reading for key stages three and four (ages eleven/twelve to fourteen and fourteen to sixteen) we included the following vital paragraph about the importance of the English cultural heritage:

> Pupils need to be aware of the richness of contemporary writing, but they should also be introduced to pre-twentieth century literature. Teachers should introduce pupils to some of the works which have been most influential in shaping and refining the English language and its literature – for example, the Authorized Version of the Bible, Wordsworth's poems, or Dickens's novels. In particular, they should give pupils the opportunity to gain some experience of the works of Shakespeare. (16.31)

We deliberately kept these examples to the minimum to avoid controversy, and to leave teachers free to use their professional judgment in selecting texts suitable for the needs of their own pupils.

On this occasion there were objections that we should have included more names. What about Jane Austen, Dr Sheila Lawlor demanded, in the response to our Report sent in to the National Curriculum Council by the right-wing Centre for Policy Studies. We knew that if we mentioned such additional names, even only as examples, the media would highlight these, and demand to know why other names were excluded. If we published a list of set texts, their names would be engraved in stone, and the canon would become unchangeable, reflecting out-of-date literary and social opinions. When I was at Nunsthorpe and Wintringham, the canon would have included Kinglake's *Eothen*, Thomas Hughes's *Tom Brown's Schooldays*, Charles Kingsley's *The Water Babies* and the essays of Charles Lamb, all little read by the young today.

A major problem in writing our Report was to prevent it from being miscontrued by the media, always deliberately intent on stirring up trouble. In this task of stopping the newspapers from distorting our recommendations we were singularly unsuccessful. Perhaps it was impossible to suppress their determination to misread in the search for sensational copy. When the Report was finalized by the National Curriculum Council, Jane Austen and the Brontës were added to our list, and I was very happy with this.

My Working Group began its task by recognizing that teachers of English vary widely in their views of the purpose of teaching English. In our second chapter, therefore, we listed five different 'views' of the subject, insisting that they are not the only possible views, that they are not sharply distinguishable, and that they are certainly not mutually exclusive. These are the five 'views' representing, I believe, the balance I had been advocating for so many years:

1. A 'personal growth' view focuses on the child; it emphasizes the relationship between language and learning in the individual child, and the role of literature in developing children's imaginative and aesthetic lives.

2. A 'cross-curricular' view focuses on the school; it emphasizes that all teachers (of English and other subjects) have a responsibility to help children with the language demands of different subjects on the school curriculum: otherwise areas of the curriculum may be closed to them.

3. An 'adult needs' view focuses on communication outside the school; it emphasizes the responsibility of English teachers to prepare children for the language demands of adult life, including the workplace, in a fast-changing world. Children need to learn to deal with the day-to-day demands of spoken language and of print; they also need to be able to write clearly, appropriately and effectively.

4. A 'cultural heritage' view stresses the responsibility of schools to lead children to an appreciation of those works of literature that have been widely regarded as amongst the finest in the language.

5. A 'cultural analysis' view gives greatest importance to the role of English in helping children towards a critical

understanding of the world and cultural environment in which they live. Children should know about the processes by which meanings are conveyed, and about the ways in which print and other media carry values.

The 'cultural heritage' and 'cultural analysis' views led us into central disagreements about the canon, about the choice and treatment of texts. My Conservative friends wished to keep at the centre of the school curriculum the well-known traditional canon from Chaucer to T.S. Eliot. The most dynamic English today, however, is often found outside England: from Saul Bellow, Alice Walker and Toni Morrison from the United States, Anita Desai from India, Nadine Gordimer from South Africa, V.S. Naipaul from Trinidad, Chinua Achebe from Nigeria, for example. All pupils, we argued, need to be aware of the richness of experience offered by writing in English from different countries. They are thus introduced to the ideas and feelings of countries different from their own, and so we shall help the cause of racial tolerance. In Britain today our multi-cultural society must be taken into account by anyone establishing texts for a national curriculum.

So we wanted to preserve our cultural heritage, and yet also awaken pupils to the vitality of literature in English written in other countries. We were also worried that too often British schools concentrate in their choice of texts almost entirely on the contemporary novel. We put forward *three* criteria for teachers in their choice of texts for a national curriculum. Programmes of study should be constructed to give all pupils the opportunity:

a.  to enjoy work in a wide range of literary forms. They should read a selection of material that includes short stories, novels, plays and poems. They should also be given the opportunity to encounter types of writing drawn from a variety of other genres – such as letters, biographies, autobiographies, diaries, film or TV scripts and travel books and other non-fictional literature;

b.  to encounter and find pleasure in literary works written in English – particularly new works – from different parts of the world;

c.   to gain pleasure and critical awareness from the study of pre-twentieth century writing. As many pupils as possible should have contact with some of the great writing which has been influential in shaping our language and culture. Rich and rewarding as the study of contemporary material undoubtedly is, it should not dominate in the class-room to the exclusion of all else. In particular, every pupil should be given some experience of the plays or poetry of Shakespeare. Whether this is through the study, viewing or performance of whole plays or of selected poems or scenes should be entirely at the discretion of the teacher.

In writing that last sentence we were very much aware that we were recommending knowledge of Shakespeare for *every* pupil, including the bottom forty per cent in ability; this would often best be achieved by introducing them to dramatic performances either in the theatre or on film.

Rex Gibson of the 'Shakespeare and Schools' project at the Cambridge Institute of Education visited the Working Group to explain his methods for teaching Shakespeare to children of low ability. He divided the committee into two groups, placed opposite each other, and made us curse each other, providing us with quotations from the words of Prospero and Caliban in *The Tempest*. Soon loud shouts of 'poisonous slave', 'hag-seed', and 'a south-west blow on ye and blister you all o'er' resounded down the corridors of Elizabeth House. I hoped the suppressed feelings of the Working Group were not being revealed.

Our most difficult task was to formulate the right proposals for the teaching of grammar. Our problem was that many older people felt very deeply that the teaching of Latinate grammar in the period before 1950 underpinned the stability, order and discipline which they considered so lacking in our society today. In a speech just before the Kingman Committee's deliberations, Norman Tebbit, previously a member of Mrs Thatcher's Cabinet, pronounced that the decline in the teaching of grammar in the 1950s and 1960s was responsible for football hooliganism. Such members of the older generations reacted with anger to the Kingman Committee's arguments that there must be no return to teaching about language based on Latin. A middle-aged teacher told me that when he was at school he was cuffed for writing 'a dilapidated wooden shed'. '*Lapis* means a stone,' proclaimed the teacher, tweaking his ear. 'You foolish boy; you can't call something wooden "dilapidated".' Katharine Perera told me her Professor at Bedford College in the 1960s insisted that 'companion' must be used only for a person with whom one eats (*com panis* with bread, food).

In the first chapter of the Kingman Report we included this crucial paragraph:

> Nor do we see it as part of our task to plead for a return to old-fashioned grammar teaching and learning by rote. We have been impressed by the evidence we have received that this gave an inadequate account of the English language by treating it virtually as a branch of Latin, and constructing a rigid prescriptive code rather than a dynamic description of language in use. It was also ineffective as a means of developing a command of English in all its manifestations. Equally, at the other extreme, we reject the belief that any notion of correct or incorrect use of language is an affront to personal liberty. We also reject the belief that knowing how to use terminology in which to speak of language is undesirable. Language is, as a matter of observable fact, plainly governed by a series of conventions related to the varying audiences, contexts and purposes of its use. Successful communication depends upon a recognition and accurate use of the rules and conventions. Command of these rules and conventions is more likely to increase the freedom of the individual than diminish it. (1.11)

My Working Group's task was to build on these recommendations, and to describe in detail what children should know about language. The rage with which right-wingers greeted the Kingman Report warned us of the pitfalls ahead; we therefore decided to include detailed chapters explaining our recommendations on grammar and Standard English.

Our difficulty was that the term 'grammar' is used today in different senses. In everyday usage, 'grammar' is associated with correct Standard English. But linguists use the term differently. They use it first to refer to ways in which words are combined to make sentences (in any dialect); second, to label the body of statements they use to write about the language as they attempt to make explicit the implicit knowledge possessed by all native speakers of English. If we advocated the teaching of grammar, without such explanations, many teachers would think we were in favour of a return to Latinate grammar. For grammar to be relevant to English teaching, we explained, it should be a form of grammar which can describe language in use. It should be concerned with all levels of discourse, from the syntax of sentences through to the organization of substantial texts. We advocated a form of grammar which would be able to describe the considerable differences between written and spoken Standard English, and which would form part of a wider syllabus of language study. It would include the history of the language, the status of dialect, and the social implications of Standard English.

After these explanations we recommended that all children should be taught grammar, as we had defined the subject, and that, for example, even little children should be expected to use words such as 'noun', 'verb' or 'adjective' when discussing their own writing. Unfortunately when our first Report was published and sent out for consultation, it was introduced with comments by Mr Baker. In particular, he asked that our proposals for attainments in writing 'should be strengthened to give greater emphasis to pupils' mastery of the grammatical structure of the English language'. Apparently Mr Baker was leaning over backwards to satisfy his right-wing constituency, and, even more important to him, the Prime Minister. I was furious when I read these words, for they showed no understanding of the different uses of the term 'grammar', and they gave the education journalists just the story they needed.

In the London *Evening Standard* a photograph of me accompanied headlines proclaiming that Mr Baker's hard man had gone soft on grammar. The *Daily Telegraph* took quotations out of context that would annoy their readers, and so managed to convey an idea of the Report totally contrary to what it actually said. In the Valerie Grove interview in the *Sunday Times* (20 November 1988) the headline read: 'In plain words can a blimp turn woolly liberal?' Before I gave this interview to Valerie Grove I told her that I would charge a fee (I never received payment for any interview I gave to the Press). The fee, I told her, was that she should quote two crucial sentences from the Report, where we advocate the teaching of Standard English and the use of linguistic terminology. She dutifully obliged, and this prominent newspaper feature to some degree helped a large body of readers to hear what we actually said. The *Evening Standard* (17 November) followed its first story with a vituperative article by John Rae, previously headmaster of Westminster, a leading public school. This provided an excellent example of the ignorance of many highly educated older people. He wrote:

> I thought it was correct to write we were and incorrect to write we was. I did not realise it was just a question of dialect; I thought it was a question of grammar or, if you do not like that word, of logic. You cannot use a singular form of the verb with a plural pronoun.

Rae's appeal to logic was mistaken: *you were* is both singular and plural in Standard English. Moreover, other verbs in Standard English use the same form with both singular and plural pronouns: e.g. *I go, we go; I wanted, we wanted; I might, we might.* The verb *to be* is highly irregular in Standard English, and much more regular in non-standard dialects. John Rae did not understand that logic is a feature not of the grammar of a language or dialect, but of arguments in sentences and in texts. It is people in their use of language who are logical or illogical, not languages or dialects themselves.

The Press took out of context such explanations, particularly our insistence that dialects obey their own rules of grammar, and should not be despised. Not surprisingly the tabloid newspapers pretended this meant that children could speak as they pleased, and there was no need to speak and write Standard English. During the resulting furore I realized once again that newspaper coverage of major issues often bears little relation to what has been actually said or written. This particular controversy threw a clear light on the snobbery and arrogance implicit in the English class system. To suggest that those who speak in dialect should not be treated with disdain shocked those upper-class people who took their superiority in their use of language for granted.

The excellent coverage of our Report in the *Independent* and *The Times Educational Supplement* showed that when teachers actually read what we said there would be much support for our proposals. We also received strong support from the National Association of Teachers of English. After hard battles behind the scenes with the National Curriculum Council, our recommendations for the teaching of knowledge about language were incorporated into the final Orders that decreed what would happen in every State school. Mr Baker's irrelevant words about grammar were quietly forgotten.

We divided the English curriculum into three sections: speaking and listening, reading, and writing. In our first Report we recommended that the three profile components, as they were called, should be weighted equally in the assessment process. In his comments Mr Baker agreed that this was appropriate for seven-year-olds, but proposed that for eleven-year-olds greater emphasis should be given to the key skills of reading and writing. When the document was sent out for consultation, teachers, advisers and inspectors came down almost unanimously on our side. As the Working Group continued its deliberations on the secondary school curriculum, I was informed privately that Mr Baker would give way on this issue as long as the weighting for sixteen-year-olds gave more emphasis to reading and writing. I was happy to agree with this because it seemed to me that teachers were not ready for all the problems of assessment of speaking and listening for pupils aged fourteen and sixteen; for this profile component to be given a twenty per cent weighting would be a considerable step forward. To my surprise my Working Group insisted after a lively debate that we kept the weighting at thirty-three and a third per cent for fourteen-year-olds. When the Report was published I was amazed to discover that Mr Baker had accepted this proposal. A few months later, after the consultation process was complete, the National Curriculum Council recommended that this one-third weighting should also apply to the testing of sixteen-year-olds. Unfortunately since then this weighting has been gradually reduced.

In my subsequent talks to teachers I claimed that our recommendations on speaking would transform the English national character. The traditional view of the Englishman as reserved, taciturn and silent ('an Englishman needs time', sings Eartha Kitt) will become a thing of the past. As at Berkeley, English university students of the future will take it for granted that they must converse in their tutorials and seminars. The young man I recall so vividly from my tutorial at Hull in 1966 after I returned from California will be woken from his lethargy. Such changes in the curriculum *will* change our national identity; not surprisingly, the Press allocated most space to silly features on Enid Blyton's Noddy, in most cases failing to notice this revolutionary proposal about speaking and listening.

I was also pleased that the Working Group put so much emphasis on the vital role that drama should play in primary and secondary schools. But my greatest satisfaction, as I explained in my last chapter, came from our recommendation that children should practise the art of writing in a variety of forms. It has been my privilege to bring into reality Ted Hughes's dream that all children should be makers.

When the final draft was sent to Mr Baker he discussed it with the civil servants. I was not invited and I was never given the opportunity to explain to him our rationale. The meeting, so I understand, was like something from the television series *Yes, Minister*. When Mr Baker read out a section and made unfavourable comments, the civil servants stayed silent. When he found a passage, on spelling, for example, of which he approved, they all responded vociferously, pointing out to him similar material on other pages. Eventually he agreed to the publication of the Report, as long as it was printed back-to-front, with the statements of attainment and programmes of study in chapters 15 to 17 first, and the rationale in chapters 1 to 14 last. I found this hilarious, but I was also very cross. I decided to keep quiet in case my objections led Mr Baker to refuse to send out the whole Report to teachers.

The Report was sent to Mrs Thatcher's office with summaries

and references prepared by the civil servants at the Department of Education and Science. They naturally drew attention to our firm proposals for the teaching of spelling, punctuation, grammar and written and spoken Standard English. Mrs Thatcher agreed to allow the Report to be sent out for consultation, but asked for one alteration. In the attainment targets for Writing we had put: 'Use Standard English, where appropriate'. The Prime Minister asked for 'where appropriate' to be deleted. I presume she feared – rightly, I suspect – that in some schools where children spoke in dialect the teachers might decide it was never appropriate. I rewrote the sentence as follows: 'Use Standard English (except in contexts where non-standard forms are needed for literary purposes, e.g. in dialogue, in a story or play-script).' This was accepted, and printed in the final version. To my surprise the civil servants informed me that the revision went back to the Prime Minister, and that she herself checked it was satisfactory. I was impressed by her meticulous attention to detail.

During the fourteen months I chaired the English Working Group, I worked harder than at any other time in my life. During a typical day I would move rapidly from chairing a committee on Manchester University library finance, to a seminar on T.S. Eliot, to another urgent phone call about the latest draft from Jane Benham. Almost every week I travelled down to London, often staying the night with Tony Dyson in Hampstead. Now it is all over I am very proud of what is popularly called the Cox Report. It has created a consensus among teachers of English which should influence class-room teaching for generations. The Report has also given me deep personal satisfaction for another reason. I do not mind that Conservative newspapers now label me as a woolly liberal. For twenty years whenever I appeared before an audience of teachers they began by presuming that I was some kind of right-wing fanatic, stuck in the educational philosophy of the 1930s. On such occasions it was a common experience for me to be drawn aside by teachers afterwards to say they were surprised to find me so different from the Black Paper ogre they read about in the newspapers. During the last three years I have addressed large audiences of teachers and advisers in London, Cambridge, Oxford, Manchester, Exeter, Reading and Liverpool. They tell me how much they admire the Report. And they treat me as a human being, not a caricature. I now appear as I am: conservative (in my belief that great books express universal values), liberal (in my attitudes to class and race), radical (in my schemes to increase access to higher education) and progressive (in my advocacy of new teaching methods in universities). During the Black Paper years of struggle I was often told that once the media have attached a false label to an individual it sticks for ever. Because of the Cox Report my right-wing label has finally been discarded.

# *Postscript*

'It does not have fantasy, intuition or imagination.'
Garry Kasparov, after trouncing the most
highly rated chess computer, Deep Thought

After the National Curriculum English Report was greeted with such enthusiasm by teachers, in my fantasy I dreamt I might rest on my laurels, and retire quietly with Jean to buy a little house in the Alps near Annecy. Unfortunately I was soon reminded that education battles are never finally won.

The first person to cause me trouble was the Prince of Wales. Only a few days after our Report was published in 1989 he complained in an offhand remark at a Business in the Community function that English was taught so 'bloody' badly that even his own office staff could not speak or write it properly. This made headline news, and some Conservative newspapers suggested that he was responding to what he thought were inadequacies in our proposals for National Curriculum English. The furore soon died down. In September, however, I was alarmed to hear from an H.M.I. that the Prince on 19 December, when presenting the Thomas Cranmer Schools Prize, intended to deliver a major speech on the teaching of English. I feared that if he attacked the National Curriculum he would cause irreparable harm; I also suspected that his knowledge and that of his advisers derived from the media rather than from a reading of the actual Report. I felt I should not sit back and do nothing. I wrote a confidential letter to his Private Secretary, suggesting that he should draw the Prince's attention to what we actually said, particularly to our firm recommendations for the teaching of spelling, punctuation and grammar.

To my surprise, ten days later I received a reply from the

Deputy Private Secretary saying that the Prince was 'interested in pursuing the points which you made in your letter and wonders whether you might be prepared to contribute some passages for use in his speech'. I responded immediately, sending paragraphs which stressed the dedication of teachers in inner-city schools, and which drew attention to the National Curriculum's actual recommendations. The Prince used this material in his speech, saying he did not envy 'the task that teachers have, particularly in inner-city schools . . . They need our sympathy and support in an exhausting task.' He continued:

There is now, I think, a growing consensus on what needs to be taught and it is heartening to witness the widespread recognition of this in the new National Curriculum for English. It emphasizes the importance of spelling, listening, reading and writing. It recognises the fact that competence in English is a key to success in all other subjects in the curriculum and a pre-requisite for adult life.

These words attracted little attention, although they were reproduced in some newspapers. I was happy that no damage was done. When friends congratulated me on the Prince's support for the National Curriculum, I did not like to reveal that I had drafted these sentences myself.

In September the following year I was somewhat taken aback when I received an invitation to attend a 'brainstorming' session with the Prince and 'a small number of people whose views on language and education he respects'. We were to meet at his home at Highgrove in Gloucestershire from 10.00 to 12.00 on 2 November. The Prince was thinking of following up his Thomas Cranmer address with a 'second barrel' in the form of a further speech. After this seminar at Highgrove the event was written up in April 1991, in a four-page news item in the *Sunday Times*. I do not know how they obtained their material. When a few days before this feature was published a reporter rang me, he possessed full details of the people present and the tenor of the discussion.

The main participants at the seminar were Sir Peter Parker, previously chairman of British Rail, Anne Sloman, a BBC producer,

George Walden, a Conservative MP, and Eric Anderson, head of Eton, once the Prince's English master at Gordonstoun. I stayed the previous night at the Close Hotel in Tetbury, and then travelled by taxi the few miles to Highgrove, saddened by the necessary security when the taxi was searched and then watched by cameras as we drove through the grounds to the house. Harold Brown, the Prince's butler, served coffee, and then we sat in comfortable arm-chairs for the seminar. Many friends have asked me about the furnishings, decorations and pictures in the Prince's drawing-room. As I concentrated hard on my ideas about education, I hardly noticed, and in my memory the surroundings remain a blur.

I felt embarrassed because although I concurred with much in the Thomas Cranmer speech, I disagreed sharply with the Prince's unfair contrasts between the English of Shakespeare and the Authorized Version of the Bible and today's sloppy colloquial language in tabloids and on television. He declared that our language had become 'impoverished'. This is simply not true. Language today has not declined from a golden age in the early seventeenth century, and this kind of nostalgia is not helpful. In the poetry of T.S. Eliot, W.B. Yeats or Robert Lowell, or in the fiction of D.H. Lawrence, Saul Bellow, Toni Morrison or Nadine Gordimer, among a host of major writers, literature in English in the twentieth century has achieved wonders, both in Britain and other countries.

Fortunately the seminar kept away from these issues. We tactfully but firmly pointed out that it was extraordinary that the seminar included no teacher from State schools, and the Prince certainly made sure in subsequent weeks that he took such advice. He was very conscious that in his position he can have very little real 'feel' for the day-to-day problems of a teacher in an inner-city comprehensive. I wondered what forms of politeness were appropriate for such an occasion. I am used to fierce arguments, no quarter given, which were typical of my years at Cambridge. I was uncertain how to respond when George Walden vehemently attacked the lack of idealism among teachers in State schools. I was angry to be made to listen to such nonsense; I am proud that the strangeness of the occasion did not prevent me from making sharp rejoinders. After the seminar the Prince made an impassioned defence of Shakespeare in a speech on the 426th anniversary of the poet's birth; but so far there have been no further contributions to the debates about the teaching of English.

Meanwhile Conservative politicians were interfering once again in educational matters they often misunderstood. Extreme right-wing views, out of touch with real class-rooms, began to prevail. After my Report was submitted I heard nothing more from Conservative ministers, except for a formal letter of thanks from Mr Baker. Copies of the Report were sent to schools, but as it was not published for sale in bookshops it was rapidly becoming unobtainable. To make it available to parents, scholars and future teachers I published *Cox on Cox* (1991), the complete Report edited by me with detailed comments on the controversies and the political background.

When Kenneth Clarke became Secretary of State for Education, my decision to publish was shown to be wise. In January 1992 the recommendations of the National Curriculum Working Groups on Music and Art were radically altered by the National Curriculum Council, under the chairmanship of David Pascall, carefully selected by Mr Clarke. The two chairmen of the Working Groups, Sir John Manduell, Principal of Manchester College of Music, and Lord Renfrew, Master of Jesus College, Cambridge, protested, but apparently to little avail. Petitions from famous people in the music world, such as Simon Rattle, were treated by Mr Clarke with scant respect. I was relieved that my Report had been validated by the Statutory Orders of the House of Commons, but I remain fearful that in the future our proposals will be emasculated either by changes in the Orders or by inappropriate arrangements for testing and assessment of pupils.

My decision to publish *Cox on Cox* was also proved right when in June 1991 the Conservative government decided to suppress the publication of 500 pages of materials designed to help teachers improve their pupils' knowledge about language. The government had spent £21 million on the Language in the National Curriculum (LINC) project, mostly on teacher training, but now refused to pay for the materials to be available in the class-room. Presumably the ministers wanted a return to old-fashioned teaching of grammar. Professor Ronald Carter, the leader of the project, protested vigorously, but he was even denied the right to find a commercial publisher for his work. The LINC materials tried to put into practice my own Working Group's recommendations for the teaching of grammar and knowledge about language. From Kingman to Cox to LINC a revolution had taken place in schools, with teachers after so many years of neglect now enthusiastic about new ways of teaching English language. The suppression of these class-room materials was a great blow to the morale of the best teachers of English in the profession.

This kind of censorship made my commitment to *Critical Quarterly* of great importance, and I am glad that in the 1990s I remain involved in editing the journal. Such little magazines are vital for the free dissemination of new ideas. By the late 1980s I had been editing *C.Q.* for almost thirty years, and we needed new blood. Younger people must take over, and I could not expect them simply to replicate my views. I persuaded Kate Pahl, a young graduate from Cambridge, and Colin MacCabe, to assume the main burden of the editing. Colin MacCabe became famous in the early 1980s when his appointment as Lecturer at Cambridge University was terminated supposedly because he was a 'structuralist'. His dismissal provoked a huge newspaper debate about 'structuralism', and how it was upsetting the traditional values of English scholarship. Colin was fixed into a stereotype. For him the mid-1960s in Paris were an astonishingly creative period which rocked the foundations of both the humanities and the social sciences. In a recent *C.Q.* essay he wrote: 'Lacan, Barthes, Derrida, Foucault, Althusser: the names roll off the tongue like a summons to some epic battle of the intellect.' In the 1980s we witnessed a great shift in our concepts of English national identity, as feminism and multi-cultural values transformed scholarly thinking. But MacCabe's response to this ferment of ideas has always been independent; recent issues of *C.Q.* (now published by Blackwell's) have been devoted to evaluating these cultural changes. Colin MacCabe (who teaches part-time at Pittsburgh University and also works for the British Film Institute) believes that the traditional canon of English literature still needs to be studied and evaluated, for it is crucial to our understanding of our contemporary situation. Only ridicule and scorn is appropriate, he says, for those 'who claim they are serving the class struggle by teaching students not to read Shakespeare'.

We often hold our editorial meetings in the Groucho Club, where wine and ideas flow freely. Colin is a large, ebullient man who laughs a great deal. His liberalism (seen in his support for Salman Rushdie), his festivities, make him a splendid editor to continue *C.Q.* traditions.

My heroes and heroines are the class-room teachers in State schools. In the 1960s and 1970s many were badly trained by utopian colleges of education lecturers, deceived by egalitarian ideas unsuited to real class-rooms, particularly in the inner cities. They are put under immense strain, and the crisis in education continues. I think of the hundreds of teachers who wrote to the *C.Q.* office in 1969 to thank us for speaking up for the disciplines of study which educationalists and politicians, like Edward Short, were pressing them to abandon. The Plowden Report of 1967 caused so much damage because, as I have explained, it claimed that research had proved the traditional teachers were wrong, and that new child-centred learning would raise standards. There was no validity to such claims.

Today the best teachers have escaped from such excesses, but in 1991 Professor Robin Alexander's Leeds Report showed that too many ordinary class-room teachers still have too low expectations of their pupils. He led a team which surveyed what teachers and pupils actually did in 231 primary schools. They found that excessive reliance on unshaped discovery methods meant that children wasted considerable amounts of time during each working day. This is not a minor matter. In a press interview, Professor Alexander talked about how schools have placed too much emphasis on 'exploratory learning':

> There is now overwhelming evidence that some of these central beliefs are questionable, to say the least, and that many of the most widely endorsed practices simply don't work. As a result, millions of children have had a raw deal – they've wasted such a hell of a lot of time.

This is exactly what was said in the Black Papers. For twenty-five years, standards in State education have been unnecessarily low, and this is still true today.

In the *T.E.S.* on 31 January 1992, Professor Alexander wrote that a 'new consensus now seems within reach, but it is certainly not a soft option'. There are now many excellent class-rooms where formal instruction is balanced with exploratory learning, and the best hope for the 1990s is that such good sense will lead to a transformation of class-rooms in English primary schools.

Comprehensive schools still create major problems, however. In the 1960s the Labour Party's plans for comprehensive schools were introduced thoughtlessly and without proper research. Objections to comprehensives still provoke rage among their supporters. Their criticisms of the inadequacy of the eleven-plus selection system, their passion for justice for all children, deserve every sympathy. As I have shown, however, in many places the comprehensive system does not work, mainly because the ethos of each school depends so much on its neighbourhood.

The progressive ideology of the 1960s, still dominant in some comprehensives, is ambiguous and philosophically inconsistent. I have already quoted G.H. Bantock's essay in *Black Paper 1975*. The central confusion, he says, is that progressives believe in the importance of the individual; this should persuade them to allow able children to advance as fast as possible. They also believe in equality, however, and this leads to collectivism, uniformity, instinctive faith in non-streaming. This affects both the able children and those without commitment to academic studies. Many of them succumb to peer group pressure, and leave school at sixteen. At the same time the discipline problems of such schools reflect the dissatisfactions of all pupils. Recently a teacher told me how he took a group of secondary school pupils, including several of low academic attainment, on a trip to Spain where they enjoyed well-organized outdoor courses in swimming, canoeing and windsurfing. Children who were recalcitrant and surly in their class-room changed quite remarkably, becoming enthusiastic and co-operative. Children only learn if they are motivated to do so, and schools must adapt to their real needs and aspirations.

How should this be done? The arrangement of schools now varies so much in different parts of Britain that it is difficult to put forward a simple programme of reform. We need to move towards a system in which children at the age of thirteen or so are offered various choices, academic or vocational. These might be in separate schools, or in the same large comprehensive. Teachers should agree with parents and children on the appropriate courses. But opportunities should be created for transfer at later ages. Children at sixteen who at an earlier stage chose vocational or technological courses should be able to change their minds and opt for a more academic programme, and vice versa. As different areas in Britain make plans for the future of their schools, these should be the guiding principles. We urgently need to persuade more young people to stay on at school after the age of sixteen, and this can only be achieved if we offer them appropriate programmes of study.

After the Conservatives won the Election in April 1992, Mr John Patten, the new Secretary of State for Education, devoted his first Press conference to the problems of comprehensive schools. He announced that schools will specialize increasingly in fields of learning, rather than revert to the eleven-plus grammar school form of selection. Greater diversity in schools will come from those concentrating in specific areas, such as music, technology, languages or the arts, in addition to delivering the National Curriculum. I welcome this proposal. It should provide children with a flexible variety of courses adapted to their individual needs and abilities.

Further opportunities should be available later in life. I am in favour of the introduction of modular degrees, as at Berkeley. All polytechnics and universities should retain their present full-time three- or four-year degree structures, but as an alternative allow students to build a degree brick by brick, with modules at one institution valid for transfer to another. Part-time study should be common, with older students who start degrees at evening classes allowed, if they wish, to transfer to full-time study. Open University modules could easily be fitted into a national plan. In many ways we all remain half-educated throughout our lives, and new educational opportunities should be available even after we have retired.

I have described the wasted postgraduate years I spent at Pembroke College, in almost complete isolation from other students and teachers who might have discussed with me my thesis on Henry James. This is still happening in some universities.

Postgraduate degrees should also be modular, with students working together in seminars and sharing their drafts with each other. All these innovations are already being introduced in some institutions of higher education, and should become the norm.

I look forward to a vast expansion in higher education, and, of course, that will cost money.

I have long been in favour of some kind of National Council of Teachers, charged with maintaining high standards in education, and raising public esteem for the profession. Teachers will only gain proper financial support when their professional stature attracts more public recognition. Millions of children are still getting a raw deal in our State schools, and we must invest in their future.

Behind all these arguments about resources and organization lies the question of how far we retain the faith of Matthew Arnold in the civilizing power of the Humanities. My life-long enthusiasm for teaching literature testifies to my own commitment. I still hold to the words Tony Dyson and I wrote in 1968 at the end of our editorial for the tenth anniversary issue of *Critical Quarterly*: 'Great literature helps to keep alive our most subtle and delicate feelings, our capacity for wonder, and our faith in human individuality.'

While I was preparing this book Jean and I watched a brilliant performance of Tennessee Williams's *The Glass Menagerie* at the Royal Exchange Theatre in Manchester. The production captured the fragility of the Wingfield family, the crippling repression enforced on son and daughter by the mother's foolish nostalgia for her youth in Blue Mountain and her gentlemen callers. I do not see how this performance could fail to enhance the sensitivities of the audience. As we drove home through the November night, past the ugly modern University buildings, I consoled myself by thinking of the numerous aesthetic experiences I have created for other people. I recalled the many occasions when I have read poems to large audiences, the poetry readings I have organized, the many new poems I have published in *C.Q.* which otherwise my readers might never have seen, the pleasure of introducing the literature I enjoy to my students. When all my literary criticism is forgotten, these living moments will remain in the memory of so many people. To teach so many wonderful students has been for me a great privilege.

# *Appendix A*

'Freedom in the Academic Community' was published in *The Times* on Monday 23 November 1970, together with the names of 154 members of university staff who had agreed to sign the document. Many more added their names after publication.

## Freedom in the Academic Community

The central functions of an academic community are learning, teaching, research and scholarship. They must be characterized by free expression, particularly freedom from political interference, by intellectual honesty and respect for the opinions and dignity of others.

1. All the members of a university have the right to express political views and to press for action on matters of concern by any legal and non-violent means. Such means include the rights to organize and join political groups and associations, to convene and conduct meetings on all public and political issues, to petition in writing and in person, to demonstrate in a peaceful fashion, and to publicize opinions by any legal means.

   Possession of these rights imposes the obligation to respect the basic rights of others. We regard the following activities as unacceptable because they prevent or impede the performance of the essential tasks of the universities, and are incompatible with the shared purposes of an academic community:
   a) violence or intimidation against any member or guest of a university including the families or associates of any member of the community.

b) forcible interference with the freedom of movement of any member of a university, or any invited guests of a university.

c) deliberate interference with academic freedom and freedom of speech, including any disruption of lectures and classes, and any attempt to prevent a speaker invited by any section of a university community from expressing his views.

d) wilful destruction or damage or theft of university property or of the property of members of the university.

e) obstruction of the normal processes and activities essential to the functions of the university community, including trespass on or unauthorized occupation of university buildings or any part of them.

f) the effort to align the university or any of its constituent bodies with any political party or political doctrine.

We believe that the 'sit-in' is an unacceptable form of protest in a university community. Sit-ins necessarily involve the use of physical force. If sit-ins are accepted, any group or groups of dissidents, small or large, can disrupt the life of the university. This method has already done great harm to the reputation of universities, and jeopardized the future welfare and freedoms of both students and staff. University authorities should not negotiate under duress.

2. We think that too little attention has been given to problems that occur when students are brought on to executive and decision-making bodies in universities. We believe there are some issues, including everything involved in the general determination of academic standards, on which, while consultation with students may be welcomed, the ultimate decision-making responsibility must rest and be seen to rest entirely on the appointed staff of the university. Matters for which the staff must be finally responsible include appointments, setting and marking of examinations, assessments of progress, the content of courses, the formulation of curricula and syllabuses, the direction of research, and the conduct of academic and library policy.

Students lack the knowledge and experience for making informed judgements about the university's work. Financial problems in particular have to be explained in detail, and the time academics can devote to teaching their students and to research is being seriously reduced. Universities are thus becoming less and less efficient at their prime functions and more, not less, 'bureaucratic'.

3.  A further need is for universities to draw up disciplinary codes to maintain freedom and order. Students should be required to agree to the code before admission. Infringement should lead to penalties, and those who persistently break the rules must be rusticated or sent down. Some universities have already established such procedures, and are putting them into practice. We urge all other universities to accept the principles outlined in this document and to take steps to implement them.

    For many decades British universities have maintained the highest reputation for academic freedom. People with extreme political views, both left and right wing, have been given a fair hearing at public lectures, accepted without question as undergraduates, and appointed when properly qualified to administrative and teaching posts. We believe that traditional British values of free enquiry can be maintained only if the standards set out in this document are firmly subscribed to by members of the academic profession in this country.

# *Appendix B*

## Black Paper Basics: Ten Points

1. Children are not naturally good. They need firm, tactful discipline from parents and teachers with clear standards. Too much freedom for children breeds selfishness, vandalism and personal unhappiness.
2. If the non-competitive ethos of progressive education is allowed to dominate our schools, we shall produce a generation unable to maintain our standards of living when opposed by fierce rivalry from overseas competitors.
3. It is the quality of teachers which matters, rather than their numbers or their equipment. We have sacrificed quality for numbers, and the result has been a lowering of standards. We need high-quality, higher-paid teachers in the class-room, not as counsellors or administrators.
4. Schools are for schooling, not social engineering.
5. The best way to help children in deprived areas is to teach them to be literate and numerate, and to develop all their potential abilities.
6. Every normal child should be able to read by the age of seven. This can be achieved by the hard work of teachers who use a structured approach.
7. Without selection the clever working-class child in a deprived area stands little chance of a real academic education.
8. External examinations are essential for schools, colleges, polytechnics and universities. Without such checks, standards decline. Working-class children suffer when applying for jobs if they cannot bring forward proof of their worth achieved in authoritative examinations.

9. Freedom of speech must be preserved in universities. Institutions which cannot maintain proper standards of open debate should be closed.
10. You can have equality or equality of opportunity; you cannot have both. Equality will mean the holding back (or the new deprivation) of the brighter children.

(Printed at the front of *Black Paper 1975*)

# *Appendix C*

## Association for Verbal Arts

*The association for verbal arts presents its manifesto, arguing that verbal skills are neglected by the education system*

Urgent reforms are needed in the teaching of English, particularly in secondary schools and higher and further education. For most people, training in the verbal arts is a missing subject.

Other arts, such as music, painting, sculpture or drama, include practice as an essential component. In contrast, courses in literature usually concentrate on the understanding, description and evaluation of texts, with some attention to critical method. Courses in language are mainly concerned to introduce students to the analysis of speech acts and to linguistic theory. Most literature and language courses do not require students to develop their skills in non-discursive modes of prose or in verse. This is an extraordinary situation.

It is an unfortunate anomaly that verbal arts as part of the discipline of classics were not carried over into the study of English when this became a major academic area in the early years of the century. It is time to return to a more effective and longer established tradition. English, at all levels, should involve the study and practice of a wide range of modes, written and oral, literary and non-literary.

Too often, writing by children after they leave the primary school is unimaginative and unadventurous. What most secondary school teachers are expected to ask from children is 'fair copy' work, safe writing with predictable and imposed subject matter. There are notable exceptions. Some teachers have achieved great success in developing imaginative writing, but they are in a minority. What is sown at O level is reaped at A level and beyond. Students of English at polytechnics and universities often write dull, secondhand discursive prose and are taught to do nothing else. This is particularly unfortunate because many of these students privately attempt to develop creative abilities in language, and all must be counted among the most verbally gifted of their generation. English, as at present constituted, neither meets their needs nor, arguably, fulfils its duty to the community, to which verbal skills are so vitally necessary.

Many teachers in Britain regard verbal arts, under the guise of 'creative writing', with suspicion because often there has been too much emphasis on free expression. True creativity in any art can best be developed within the framework of a thorough understanding of the nature and history of that art. The notion that verbal creation is somehow more self-indulgent, undisciplined or easy than other forms of creation is false. Responsible teaching is that which develops purposeful artistry in the handling of the medium. Verbal skill must be taught and practised in the curriculum, not left to chance, for it is one of the most important requirements for membership of a modern community. Precise and creative use of language is of major importance for the maintenance of our complex intellectual, industrial and democratic structures. Practice in verbal arts develops emotional and intellectual discrimination and provides the individual (and through the individual, society) with a vital tool of discovery and communication.

In recent years many English teachers have grown uneasy at the split between academics and professional writers. No discipline concerned with an art should divide those who study from those who practise it. The number of writers' fellowships, residences and part-time posts should be increased, on a par with the situation that obtains in other arts, while the role of academics in the encouragement of verbal skill and creativity should be greatly expanded.

Practice in the verbal arts is valuable not only for its own sake, but because it helps students appreciate the achievement of writers of the past and take an informed interest in contemporary writing. It provides an intimate and practical insight into how language works, so acting as the ideal bridge between literary and linguistic concerns. Modern literary theory, too, is most easily understood by students who have made their own raids on the inarticulate.

No doubt intending writers may benefit from an expansion of English to include verbal arts. And it is proper that teachers of an art should contribute to its development. The aim of verbal arts courses, however, is not to train professional writers (any more than courses in criticism aim to train professional critics). Their aim is, more centrally, to expand the range and improve the quality of the language used by students.

Verbal arts should become an essential component of all school examinations and courses in English in higher, further, part-time and community education. Courses in this aspect of literacy should be made available to students of other subjects, including the sciences and technology. Teacher training should be adapted accordingly.

Changes in the teaching of English are necessary and urgent if English is not only to survive the present difficult period but fulfil its promise as a major area of study and practice in the future.

**Signatories**
Peter Abbs; Mavis Ainsworth; Susan Basnett;
Malcolm Bradbury; John Broadbent; John Brown;
Christopher Butler; Anne Cluysenaar; Diana Collecot;
Richard Cooper; C. Brian Cox; John Cox; David Craig;
Douglas Dunn; Roy Fisher; David Fuller; Terry Gifford;
Damian Grant; John Haffenden; Barry Hines;
Philip Hobsbaum; Richard Hoggart; David Holbrook;
Ted Hughes; Aileen Ireland; Roger Knight; David Lodge;
Ian McMillan; John Mole; A.D. Moody; Roy Niblett;
David Orme; Malcolm Povey; Peter Redgrove; Ann Ridler;
Ken Robinson; John Saunders; Sir Roy Shaw;
Jon Silkin; Anne Stevenson; Raymond Williams;
Clive Wilmer; Alan Young.
(Printed in *The Times Higher Education Supplement*, 21 October 1983)

# Index

277